wild
fermentation

wild
fermentation

The Flavor, Nutrition, and Craft
of Live-Culture Foods

Updated and Revised Edition

Sandor Ellix Katz

Chelsea Green Publishing
White River Junction, Vermont

Project Manager: Patricia Stone
Developmental Editor: Makenna Goodman
Copy Editor: Laura Jorstad
Proofreader: Helen Walden
Indexer: Shana Milkie
Designer: Melissa Jacobson

Printed in the United States of America.
First printing August, 2016.
10 9 8 7 6 5   20 21 22 23

Our Commitment to Green Publishing

Chelsea Green sees publishing as a tool for cultural change and ecological stewardship. We strive
to align our book manufacturing practices with our editorial mission and to reduce the impact of
our business enterprise in the environment. We print our books and catalogs on chlorine-free
recycled paper, using vegetable-based inks whenever possible. This book may cost slightly more
because it was printed on paper that contains recycled fiber, and we hope you'll agree that it's
worth it. *Wild Fermentation* was printed on paper supplied by LSC Communications that contains
at least 10% postconsumer recycled fiber.

Library of Congress Cataloging-in-Publication Data
Names: Katz, Sandor Ellix, 1962– author.
Title: Wild fermentation : the flavor, nutrition, and craft of live-culture foods / Sandor Ellix Katz.
Description: Revised and updated edition. | White River Junction, Vermont
Chelsea Green Publishing, [2016] | Includes bibliographical references and index.
Identifiers: LCCN 2016019260| ISBN 9781603586283 (pbk.) | ISBN 9781603586290 (ebook)
Subjects: LCSH: Fermented foods.
Classification: LCC TP371.44 .K37 2016 | DDC 664/.024—dc23
LC record available at https://lccn.loc.gov/2016019260

Chelsea Green Publishing
85 North Main Street, Suite 120
White River Junction, VT 05001
(802) 295-6300
www.chelseagreen.com

Dedicated to Jon Greenberg (1956–1993)

This beloved ACT UP comrade first articulated to me the idea of peaceful coexistence with microbes rather than warfare. I honor Jon and all our fellow skeptics, rebels, and iconoclasts who question prevailing wisdom and authority. Believe in the future and keep change fermenting.

contents

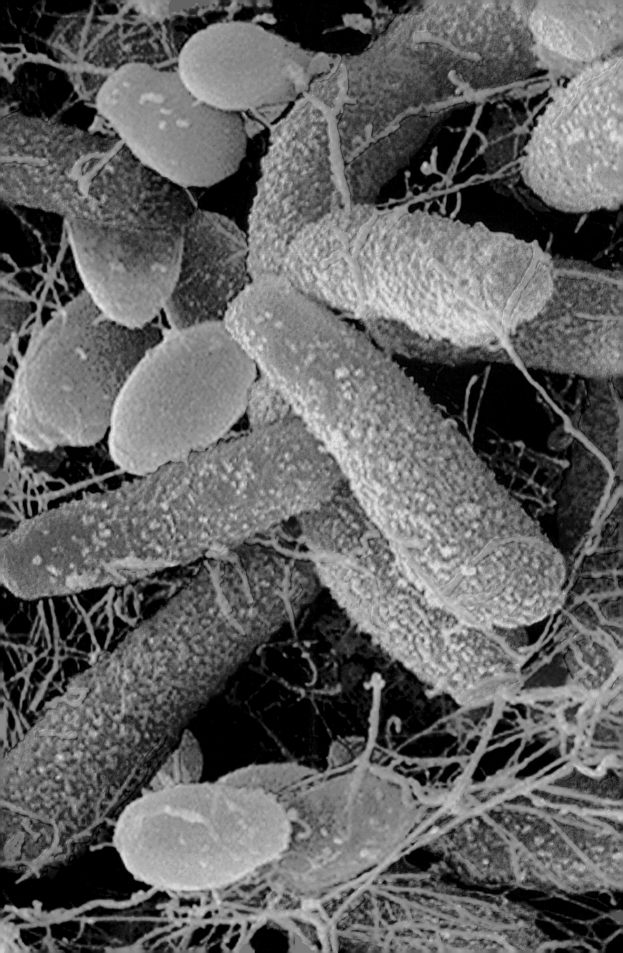

foreword

The process of fermenting foods—to preserve them and to make them more digestible and more nutritious—is as old as humanity. From the tropics—where cassava is thrown into a hole in the ground to allow it to soften and sweeten—to the Arctic—where fish are customarily eaten "rotten" to the consistency of ice cream—fermented foods are valued for their health-giving properties and for their complex tastes.

Unfortunately, fermented foods have largely disappeared from the Western diet, much to the detriment of our health and economy. Fermented foods are a powerful aid to digestion and a protection against disease. And because fermentation is, by nature, an artisanal process, the disappearance of fermented foods has hastened the centralization and industrialization of our food supply, to the detriment of small farms and local economies.

The taste for fermented foods is usually an acquired taste. Few of us can imagine eating fermented tofu crawling with worms, which is relished in parts of Japan; or bubbly sorghum beer, smelling like the contents of your stomach, which is downed by the gallons in parts of Africa. But then, few Africans or Asians can enjoy the odiferous chunks of rotten milk (called cheese) that are so pleasing to Western palates. To those who have grown up with fermented foods, they offer the most sublime of eating experiences—and there are many that will appeal to Western tastes even without a long period of accustomization.

In the spirit of the great reformers and artists, Sandor Katz has labored mightily to deliver this magnum opus to a population hungry for a reconnection to real food and to the process of life itself. For fermented foods are not only satisfying to eat, but also immensely satisfying to prepare. From the first successful batch of kombucha to that thrilling taste of homemade sauerkraut, the practice of fermentation is one of partnership with microscopic life. This partnership leads to a reverence for all the processes that contribute to the well-being of the human race, from the production of enzymes by invisible bacteria to the gift of milk and meat from the sacred cow.

The science and art of fermentation is, in fact, the basis of human culture: Without culturing, there is no culture. Nations that still consume cultured foods, such as France with its wine and cheese, and Japan with its pickles and miso, are recognized as nations that have culture. Culture begins at the farm, not in the opera house, and binds a people to a land and its artisans. Many commentators have observed that America is a nation lacking culture—how can we be cultured when we eat only food that has been canned, pasteurized, and embalmed? How ironic that the road to culture in our germophobic technological society requires, first and foremost, that we enter into an alchemical relationship with bacteria and fungi, and that we bring to our tables foods and beverages prepared by the magicians, not machines.

Wild Fermentation represents not only an effort to bring back from oblivion these treasured processes but also a road map to a better world, a world of healthy people and equitable economies, a world that especially values those iconoclastic, free-thinking individuals—so often labeled misfits—uniquely qualified to perform the alchemy of fermented foods.

—Sally Fallon Morell

preface to
the revised edition

This revised edition is a book I could not possibly have written when I first wrote *Wild Fermentation* 15 years ago, because writing this book changed my life.

When *Wild Fermentation* was first published in 2003, and for a decade before, I was living in the community I refer to in these pages (where I no longer live, though I live just down the road). *Wild Fermentation* grew out of my experience in this community. During those many years, my days were devoted to the land and the people and the animals and the plants there, and I became a fervent student in seeking to learn the practical skills of the homestead. My exploration of fermentation emerged as an element of this.

I also gardened. I started learning about the forest we were in, the plants I could find in it, and how to wildcraft herbs, dry them, and make tinctures. I learned to cook for large groups, and did a lot of the community food purchasing. I learned to operate a chain saw, and cut, moved, split, and burned a lot of wood. I was canning and pickling. I learned to build, and (along with others) built a house, for less than $10,000, out of mostly salvaged or locally harvested materials. I was milking goats, drinking raw goat's milk, and making yogurt and cheese. I was baking sourdough bread. I started making sauerkraut and country wines. My fermentation obsession developed in this larger context.

It was just a personal obsession for a while, though always shared with (some might say inflicted upon) my friends, fellow communards, neighbors, and family. I was first invited to teach a sauerkraut-making workshop in 1998 at the nearby Sequatchie Valley Institute, after which the workshop became an annual ritual. But meanwhile, I was struggling with my health. Though I had moved to Tennessee from New York City in the hope that active country living would keep me healthy, I was experiencing HIV-related symptoms and spiraling downward. After a health crisis in 1999–2000, I began taking anti-retroviral drugs, and my health stabilized and began to improve. The following year is when I originally wrote *Wild Fermentation*. "This project has given me back a sense of the future as expansive and full of possibilities," I wrote. And expansive it has been! My experience since the publication of the first edition has been beyond my wildest dreams.

What began as a series of self-organized grassroots book tours just never quite stopped, because there was so much interest, so many opportunities, and I was having so much fun. I have now taught many hundreds of workshops, at farms and farmers markets, universities, museums, and libraries, culinary schools and galleries, cafés, restaurants, breweries, wineries, community centers, conferences, festivals, private homes, and churches, in big cities and rural areas alike, mostly around the United States but increasingly beyond. I find that I have become an international teacher and lecturer on the broad topic of fermentation, just at a time when fermentation is getting hot, cited as the latest food trend as if bread, cheese, beer, wine, chocolate, coffee, yogurt, salami, vinegar, olives, sauerkraut, and kimchi hadn't been there all along.

In February 2015, as I embark upon this revision, I reflect upon a year that brought me to four continents, with presentations in Australia, New Zealand, Ireland, the UK, Belgium, Sweden, Canada, India, Mexico, Costa Rica, and a dozen states of the United States. I love to travel and get to see all these places and learn from them, to see fermentation in context, to be wined and dined, and to meet the wonderful and passionate people whom I do meet, everywhere. I feel lucky to be seeing the world in this extraordinary way, making so many connections, and sharing important information and skills for which people are, quite literally, hungry. I feel fulfilled to know that my books are making a difference, and to be a catalyst in a broad fermentation revival.

And yet I cannot help but have some ambivalence. It is truly dizzying to travel so much and meet so many people. And traveling means not being at home, in the kitchen and the garden and the forest, and with my beautiful family and friends. My interest in fermentation grew out of the practicalities of living on and from the land. My life as a fermentation revivalist, and especially traveling to all these places, takes me away from all of this. As I said, this book changed my life.

Life is full of trade-offs and I have no regrets. As a result of talking to people in so many different places about fermentation, and tasting, hearing about, and learning to make an ever-broader repertoire of ferments and variations, my experience and understanding of fermentation have been broadened and deepened immeasurably. I know a lot more now than I did in 2001 when I first wrote *Wild Fermentation*, and I decided that it was time to update and improve the first edition, to make it a better and clearer book of fermentation basics, informed by all that I have learned, but not including it all (for that readers can turn to *The Art of Fermentation*, where I go deeper into the concepts and processes).

The book is somewhat reorganized. Many of the original recipes have been revamped or revised. Some recipes (and digressions) that now seem superfluous have been removed, in order to make space for others that are more relevant. I hope that this book contains the information you are looking for, and helps empower you to feel confident to experiment in the realm of fermentation. Welcome to the fermentation revival!

acknowledgments

Sometimes I wonder whether my life could be an elaborate dream. Could my personal obsession with fermentation really have turned into bestselling books and invitations to teach around the world? Could this interest, considered arcane, weird, or even disgusting by many friends as it first developed, have turned out to be of interest to so many people? Will I wake up and learn that this is all a dream, too good to be true? More than anything, I feel very lucky. I wish to acknowledge this, and to offer proof that sometimes pursuing some weird passionate interest turns out to be the best thing you could possibly do. May it happen to you, too!

This revised and improved edition of *Wild Fermentation* is possible only because of all the incredible people I have met in my work as a fermentation revivalist. My learning curve has been ongoing for nearly a quarter century, and this revision is a book I could not possibly have written in 2001 when I first wrote *Wild Fermentation*. Thanks to all of you who have shared homemade foods and beverages, stories, information and context, recipes and methods, and questions that made me think and seek out more information. I cannot possibly list all the people who have contributed to my education, because it is literally thousands, from my earliest mentors to encounters on my most recent travels. A few of these people you will meet in these pages, but there are many more. I thank all the generous people everywhere I have gone for always broadening my knowledge of fermentation.

I appreciate the people who have shared their photos and artwork and allowed them to be included in this book. Thanks to Kate Berry, Barry Blitt, Bread and Puppet Press, Noah Church, Milos Kalab, Jessieca Leo, Alison LePage, Catherine Opie, Eileen Richardson, Joseph Shuldiner, and especially Shane Carpenter and Jacqueline Schlossman for their many gorgeous images.

I am grateful for my wonderful publisher, Chelsea Green. I always felt like I'd found a good niche with them, and they have just gotten better and better since they took a chance on me in 2001. I applaud their transition to worker-ownership and I thank the whole team there, now and since the beginning, especially Margo Baldwin, Ben Watson, Shay Totten, and my editor, Makenna Goodman. I also thank my agent, Valerie Borchardt.

I am ever grateful to my family of birth, who gave me my love of food, and have been such steady sources of ease, love, and devotion. I am no less grateful for the embrace of my family of choice. I am part of a vibrant queer extended community over two rural counties, what we call the baberhood, or faeborhood, or gayborhood. I feel so lucky to live in a rural area with so much and such vibrant queer culture, and so many old and dear friends as well as interesting new people all the time. I am always especially appreciative of the food producers and procurers among us, who grow, raise, milk, and forage such bounty from the land (and rescue the best of the dumpster waste stream). But what I am most grateful for is simply the love, care, and consideration that we show to one another, and our willingness to do the hard work of caring for one another through illness, death, and other life challenges. Building community is about taking care of one another over the long haul, or at least trying.

The people I rely on day-to-day are all part of this community. I thank Caeleb for helping me manage so much. I thank Kassidy and the whole amazing Walnut Ridge team for creating a space that is such a joy to ferment, teach, write, and just be in. I thank Dashboard, Mati, MaxZine, and Simmer for devoting their time and wisdom to the Foundation for Fermentation Fervor. I thank Spiky for geeking out with me on fermentation, formats, and more. I thank Lisa and Tom for sharing their cultures with me, and Lisa for sharing her yeast soda methods. I thank Surprise for descending with me into test kitchen madness. I thank Shopping Spree for his relentless positivity, and for taking such excellent care of me. I am ever grateful to Leopard for being such a constant in my life.

I thank you for your interest in my book.

introduction:
cultural context
The Making of a Fermentation Fetish

This book is my song of praise and devotion to fermentation. For me, fermentation is part health regimen, part gourmet art, part practical food preservation, part multicultural adventure, part activism, even part spiritual path as it affirms again and again the underlying interconnectedness of all. My daily routine is structured by the rhythms of these transformative life processes.

Sometimes I feel like a mad scientist, tending to as many as a dozen different bubbly fermentation experiments at once. Sometimes I feel like a game show host: "Would you like to taste what's in Crock Number One, or trade it for what lies buried in Crock Number Two?" Sometimes I feel like a Holy Roller evangelist, zealously spreading the word about the glorious healing powers of fermented foods. My friends tease me about my single-mindedness as they sample my fermented goodies. One friend, Dashboard, even wrote a song about my obsession:

> Come on friends and lend me an ear,
> I'll explain the connection between wine and beer,
> And sourdough and yogurt and miso and kraut,
> What they have in common is what it's all about.
> Oh the microorganisms,
> Oh the microorganisms . . .

Fermentation is everywhere, always. It is an everyday miracle, the path of least resistance. Microscopic bacteria and fungi are in every breath we take and every bite we eat. Try as we may—and many do—to eradicate them with antibacterial soaps, antifungal creams, and

antibiotic drugs, there is no escaping them. They are ubiquitous agents of transformation, feasting upon decaying matter, constantly shifting dynamic life forces from one miraculous and horrible creation to the next.

Bacteria are essential to life's most basic processes. Organisms of every description rely upon them and other microorganisms to accomplish many aspects of self-maintenance and self-protection. We humans are in a symbiotic relationship with these single-cell lifeforms and could not possibly exist without them. This microbiota, as the trillion-cell collective entity of microbes associated with each of us is known, digests food into nutrients our bodies can absorb, synthesizes essential nutrients so we don't have to obtain them from food, protects us from potentially dangerous organisms, teaches our immune systems how to function, and regulates many of our physiological systems in ways that we are just beginning to recognize. Not only are we dependent upon microorganisms, we are their descendants: There is widespread agreement that all forms of life on Earth spring from bacterial origins. Microorganisms are our ancestors and our allies. They keep the soil fertile and are an indispensable part of the cycle of life. Without them, there could be no other life.

Certain microorganisms can manifest extraordinary culinary transformations. Tiny beings, invisible to us, bring us compelling and varied flavors. Fermentation gives us many of our most basic staples, such as bread and cheese, and our most pleasurable treats, including chocolate, coffee, wine, and beer. Cultures around the globe enjoy countless exotic fermented delicacies. Fermentation is also used to make food more stable for storage, and more digestible and nutritious. Live, unpasteurized, fermented foods carry beneficial probiotic bacteria directly into our digestive systems, where they can help to replenish and diversify our microbiota.

In this book, I explain simple methods for making a variety of fermented foods and beverages. Over more than two decades, I have explored and experimented widely in the realm of fermentation. I want to share what I have learned. Truth be told, I am more a generalist than an expert. The experts find my techniques primitive. Because they are. Fermentation is easy. Anyone can do it, anywhere, with the most basic tools. Humans have been fermenting longer than we've been writing words, making pottery, or cultivating the soil. Fermentation does not require state-of-the-art facilities, vast expertise, or laboratory conditions. You do not need to be a scientist able to distinguish specific organisms and their enzymatic transformations, nor a technician maintaining sterile environments and exact temperatures. You can do it in your kitchen using equipment you already have.

The focus of this book is the basic processes of transformation, which mostly involve creating conditions in which naturally occurring wild organisms thrive and proliferate. Fermentation can be low-tech. These are ancient rituals that humans have been performing for many generations. They make me feel connected to the magic of the natural world, and to our ancestors, whose clever observations enable us to enjoy the benefits of these transformations.

When I try to conjure the origin of my fascination with this natural phenomenon, it leads me to my taste buds. I have always been crazy about brined sour pickles and sauerkraut. I am a descendent of Jewish immigrants from Poland, Russia, and Lithuania. These foods and their distinctive flavors are part of my cultural heritage. In Yiddish, these sour vegetables are known as *zoyers*. Sour flavors from fermentation are prominent in the food of Eastern Europe (as in many regions of the world), and carried over into the distinctive culinary identity of New York City, where I grew up. We lived on the Upper West Side of Manhattan, two blocks from Zabar's, an icon of New York food, and my family regularly feasted on their *zoyers*. I recently learned that

Lithuanian tradition worships Roguszys, a god of pickled food. Just a couple of generations out of Eastern Europe, my taste buds still salivate at Roguszys's temple.

I started experiencing and thinking about the health benefits of bacterially rich foods when I was in my mid-20s, when dietary exploration led me to macrobiotics, a dietary movement with roots in simple Japanese Zen Buddhist cuisine that emphasizes regular consumption of miso, live unpasteurized sauerkraut, and other live pickles as an aid to digestion. I began to notice that every time I ate my beloved pickles or sauerkraut I could feel my salivary glands squirt saliva—quite literally getting my digestive juices flowing.

Unbeknownst to me as I began regularly eating live-culture ferments as a health practice, at some point I became HIV-positive; I tested positive in 1991, long before effective medical treatments were available. I was seeking strategies for resilience and survival, and nutrition became very important to me. Fermented foods made my body feel well nourished, and I became even more devoted to eating them regularly.

I think it is imperative that I emphasize that fermented foods are not a cure for HIV or any other specific disease. They certainly may help, with many varied conditions, and people tell me all the time about their successful treatment regimes that include fermented foods

and beverages. But how, in any single case, can we know whether it was fermented foods that made the difference, or a combination of factors? Who knows without controlled trials? Sadly, in our system, such trials are almost entirely profit-driven, and just not being done for traditional foods and beverages.

As for my own health, despite my hope that good living, including but not limited to fermented foods, would keep me healthy, I've lived through harrowing downward spirals, as well as miraculous recoveries. I feel very lucky to be alive and relatively healthy, awed by my body's recuperative powers. I take anti-retroviral drugs every day, but many different factors, including regular consumption of live fermented foods, contribute to my present robust and relatively energetic state. Fermented foods can improve digestion, immune function, mental health, and possibly much more, contributing in important ways to overall health even if they do not necessarily cure particular diseases.

What drove me to finally start making sauerkraut for myself was not my health as much as the practical value of preserving the bounty of the garden. When I moved from New York City to rural Tennessee in 1993, I immediately got involved in keeping a garden. When the cabbage in our garden was ready for harvest that first year, I learned how to make sauerkraut. I found an old crock buried in our barn, chopped up the cabbage, salted it, pounded it into the crock, and waited. That first kraut tasted so alive and powerfully nutritious! Its sharp flavor sent my salivary glands into a frenzy and got me hooked on fermentation. I have made sauerkraut ever since, earning the nickname Sandorkraut, even as my repertoire has expanded. After kraut, I learned how easy it was to make yogurt and cheese with the steady supply of fresh milk from our small herd of goats. And, as I described earlier, sourdough baking, beer- and wine-making, and miso-making followed.

My experimentation has never really stopped. Bubbling crocks have become a permanent feature of my kitchens. Some of these projects are finished in a few hours, some take months or even years, and others are ongoing, as I feed and stir the crocks and jars, developing a symbiotic rhythm with these tiny fermenting organisms, nurturing them so that they will nourish us.

A fetish, according to *Webster's*, is anything "supposed to possess magical powers" and thereby worthy of "special devotion." Fermentation is magical and mystical, and I am deeply devoted to it. I have indulged this arcane fetish (and been indulged). This book is the result. Fermentation has been an important journey of discovery for me, and I invite you to join me along this effervescent path, well trodden for thousands of years yet largely forgotten in our time and place, bypassed by the superhighway of industrial food production.

1: cultural rehabilitation

The Many Benefits of Fermented Foods

Fermented foods and drinks are quite literally alive with flavor and nutrition. Their flavors tend to be strong and pronounced. Think of stinky aged cheeses, tangy sauerkraut, rich earthy miso, smooth sublime wines. Though not everyone loves every flavor of fermentation, humans have always appreciated the unique, compelling flavors resulting from the transformative power of microscopic bacteria and fungi.

One great practical benefit of fermentation is that it can preserve food. Fermentation organisms produce alcohol, lactic acid, and acetic acid, all "bio-preservatives" that retain nutrients while preventing spoilage and the growth of pathogenic organisms. Vegetables, fruits, milk, fish, and meat are highly perishable, and our ancestors used whatever techniques they could discover to store foods from periods of plenty for later consumption. From the tropics to the Arctic, fermentation has been used to preserve food resources.

Captain James Cook, the 18th-century English explorer who extended the far reaches of the British Empire, was recognized by the Royal Society for conquering scurvy (vitamin C deficiency) among his crews by sailing with large quantities of sauerkraut. Among the many lands Cook "discovered" and delivered into the Crown's realm were the Hawaiian Islands (where Cook later lost his life). I find it an interesting parallel that the Polynesian people who crossed the Pacific

Ocean and populated Hawai'i more than 1,000 years before Captain Cook also sustained themselves through the long voyage with fermented food, in this case poi, a thick starchy taro root porridge still popular in Hawaii and throughout the South Pacific.

Fermentation doesn't only preserve nutrients, but generally breaks them down into more easily accessible forms. Soybeans are a good example. This extraordinarily protein-rich food is largely indigestible (and some would say toxic) without fermentation. Fermentation breaks down the soybeans' dense complex protein into readily digestible amino acids (and simultaneously breaks down the potential toxins), giving us traditional fermented soy foods such as soy sauce, miso, and tempeh.

Milk, too, is difficult for many people to digest. Lactic acid bacteria transform lactose, the milk sugar that so many humans cannot tolerate, into easier-to-digest lactic acid. Likewise, gluten that has undergone bacterial fermentation (as opposed to the pure yeast fermentation most commonly used in contemporary breads) is broken down and easier to digest than unfermented gluten. According to the United Nations Food and Agriculture Organization, which actively promotes fermentation as a critical source of nutrients worldwide, fermentation improves the bioavailability of minerals present in food.[1] Bill Mollison, author of *The Permaculture Book of Ferment and Human Nutrition*, calls the action of fermenting foods "a form of pre-digestion."[2]

This pre-digestion action of fermentation also breaks down certain toxic compounds found in foods into benign forms, as mentioned in the case of soybeans. Another vivid illustration of this is cassava (also known as yuca or manioc), the tuber native to the tropical Americas that has also become a staple food in equatorial Africa and Asia. Cassava grown in certain soils contains high levels of cyanide and is poisonous without removal of the toxin. One common method of doing this is a simple soaking fermentation—peel and coarsely chop the tubers and submerge them in water for about five days—which breaks down the cyanide and renders the cassava safe and nutritious.

Not all food toxins are as dramatic as cyanide. Grains and legumes contain a compound called phytic acid, which binds with zinc, calcium, iron, magnesium, and other minerals, blocking their absorption and potentially leading to mineral deficiencies. Fermenting grains by soaking them before cooking breaks down phytic acid, rendering the grain far more nutritious.[3] Nitrites, prussic acid, oxalic acid, nitrosamines, and glucosides are some other potentially toxic compounds found in foods that can be reduced or eliminated by fermentation.[4]

Fermentation also creates new nutrients. As they go through their life cycles, microbial cultures create B vitamins, including folic acid, riboflavin, niacin, thiamin, and biotin. (Ferments have often been credited with creating vitamin B_{12}, otherwise absent from plant-source foods; however, some argue that what had been identified as B_{12} in fermented soy and vegetables are actually inactive "analogues" known as *pseudo*vitamin B_{12}.)[5]

Some ferments have been shown to function as antioxidants, scavenging cancer precursors known as free radicals from the cells of your body.[6] Lactic acid bacteria create omega-3 fatty acids, essential for cell membrane and immune system function.[7] The fermentation of vegetables produces isothiocyanates and indole-3-carbinol, both regarded as anticarcinogenic.[8] A marketer of "cultured whole food supplements" boasts that "the culturing process generates copious amounts of naturally occurring ingredients like superoxide dismutase, GTF chromium, detoxifying compounds like glutathione, phospholipids, digestive enzymes, and beta 1,3 glucans."[9] Frankly, nutritional factoids like this make my eyes glaze over. You don't really need molecular analysis to tell you what foods are healthy. Trust your instincts, your taste buds, and how it makes you feel. The data adds up to this: Fermentation makes food more nutritious.

Perhaps the most profound benefit of eating fermented foods is the bacteria themselves, which are probiotic, meaning they can be beneficial to us. Many different fermented foods are embodiments of dense and biodiverse microbial communities, which interact with our microbiome in ways we are just beginning to recognize. This interaction can improve digestion, immune function, mental health, and many other aspects of our well-being.

Making sauerkraut with a group of nuns in Tecate, Mexico.

Not all fermented foods, however, are still alive when you eat them. Certain foods, by their nature, cannot contain live cultures. Breads, for instance, must be baked, thereby killing the organisms present in them. However, many fermented foods can be consumed live, and alive is the most nutritious way to eat them.

Read labels and be aware: Many commercially available fermented foods are pasteurized or otherwise heat-treated, which extends shelf life but kills microorganisms. Ferments that are still alive generally include in the label words to the effect that they "contain live cultures." If you want live-culture fermented foods in our world of pre-packaged mass-produced food commodities, you have to seek them out or make them yourself.

By promoting digestive health, live fermented foods can help control digestive disease processes such as diarrhea and dysentery. Live-culture foods have been shown to improve infant survival rates. A study conducted in Tanzania compared mortality rates between infants fed different "weaning gruels," some fermented, some not. The infants eating fermented gruels had half as many "diarrhea episodes" as the infants fed non-fermented gruels.[10] Lactic acid fermentation inhibits the growth of diarrhea-related bacteria.[11] Another study, reported in the journal *Nutrition*, concludes that thriving microbiota prevent disease because lactic acid bacteria "competes with . . . potential pathogens for receptor sites at the mucosal cell surfaces" of the intestines and proposes a treatment strategy of "ecoimmunonutrition."[12]

As 18-letter words go, I like the word *ecoimmunonutrition*. It recognizes that an organism's immune function occurs in the context of an ecology, an ecosystem of different microbial cultures, and that it is possible to build and develop that cultural ecology in oneself through diet. Eating bacteria-rich foods is one way to do this; eating lots of plant fibers (prebiotics) is another. A huge body of research reaffirms the fact that bacteria play an important role in protecting us, as organisms among organisms, from disease.

The Case for Microbial Coexistence

Western culture is terrified of germs and obsessed with hygiene. We live in the midst of the war on bacteria, and our bodies are major battlegrounds. We are taught to fear exposure to all forms of microscopic life. Every new sensationalized killer microbe gives us more reason to defend ourselves with vigilance. Nothing illustrates this more vividly than antibacterial soap. A few decades ago, mass marketing of soap

with antibacterial chemicals was but a glimmer in some pharmaceutical executive's eye. It has quickly become the standard hand-washing hygiene product. Are fewer people getting sick as a result? "No data support the efficacy or necessity of antimicrobial agents in such products, and a growing number of studies suggest increasing acquired bacteria resistance to them," warns the American Medical Association's Council on Scientific Affairs. "It is prudent to avoid the use of antimicrobial agents in consumer products."[13]

The antibacterial compounds in these soaps, most commonly triclosan, kill the more susceptible bacteria but *not* the heartier ones. "These resistant microbes may include bacteria . . . that were unable to gain a foothold previously and are now able to thrive thanks to the destruction of competing microbes," according to Dr. Stuart Levy, director of the Tufts University Center for Adaptation Genetics and Drug Resistance.[14] Hygiene is important. Wash your hands often with soap and water, hot if possible. But we don't need more and more chemicals to make us safe. Antibacterial soap is just another exploitative and potentially dangerous product being sold by preying on people's fears.

In our bodies, microorganisms we are host to vastly outnumber our bodily cells. They are present in mind-boggling numbers, comprising elaborate communities that vary according to each ecological niche, inhabiting our skin with its diverse moisture conditions, all our orifices, in greatest concentration throughout our intestinal tracts, and increasingly we are finding them in places where previously they were presumed not to be, such as the womb.

These organisms provide us with an incredible array of services. Bacteria enable us to effectively digest our food and assimilate its nutrients. They synthesize essential nutrients so that we do not need to obtain them via food. It has become clear that serotonin and other chemicals that influence how we think and feel are regulated by gut bacteria. Our immune function is largely the work of bacteria, and bacteria that we come into contact with stimulate immunity.

A growing number of researchers are finding evidence to support what is known as the hygiene hypothesis, which attributes the dramatic rise in prevalence of asthma and other allergies to lack of exposure to diverse microorganisms. The more "germ-free" we try to be, the more vulnerable we become. Well-informed hygiene is very important, but it is impossible to avoid exposure to microbes. They are everywhere.

Much of Western chemical medicine aims to eradicate pathogenic organisms. In the case of my HIV drugs, the treatment strategy is called highly active anti-retroviral therapy. Having benefited from the miracles of high-tech pharmaceuticals, I'm in no position to argue against the value of this approach. I firmly believe, however, that microbial warfare is not a sustainable practice, and that the war on bacteria is not a war we will win. "Bacteria are not germs but the germinators—and fabric—of all life on Earth," writes Stephen Harrod Buhner in *The Lost Language of Plants*. "In declaring war on them we declared war on the underlying living structure of the planet—on all life-forms we can see—on ourselves."[15]

Health and homeostasis require that humans coexist with microorganisms. Bacteria-counting scientists have quantified this simple fact, estimating that each person's body is host to a bacterial population in excess of 100 trillion, and noting that "the interactions of these colonizing microbes with the host are nothing if not complex."[16] Humans and all other forms of life evolved from and with these organisms, and we cannot live without them. "Nature appears to maximize mutual cooperation and mutual coordination of goals," writes ethnobotanist Terence McKenna. "To be indispensable to the organisms with which one shares an environment—that is the strategy that ensures successful breeding and continued survival."[17]

Bacterial cells are "prokaryotes," without nuclei; their genetic material is free floating in the cells. "Genes from the fluid medium, from other bacteria, from viruses, or from elsewhere enter bacterial cells on their own," write biologists Lynn Margulis and Karlene V. Schwartz.[18] By incorporating DNA from their environment into themselves, prokaryotes assimilate genetic traits. They are thought to have evolved first into structured cells with nuclear membranes and eventually into complex organisms such as ourselves. But they never left their progeny; they are with us always.

"Prokaryotes are the master engineers of our complexity," explains my excited scientist friend Joel Kimmons, a PhD nutritionist. Inside our bodies, most dramatically in the gut, bacteria absorb genetic information that informs our function as organisms; they are an integral part of our sentient experience. "We eat and thus we know," says Joel. Humans are in mutually beneficial and mutually dependent relationships with these and many different microbes. We are symbiotic, inextricably woven together, in a complex pattern far beyond our capacity to comprehend completely.

Microbiodiversity and Incorporating the Wild

By eating a variety of live fermented foods, you promote microbial diversity in your body. The live bacteria in those ferments not heated after fermentation enter our bodies, where some of them survive the stomach and find themselves in our already densely populated intestines. There, they help to digest food and assimilate nutrients, as well as stimulate immune responses. There is no one particular strain that is uniquely beneficial; rather the greatest benefit of eating bacteria lies in biodiversity. Few if any of the bacteria we eat take up residence in our intestines, but even so they have elaborate interactions with the bacteria that are there, and with our bodily cells, in ways that we are just beginning to recognize and that remain little understood.

Biodiversity is increasingly recognized as critical to the survival of larger-scale ecosystems. Earth and all its inhabitants comprise a single, seamless matrix of life, interconnected and interdependent. The frightening repercussions of species extinctions starkly illustrate the impact of the loss of biodiversity all over our planet. The survival of our species depends upon biodiversity.

Biodiversity is just as important at the micro level. Call it microbiodiversity. Your body is an ecosystem that can function most effectively when populated by diverse microorganisms. Sure, you can buy "probiotic" supplements containing specific strains. But by eating traditional fermented foods and beverages, especially those you ferment yourself with wild microorganisms present in your environment, you become more interconnected with the life forces of the world around you. Your environment literally becomes you, as you invite the

microbial populations you share the Earth with to enter your diet and your intestinal ecology.

Wild fermentation is a way of incorporating the wild into your body, becoming one with the natural world. Wild foods, microbial cultures included, possess a great, unmediated life force, which can help us lower our susceptibility to disease and adapt to shifting conditions. These microorganisms are everywhere, and the techniques for fermenting with them are simple and flexible.

Are live fermented foods the answer to a long, healthy life? The folklores of many different cultures associate longevity with foods such as yogurt and miso. Many researchers have found evidence to support this causal connection. Pioneering Russian immunologist and Nobel laureate Elie Metchnikoff studied yogurt-eating centenarians in the Balkans early in the 20th century and concluded that lactic acid bacteria "postpone and ameliorate old age."[19]

Personally, I'm not so inclined to reduce the secret of long life and good health to any single food or practice. Life consists of multiple variables, and every life is unique. But very clearly fermentation has contributed to the well-being of humanity as a whole. The methods of fermentation are many and varied; it is practiced on every continent, in thousands of different ways. As you proceed through these pages, you will see how simple it is for you to share in the nutritional and healing powers of fermented foods and drinks that humans have enjoyed for thousands of years.

2: cultural theory
Human Beings and the Phenomenon of Fermentation

Human beings have recognized the magic and power of fermentation for as long as we have been human. Mead, a honey wine, is generally regarded as the most ancient fermented pleasure. Archaeologists believe that human collecting of honey predates cultivation of the soil. Cave paintings in locations as geographically dispersed as India, Spain, and South Africa depict images of people gathering honey as long as 12,000 years ago.

When by chance or intention honey is mixed with water, fermentation happens. The honey already has yeast in it, but when the honey is pure, the yeast is in a state of dormancy, lacking the water it needs to be active. Add a little water and honey becomes a stimulating medium for the newly awakened yeast, which feast upon it and reproduce rapidly, making the honey-water bubbly and vividly alive. Within a short time, the honey-water will become mead, its sugars converted to alcohol and carbon dioxide by the action of tiny beings invisible to the human eye.

According to Maguelonne Toussaint-Samat's vast survey, *A History of Food*, "The child of honey, the drink of the gods, mead was universal. It can be regarded as the ancestor of all fermented drinks."[1] Our hunter-gatherer forebears, at least some of them, some of the time, enjoyed mead. The production of mead does not require heat, and possibly it has been part of human life for even longer than controlled fire. Imagine the wonder and awe our ancestors must have felt as they first encountered fermenting honey-water in the hollow of a tree. Were they scared by the bubbling, or just curious? Once they tasted it, they must have liked it and drunk more. Then they started to experience a light, giddy feeling. Surely some divine spirit granted them this substance and the state it induced.

The anthropologist and cultural theorist Claude Levi-Strauss suggests that mead-making marks the passage of humanity from nature to culture. He illustrates this distinction by describing the transitional role of a hollow tree, "which, as a receptacle for honey, is part of nature if the honey is fresh and enclosed within it, and part of culture if the honey, instead of being in a naturally hollow tree, has been put to ferment in an artificially hollowed out trunk."[2] The development of techniques and tools to ferment alcohol is a defining characteristic of human culture, made possible by the ubiquitous presence of wild yeasts. "What seems clear," writes Stephen Harrod Buhner in his *Sacred and Herbal Healing Beers*, "is that human knowledge of fermentation arose independently throughout human cultures, that each culture attributed its appearance to divine intervention, and that its use is intimately bound up with our development as a species."[3]

Fermentation-induced altered states have long been associated with oral storytelling, mythical traditions, and poetry in many different cultures. The Papago people of the Sonoran Desert region of northern Mexico and southern Arizona ferment a drink called *tiswin* from the fruit of the saguaro cactus. Buhner cites the traditional song the Papago sing as they drink tiswin:

> Dizziness is following me!
> Close it is following me.
> Ah, but I like it.
> Yonder far, far
> On the flat land it is taking me.
> Dizziness I see.
> High up there I see it.
> Truly I like it.
> Yonder they lead me.
> And dizziness they give me to drink.
>
> 'Tis at the foot of little Gray Mountain
> I am sitting and getting drunk.
> Beautiful songs I shall unfold.[4]

This same inspirational quality is often attributed to fermented alcohol, across cultures. Inebriation is the state "of which the hymns of all primitive peoples tell us," condescended Friedrich Nietzche.[5]

Language, the most fundamental faculty that distinguishes our species, has been developed, exercised, and elaborated "under the influence." Meads, wines, and beers have been held sacred in many different traditions for thousands of years. Prohibitions notwithstanding, alcohol ferments have always been worshiped, invested with important symbolic meaning, and offered to deities.

The Sumerians, beer makers with written recipes dating back nearly 5,000 years, worshiped a goddess of beer, Ninkasi, whose name means "you who fill my mouth so full."[6] Egyptians buried great ceramic casks of wines and beers with their mummified royals in the pyramids, and in *The Egyptian Book of the Dead*, prayers for the souls of the deceased are addressed to "givers of bread and beer."[7] Ancient Mayan ceremonies involved a honey ferment called balché, used in enema form to maximize its inebriating effect. Perhaps because of this unfamiliar mode of consumption, their conquerors saw the devil lurking in balché, in order to "turn into snakes and worms that gnawed at the souls of the Maya."[8] It was banned in the name of Christendom. Nevertheless, in the Catholic magic of transubstantiation, wine becomes the blood of Jesus Christ. In my own Jewish tradition, repeated recitations of the prayer "Blessed is the creator of the fruit of the vine" are accompanied by sacramental drinks of wine.

Other forms of fermentation seem to have developed in tandem with the domestication of plants and animals as human cultures evolved. It is no accident that the word *culture* has such broad connotation. It derives from the Latin *colere*, to cultivate. Fermentation cultures are cultivated no less than plants are cultivated, and for that matter no less than the "socially transmitted behavior patterns, arts, beliefs, institutions, and all other products of human work and thought" that constitute the dictionary's first definition of *culture*.[9] The various cultures are inextricably intertwined.

Agriculture itself would not be practical without fermentation, given natural seasonal rhythms of scarcity and overabundance. How could people in temperate regions with limited growing seasons invest their energies in crops that are ready at certain moments of the year without effective techniques to preserve and derive ongoing sustenance from the harvest? Historically, and to the present day, the most widespread and prominent means of this is fermentation. Fermentation enables us to preserve summer and autumn vegetable harvests for winter survival, and turn fleeting overabundances of fruit into alcohol. Fermentation enables us to better digest and assimilate nutrients from grains, legumes, and many other foods. Fermentation enables highly perishable milk to become more stable yogurt and kefir as well as cheeses, some of which can be preserved for years. Fermentation preserves meats in salamis and myriad other cured meat products.

Fermentation practices have long illustrious histories that stretch deep into prehistory and appear to have evolved together with the crops and animals themselves. For instance, bread and beer both are born of grain fermentation, and historians debate which came first. The conventional wisdom is that humans settled into grain agriculture as a means of producing reliable, storable foodstuffs. "Are we to believe that the foundations of Western civilization were laid by an ill-fed people living in a perpetual state of partial intoxication?" asked botanist Paul Manglesdorf, incredulously, in a much-cited 1953 symposium on this question organized by the journal *American Anthropologist*. But in fact indigenous beers are starchy suspensions that are quite nutritious and often not very strong; an alternative hypothesis poses the question: Is it not possible that beer provided a more compelling incentive than mere food for well-fed migratory peoples to settle?[10] Either way, fermentation is an important part of the story.

Science Puzzles Over a Perplexing Phenomenon

Though many peoples throughout history have recognized fermentation as a mystical life force, in the Western scientific tradition it was long shrouded in confusion. Since at least Roman times, natural historians such as Pliny the Elder described what they called "spontaneous generations." The theory of spontaneous generation viewed certain forms of life as phenomena occurring independent of any reproductive process. This belief was not limited to the bubbling action of fermentation.

European fermentation enthusiasts I met at Terra Madre, the international Slow Food event in Torino, Italy, in 2008. We served fermented vegetables that they brought and collected this list of names for sauerkraut in different languages.

Scientists were earnestly trying to elucidate the spontaneous generation of mice as late as the 17th century, when Jean Baptista van Helmont reported that "if one presses a dirty shirt into the opening of a vessel containing grains of wheat, the ferment from the dirty shirt does not modify the smell of the grain but gives rise to the transmutation of the wheat into mice after about twenty-one days."[11]

He also had a recipe for creating scorpions by carving a hole into a brick, filling it with dried basil, and placing it in the full sun.

As van Helmont was exploring spontaneous generation, a Dutchman, Anton van Leeuwenhoek, developed the microscope and first observed microorganisms in 1674:

> I now saw very plainly that these were little eels, or worms, lying all huddled up together and wriggling; just as if you saw, with the naked eye, a whole tubful of very little eels and water, with the eels a-squirming among one another: and the whole water seemed to be alive with these multifarious animalcules. This was for me, among all the marvels that I have discovered in nature, the most marvelous of all; and I must say, for my part, that no more pleasant sight has ever yet come before my eye than these many thousands of living creatures, seen all alive in a little drop of water, moving among one another, each several creatures having its own proper motion . . .[12]

Meanwhile, French philosopher René Descartes had expounded his revolutionary view that all natural phenomena could be reduced to mechanical processes. Descartes ushered in a period of scientific inquiry focused on describing natural processes by causal mechanisms. Chemistry flourished in the 18th and 19th centuries, and a sort of chemical reductionism came into vogue, which held that all physiological processes were ultimately reducible to a series of chemical

reactions. Chemists of this period dismissed the idea that fermentation was caused by living organisms as "retrograde."[13]

The chemists were aware of the "animalcules" revealed by the microscope, but they stubbornly dismissed their importance and constructed elaborate theories to explain them away. The chemist Justus von Liebig, a 19th-century pioneer in the development of chemical fertilizers, was a major proponent of fermentation as a chemical rather than biological process. Von Liebig believed that the importance of the yeast in the fermentation process was its decomposition as dead matter. In an 1840 treatise, he wrote: "It is the dead part of the yeast, the part that is no longer alive and undergoing alteration, that acts on the sugar."[14]

Louis Pasteur and the Advent of Microbiology

Enter Louis Pasteur, a French chemist who turned his attention to fermentation processes at the behest of a Lille industrialist, a beetroot alcohol manufacturer whose factory was experiencing inconsistent results and whose son was enrolled in Pasteur's class at the university.

Fermentation-inspired mural by my extremely talented friend Noah Church.

Pasteur's methodical study of beetroot fermentation quickly convinced him that fermentation was a biological process. His first study on fermentation, "Memoire sur la fermentation appelée lactique," was published in April 1857: "Fermentation is a correlative of life and of the production of globules, rather than of their death or putrefaction."[15] Pasteur solved the beetroot alcohol manufacturer's problem by heating the beet juice to destroy naturally occurring lactic-acid-producing microorganisms and reseeding it with alcohol-producing yeast. This was the earliest application of the heating process now credited on every carton of milk: pasteurization.

Pasteur's findings contradicted the chemistry establishment of the time, and he spent the rest of his life studying the life cycles of various types of microorganisms, spawning the field of microbiology. Though the academic chemists reacted defensively to his findings, the burgeoning fermentation industries gratefully incorporated Pasteur's innovations. His discoveries gave a great boost to the mass production of fermented foods and drinks. These products had been enjoyed for thousands of years, created using processes learned from observation and experimentation, and passed down through the generations, often accompanied by prayers, rituals, and offerings to deities. Now, with scientific precision and without elaborate ritual, they could be reliably manufactured in mass quantities.

The advent of microbiology gave rise to a sort of colonial outlook toward microorganisms, that they, like other elements of nature and other human cultures, must be dominated and exploited. One book that expressed this attitude especially starkly is *Bacteria in Relation to Country Life*, published in 1908, midway between Pasteur's research and the development of antibiotic drugs.

> The deepening current of human existence now forces us to study the bacteria and other microorganisms. In so far as they are dangerous to our health and happiness we must learn to defend ourselves; we must learn to destroy them or to render them harmless. In so far as they are beneficial, we must learn to control them and to make their activities widely useful to human society.[16]

Homo sapiens prone to feeling overly confident of our superiority and ability to dominate would do well to ponder a small bit of wisdom attributed to Louis Pasteur himself: "It's the microbes that will have the last word."[17]

3: cultural homogenization

Standardization, Uniformity, and Mass Production

Part of the pleasure those [McDonald's] fries gave me was how perfectly they conformed to my image and expectation of them—to the idea of Fries in my head, that is, an idea that McDonald's has successfully planted in the heads of a few billion people around the world.

—Michael Pollan, The Botany of Desire

Cultures around the world have evolved as specific localized phenomena. This is true of both microbial cultures and human cultures. In varied locales with dramatically different climate, geography, natural resources, and migratory lineages, cultural practices such as languages, beliefs, and food (including fermentation) are incredibly diverse. But that rich diversity is threatened by the expansion of trade into a unified global market. Where once beer, bread, and cheese were quirky local products varying from place to place, we lucky 21st-century consumers can buy fermented commodities such as Bud Lite, Wonder Bread, or Velveeta that look and taste the same everywhere. Mass production and mass marketing demand uniformity. Local identity, culture, and taste are subsumed by the ever-diminishing lowest common denominator, as McDonald's, Coca-Cola, and other corporate behemoths permeate minds on a global scale to create desire for their products.

This is the homogenization of culture, a sad, ugly process by which languages, oral traditions, beliefs, skills, and practices are becoming

extinct every year, while ever-greater wealth and power is concentrated in fewer hands. Wild fermentation is the opposite of homogenization and uniformity, a small antidote you can undertake in your home, cultivating broad communities of organisms indigenous to your food, and also contributing those of your hands and your kitchen, to produce unique fermented foods. What you ferment with the organisms around you is a manifestation of your specific environment, and it will always be a little different. Perhaps your homemade sauerkraut or miso will conform perfectly to your image and expectation of them, as the McDonald's fries do for Michael Pollan. More likely, they will possess some quirky anomaly that will force you to adjust your image and expectation. Do-it-yourself fermentation departs from the realm of the uniform commodity. Ironically, some of the earliest commodities exchanged on a global scale were fermented foods.

Alejandro Solano-Ugalde of the Mashpi agroecological farm project in Ecuador, showing me a ripe cacao fruit.

Specifically, chocolate, coffee, and tea were among the first agricultural products shipped in vast quantity around the world; and each involves fermentation in its processing.

In 1985 I spent several months traveling with a friend in Africa. In Cameroon, not far from a town called Abong-Mbang, we met native people who took us on a trek through the jungle where they lived. We used bamboo poles for walking sticks as we waded through knee-high swamps. These people have carried on a long tradition of subsistence in that jungle. In the course of our hike, we came across several settlements engaged in cacao farming. One cacao worker we spoke with told us he had never tasted chocolate! We came to understand that the government was trying to force these people to settle in order to tend cacao monocultures. Their migratory lifestyle was being outlawed, phased out because it was of no value to a state in desperate pursuit of tax revenue and foreign exchange, and replaced by forced settlement producing an export commodity that they never even got to enjoy.

When traditional cultures are outlawed, that is the homogenization of culture. It's an old story, which could be told by any Native American, or by my grandparents, who fled pogroms and saw the Eastern European Yiddishkeit they were born into disperse and disappear in a single generation. When people are forced to change cultural course much is lost, and this includes fermentation practices. Specific local fermentation practices, manifestations of the uniqueness of place, are disappearing every year. Yet ironically, fermented stimulants were among the earliest of food commodities transported around the world, laying the groundwork for the globalized economy.

Fermented Stimulants and the Rise of Globalization

Chocolate is made from the seeds of a tree native to the Amazon rain forest, *Theobroma cacao* (*theobroma* is Greek for "food of god"). The seeds develop in much larger seedpods, each seed encased in delicious sweet pulp. After harvest, the seeds and pulp are removed from the pods; then they ferment spontaneously, with organisms naturally present, before further processing. The fermentation digests the pulp and alters the color, flavor, aroma, and chemistry of the cacao beans. The unique compelling flavor of chocolate is only achieved through fermentation. After fermentation, the cacao beans are dried, then roasted, hulled, finely ground, pressed into butter, and further processed into chocolate confections.

Humans have enjoyed cacao for thousands of years. Perhaps first enjoying the wild fruit for its juicy sweet pulp, Amazonian peoples learned to use ground roasted cacao as the basis for stimulant drinks, rather than for solid foods, as did the Mayan and Aztec cultures that brought the cacao tree to Central America and Mexico. Cacao is extremely bitter without sugar; in these cultures it was consumed unsweetened, often mixed with hot chili peppers and/or corn, as thick frothy beverages. The word *chocolate* is derived from the Aztec word *xocolatl*, a compounding of *xococ* (bitter) and *atl* (water). Cacao was an important sacrament in Mayan and Aztec religious ceremonies. Cacao beans were also used as a form of currency.

As soon as the Spanish encountered cacao, in 1519, they began exporting it to Spain. In Europe, too, cacao was consumed exclusively as a drink until the 19th century, though there cacao began to be paired with sugar. Today, global chocolate sales approach $100 billion per year. Cacao grows in the tropics, and major growing regions are in Africa, Southeast Asia, and South and Central America.[1]

Cacao is a rain forest tree, native to dense and biodiverse jungles. During a visit to Ecuador, I had the opportunity to harvest and ferment cacao at the Mashpi agroecological farm, a forest restoration project in the Mashpi valley northwest of Quito, where cacao grows among palms, bananas, and an awesome array of native and exotic fruit trees. Commercially cacao is generally grown in monocultures with "zero shading" and heavy chemical spraying. The industry is in crisis, with diseases threatening production. Researchers are using genetic modification aiming to develop resistant strains of this most cherished commodity, likely to appear soon at a store near you.[2]

Other globalized tropical stimulants also involve fermentation: The fresh, ripe, red fruits of the tree *Coffea arabica* are allowed to spontaneously ferment to digest the pulp and free the individual beans. After fermentation, the coffee beans are dried and roasted. Chances are you already know the rest of the process.

Coffee is indigenous to Ethiopia. From there it spread across the Red Sea to the Arabian Peninsula, and then throughout the Islamic world by the end of the 15th century.[3] Coffee first appeared in Europe in Venice; in Europe coffee was known as food and medicine before it became popular as a beverage. Coffee drinking was first introduced in Paris in 1643, and within 30 years there were 250 cafés there.[4] The leading coffee-producing nations in our time are Brazil, Colombia, Vietnam, Indonesia, and Mexico.[5]

Opening the cacao fruit to remove the beans and pulp.

Tea is another stimulant that is sometimes fermented. Green tea is the dried leaves of *Camellia sinensis*. Black tea is dry-cured, which intensifies the stimulant properties of the tea leaves. This curing process is often described as fermentation; while it is drying surely some incidental fermentation occurs, but most changes in the tea result from oxidation rather than the action of microorganisms. The tea that is specifically fermented is pu-er, in which moist tea leaves are packed tightly and fermented for long periods, before drying. Tea has been consumed in Asia for thousands of years. It first appeared in Europe in Lisbon in the 1550s and took 100 years to reach London, where it quickly became the rage in the 1650s, and ever since.

All tea destined for Europe and North America was exported from the Chinese port of Canton until the early 19th century. Traders were not permitted inland, and the techniques of growing and fermenting tea were guarded as trade secrets. The Chinese, self-sufficient in known resources and advanced in technology, wanted nothing the English had to offer, except gold, silver, and copper, until the British

Cacao beans embedded in sweet pulp.

hit upon opium (another product often involving fermentation) as a profitable exchange commodity. The East India Company, the British Crown's mercantile franchise, established an opium production industry in India and introduced opium into China in exchange for tea, thus initiating the global drug trade, which has grown and flourished ever since. Only in the 19th century did the British learn the techniques of tea cultivation and begin to grow it in India, East Africa, and other colonies.[6] Today China is the world's largest tea producer, followed by India, Kenya, Sri Lanka, and Turkey.[7]

The enormity of the economic and cultural changes wrought to the entire world by the mass production and global trade of chocolate, coffee, and tea cannot be overstated. These stimulants, recognized today as addictive substances, were "the ideal drugs for the Industrial Revolution," according to ethnobotanist Terence McKenna. "They provided an energy lift, enabling people to keep working at repetitious tasks that demanded concentration. Indeed, the tea and coffee break is the only drug ritual that has never been criticized by those who profit from the modern industrial state."[8]

The other related commodity that rounds out the picture is sugar. Chocolate, coffee, and tea all made their appearance in England almost simultaneously, around 1650. Though all three stimulants had been consumed as unsweetened, bitter beverages in their original cultural contexts, Europe married them to sugar and they became that important new mass commodity's marketing partner. This was the birth of marketing, the first instance of the manufacture of mass demand for a hitherto obscure commodity. Today there appears to be no end to the products consumers can be convinced we cannot live without, but it is important to know there was a beginning to this concept.

"The fashion for these hot drinks became a potent factor in the surge in sugar demand," notes historian Henry Hobhouse in his book *Seeds of Change*.[9] Between the years 1700 and 1800, per capita sugar consumption in Britain increased more than fourfold, from an average of 4 pounds a year to 18 pounds. "Sugar surrendered its place as luxury and rarity and became the first mass-produced exotic necessity of a proletarian working class," writes Sidney W. Mintz in *Sweetness and Power*.[10] Average people used more and more sugar, and desired more of it than they could afford, while "producing, shipping, refining, and taxing sugar became proportionately more effective sources of power for the powerful."[11] Chocolate, coffee, and tea consumption increased similarly.

Sugarcane, *Saccharum officinarum*, is native to New Guinea, and spread as long as 8,000 years ago to other Asian tropics.[12] Sugar was long known, traded, and used in the Middle East and, to a lesser extent, in Europe. Limited supplies were available, it was very expensive, and it was used as a medicine and as a spice, but not a food as it is today.[13] First the Portuguese and then the Spanish established their earliest colonial outposts beginning in 1418 as sugar plantations on Madeira, the Canary Islands, São Tomé, and the Cape Verde Islands in the Atlantic waters off the west coast of Africa. The location of the Atlantic island sugar plantations established and institutionalized the west coast of Africa as the primary source for slave labor.

As European empires colonized Caribbean and tropical American lands, they established much larger sugar (and later other) plantation economies with African slave labor. In the tragic course of recorded human history, it seems clear that slavery has existed in many different cultural contexts and been practiced in many different ways. Slavic people gave their name to the ancient institution of slavery, and contemporary accounts allege that slavery persists into the 21st century and can be found today on the cacao plantations of the Ivory Coast and elsewhere.[14]

But it was the sugar trade that established the systematic global racism of African slavery. As innovations in the refinement of sugar yielded a whiter and whiter product, the system of its production dehumanized people on the basis of dark skin. In symbol and in flesh and blood, sugar gave birth to the racist world order, the one that sadly persists and continues to systematically privilege white skin and penalize dark skin, devaluing black lives to such an extent that activists are forced to state the obvious, that Black Lives Matter.

Sugar and its associated stimulant commodities also gave birth to colonial rule on a global scale, with export-based agriculture. It does not make any kind of sense for the people (or the land) of any place to grow massive quantities of stimulants for export rather than diverse nutritious food for local consumption. It only happens by the exercise of force pushing people from the land that has sustained them. Initially this was accomplished through slavery and direct colonial administration. In our time, the primary mode of domination has shifted to subtler instruments of global capital such as free trade agreements, the International Monetary Fund, the World Bank, transnational corporations, and the World Trade Organization. If the people who work the fields had any measure of control over the land they worked, they would be growing food to eat, not luxury stimulants for people on other continents.

"The first sweetened cup of hot tea to be drunk by an English worker was a significant historical event, because it prefigured the

Cacao beans drying, post-fermentation.

Incredibly sweet cacao juice, delicious both fresh and fermented, draining from freshly harvested cacao.

transformation of an entire society, a total remaking of its economic and social basis," writes Mintz. "We must struggle to understand fully the consequences of that and kindred events, for upon them was erected an entirely different conception of the relationship between producers and consumers, of the meaning of work, of the definition of self, of the nature of things. What commodities are, and what commodities mean, would thereafter be forever different."[15]

We consumers of the affluent West have come to take for granted a constant flow of pleasure-gratifying products from faraway lands, at great cost of precious resources such as fossil fuels (for shipping), land (which could be used to grow real food to feed people living on it), labor (which would be better directed toward local needs), and biodiversity.

Resisting the Commodification of Culture

I have no grand plan to offer for resisting the insidious processes of globalization, commodification, and cultural homogenization. The

French sheep farmer José Bové, who became an international hero after he bulldozed a McDonald's in 1999, offers one possible model. "McDonald's is merely a symbol of economic imperialism," writes Bové. "It represents anonymous globalization, with little relevance to real food. . . . Waves of opposition to this commodification can be felt in all corners of the world." What specifically sparked his McDonald's action were the trade sanctions imposed by the United States on Europe for its ban on the import of hormone-treated beef. "We reject the global trade model dictated by the multinationals," exhorts Bové. "Let's go back to agriculture . . . People have the right to be able to feed themselves."[16]

If you tried an action like Bové's in the United States these days, it would probably be branded as terrorism. We cannot resist the homogenization of culture by overpowering it. Yet we must not resign ourselves to it. Resistance is everywhere at the margins, where the people who manage to avoid succumbing to mainstream cultural currents come together. In the margins, we create and support diverse alternative cultures that express our various needs and desires.

Resistance takes place on many planes. Sometimes it must be dramatic and public, but most of the decisions we are faced with are mundane and private. What to eat is a choice that we make several times a day, if we are lucky. The cumulative choices we make about food have profound implications.

Food offers us many opportunities to resist the culture of mass marketing and commodification. Though consumer action can take many creative and powerful forms, we do not have to be reduced to the role of consumers selecting from seductive convenience items. We can merge appetite with activism and choose to involve ourselves in food as co-creators. Food has historically been one of our most direct links to the life forces of the Earth. Bountiful harvests have always been occasions for celebration and appreciation of the divine.

In our urbanized society, the vast majority of people are completely cut off from the process of growing food, and even from the raw products of agriculture. Most Americans are used to buying and eating food that has already been processed in a factory. "Both eater and eaten are thus in exile from biological reality," writes Wendell Berry. "And the result is a kind of solitude, unprecedented in human experience, in which the eater may think of eating as first a purely commercial transaction between him and a supplier, and then as a purely appetitive transaction between him and his food."[17] Industrially produced food is dead. It severs our connection to the life forces that sustain us and deprives us of our access to the powerful magic so abundantly present in the natural world. "The time has come to reclaim the stolen harvest," writes Indian activist Vandana Shiva, "and celebrate the growing and giving of good food as the highest gift and the most revolutionary act."[18]

Not everyone can or should be a farmer. There are many ways to cultivate a connection to the Earth and buck the trend toward global market uniformity and standardization. One small but tangible way to resist the homogenization of culture is to involve yourself in the harnessing and gentle manipulation of wild microbial cultures. Rediscover and reinterpret the vast array of fermentation techniques used by our ancestors. Build your body's cultural ecology as you engage and honor the life forces all around you.

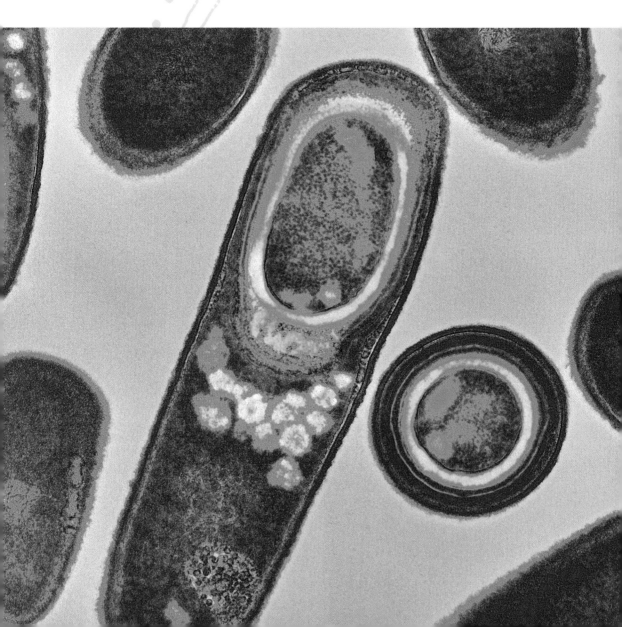

4: cultural manipulation
A Do-It-Yourself Guide

We have been taught to fear bacteria, and it is easy to project this fear upon fermentation and imagine that working with bacteria must be dangerous. This makes the prospect of fermenting at home intimidating to many people. Because microorganisms are most commonly thought of as causing disease, it is widely assumed that fermentation must be potentially dangerous, and that for these processes to be safe must require extensive expertise, thorough chemical sterilization, exacting environmental controls, and specific laboratory-bred cultures.

In fact, microorganisms (in general) are vital in all living systems, and healthy communities of microorganisms are our greatest protection. Fermentation is a strategy for food safety, and most fermented foods have long histories of use without problems. In the case of fermented vegetables, according to the US Department of Agriculture, there have been no documented cases of associated food poisoning or illness.[1] Often people project their fear of botulism onto fermented foods, but this is unfounded and mostly due to the botulism risk in canning, which is real. There is no case history of botulism associated with fermented vegetables, fruits, grains, or milk; it has only occurred in fermented meats, fish, and tofu (not covered here), and steps for preventing it are well known and easy.

Do not be afraid. Do not allow yourself to be intimidated. Reject the cult of expertise. Remember that all fermentation processes predate the technology that has made it possible for them to be made more complicated. Most fermentation does not require specialized equipment. There are gorgeous ceramic crocks for fermenting vegetables, but a jar you probably already have will do the job just fine. Carboys and air locks enable you to ferment wines and meads much longer, yielding stronger and drier beverages, but you can ferment more lightly alcoholic beverages quickly and easily in any jar, bowl, crock, or bucket. Fermentation is easy and exciting. Anyone can do it. Microorganisms are flexible and adaptable. Certainly there is considerable nuance to be learned about any of the fermentation processes, and if you stick with them, they will teach you. But the basic processes are simple and straightforward. You can do it yourself.

Do-It-Yourself

Do-it-yourself is an ethic of self-empowerment and openness to learning. Do-it-yourselfers include folks who garden, cook "from scratch," make clothes and handcrafts, build and fix things, and practice healing arts, to give just a few examples. The DIY ethos is found among old-timers anywhere who grew up with inherited land-based skills, as well as punks and other refugees from mainstream culture.

It's the do-it-yourself ethic of rural homesteading that got me first experimenting with fermentation. In the off-the-grid community where I have lived, we create and maintain all our own infrastructure, including solar electricity, phone lines, and water systems. We raise goats and chickens, grow much of our food, and build and maintain the structures we inhabit. Among us are folks who make music, spin and dye yarn, knit, crochet, sew, and fix cars. Rural homesteads are havens for those who wish to develop their breadth as generalists, acquiring skills that are themselves at risk of extinction. I find it tremendously satisfying and empowering to learn techniques for doing just about anything.

Do-it-yourself fermentation is a journey of experimentation and discovery. Rediscovery really, because, like fire or simple tools, these are some of the most basic transformative processes that our ancestors used and that form the basis of human culture. Every ferment yields unique results, influenced not only by ingredients but by environment, season, temperature, humidity, and any other factors affecting the behavior of the microorganisms whose actions make these transformations possible. Some fermentations are complete in a few hours. Some require years.

Fermentation generally requires only a little preparation or work. Most of the time that elapses is spent waiting. Do-it-yourself fermentation is about as far as you can get from fast food. Many ferments get better the longer you leave them. Use this time to observe and ponder the magical actions of invisible allies. The Chorote people of South America view the time of fermentation as "the birth of the good spirit."[2] They attract the good spirit with music and singing, exhorting the spirit to come settle into the home they have prepared. You too can prepare a comfortable environment for the spirit, the organisms, the process, however it suits you to think about it. The force is with you. It will come.

I get so excited every time my crocks start bubbling and the life forces make themselves known. But inevitably, even after decades of experience, sometimes the process doesn't go as I'd planned: Wines

Tara Whitsitt of Fermentation on Wheels aboard her fermentation education bus with Austin Durant of the Fermenters Club.

sour, yeasts become exhausted, maggots infest aging crocks. Sometimes you don't know something has gone far enough until it goes too far. None of this is *dangerous*; it's all part of the evaluation process and impossible to miss; paying attention to our senses and watching our ferments develop helps us see the deviations and learn from them. Sometimes it's just too hot or too cold for the organisms whose flavors we're after. We are dealing with fickle life forces, in some cases over long periods of time, and though we are making an effort to create conditions favorable to desired outcomes, we do well to remember that we are not, by any measure, in complete control. When your experiments go awry, as some inevitably will, learn from them and try not to be discouraged. Read, research online, or find mentors to help understand what went wrong. And remember that the prized cultures of a San Francisco sourdough or the finest blue cheese have their roots in wild fermentations that took place in someone's kitchen or farmhouse. Who knows what compelling healing flavors could be floating around in your kitchen?

"Our perfection lies in our imperfection" is one of my mantras in this life. I learned it many years ago from my friend Triscuit as we and a couple of other novice carpenters built our communal house. We used wood that we salvaged from deconstructing an old Coca-Cola bottling plant, resting on posts that we harvested from the land. We learned as we built. If uniformity was what we were after, we would have done better to shop for a double-wide trailer. Luckily, we wanted to live in something funky and woodsy, and that's what we built (and have since passed along to others in the community). Our mantra certainly holds true in the realm of fermentation, and I repeat it often. "Our perfection lies in our imperfection." If your desire is for perfectly uniform, predictable food, this is the wrong book for you. If you are willing to collaborate with tiny beings with somewhat capricious habits and vast transformative powers, read on.

Slippery Boundaries

There is no food that cannot be fermented, though not every food has an established tradition of fermentation. Fermentation processes involving meat or fish are beyond the scope of this book, though the world is full of them. Salamis and fish sauces are two prominent ones, among many. A fermented fish sauce called *garum* or *liquamen* was an important condiment in ancient Rome, not much different (less salty and more funky) from the fermented fish sauces widely used in contemporary Southeast Asian cuisines. People of the Arctic regions dig pits in the ground and fill them with whole fish to ferment for months, when they reach a cheesy consistency. The word *sushi* derives from a Japanese tradition of fermenting fish and rice together. (See my book *The Art of Fermentation* for more on fermented meat and fish.)

The idea of fermenting meat and fish (or really, anything) often raises the question of the distinction between a food that is fermented to perfection and one that is rotten. This distinction can be highly subjective. Have you noticed how polarized people are on stinky cheeses? They are either excited or repulsed. Ferments can be edgy like that.

After a goat slaughter many years ago, as I was just beginning to explore fermentation, I decided to try fermenting some of the meat. I cubed up some scrappy pieces of goat meat and placed them in a gallon jar, then filled it with a mixture of all the live ferments I had around: wine, vinegar, miso, yogurt, and sauerkraut juice. I covered the jar and left it in an unobtrusive corner of our basement. It bubbled and smelled good. After two weeks I poured the meat and its marinade into a covered pot and roasted it in the oven.

As it cooked, an overwhelming odor enveloped the kitchen. It smelled like a very strong cheese suited to only the bravest gastronome. There was some swooning and near fainting, and several folks were nauseated and had to leave the room. Lots of people complained about the smell. We had to open the windows, despite the December cold. Perhaps half a dozen of us tried the meat. It was quite tender for goat meat, and its taste was much milder than its smell. My fellow communard Mish absolutely loved it. He hovered over the pan for a long time picking at the meat, praising its strong cheesy aroma, and gloating over the rarefied "acquired taste" that only he and a few others could fully appreciate.

Many cultures have favorite fermented dishes with such strong flavors and aromas, or such unusual textures, that they become important symbols of distinctive cultural identity, all the more so because people outside the group generally find them repulsive. I got to try the Swedish low-salt fermented herring called *Surstromming* after hearing how awful many non-Swedes have reported it to be. I found the smell extremely challenging, but the taste quite pleasant, especially cushioned by flatbread, onion, and sour cream. I've now enjoyed it several times and look forward to my next encounter. Though many Asian soy ferments have gained widespread popularity in the West, slimy Japanese *natto* seems to have more limited appeal; the husband of the woman who taught me how to make natto, Betty

YES WE ACCEPT
EBT, FMNP
& WIC/SENIOR FVC

PRODUCE

CHARD 2.50	CHERRY TOMATOES 3.50
HOT PEPPERS 25¢	OKRA 2.50
SWEET PEPPERS 50¢	ZUCHINNI/ SUMMER SQUASH 50¢
TOMATOES 50¢ - 1	HERBS $2
SCALLIONS $2	EGGPLANT 50¢
BEETS $3	GARLIC $1
CARROTS $2	

Stechmeyer, who tried to get him to eat natto for health reasons, referred to it as "snottoh." Betty also taught me the word *organoleptic*, which food scientists use to describe the qualities of how food feels in the mouth (as well as subjective feels of the other sensory organs). Fermentation often transforms the organoleptic qualities of foods, and sometimes it is an organoleptic quality more than flavor that influences what we like or dislike, or passionately love or hate.

One culture's greatest gastronomic pride is another's worst nightmare. "The concept of 'rottenness'... belongs to the cultural rather than the biological sphere," notes Annie Hubert, the director of France's National Scientific Research Center. "The term defines a point where a food becomes unsuitable for consumption according to criteria associated with taste, presentation, and the concept of hygiene in different human societies."[3]

This boundary is fluid, and fermented foods have a way of making boundaries in general somewhat fluid. Take the dualism of life and death. Fermentation is the action of life upon death; living organisms consume dead plant and animal matter, in the process freeing nutrients for the further sustenance of life. Bacteria are by their very nature fluid, in that they may incorporate and discard genetic material as needed according to shifting conditions and opportunities. Bacteria are shape shifters capable of infinite and rapid adaptation.

People can be shape shifters, too. I think especially of my transgender friends, who have had to forge identities for themselves, in defiance of familial and social norms and expectations. Our society generally treats gender as fixed and binary, but there are always people whose unique selves do not conform neatly to the gender they were assumed to be, nor perhaps to any fixed gender parameters. Gender is a fluid construct that can shift over time, and gender identity is a simple right of self-determination. Transgender people are organizing, speaking out, and gaining visibility, and I see them as a positive force for change in our world. I'm for gender freedom and self-determination, and I embrace gender-blenders of diverse description. They, like any people struggling in the margins, need and deserve respect and support.

As with the spectrum of gender identity and expression, it's the fluidity of fermentation—the varied microbial ecology in different locations, varied temperature, humidity, and conditions—that makes every batch just a little bit different. Fermentation is not an easy thing to standardize. Many fermentation recipes mysteriously instruct you to ferment "until the flavor is ripe." You will have to be the judge of when that is. I advocate tasting your ferments at frequent intervals as the process progresses so you can learn about the spectrum of fermentation, discover what degree of ripeness you find most appealing, and experience the flavors of the other side of the elusive and slippery slope toward rottenness.

Sometimes people ask me whether improperly fermented foods can cause food poisoning. I have never experienced this, nor heard any reports of it from other fermentation enthusiasts. As I said before, according to the US Department of Agriculture, there is no case history of illness associated with fermented vegetables. The cases I have read about arise primarily in the realm of fermented meats, fish, and tofu, none of which are covered in this book, and to a lesser extent in cheeses (though these are generally in the context of mass production). In general, the acidic or alcoholic environments created by fermentation are inhospitable to bacteria associated with food poisoning. However, I cannot state in any absolute way that food poisoning could not result from something going wrong in a fermentation process.

Here's what I suggest: If it looks or smells disgusting, feed it to the compost. Usually I find that the funkiness is limited to the top layer, where aerobic life-forms such as yeasts and molds come into contact with the oxygen-rich air. As long as the mold is white to gray in color it is not regarded as harmful. Skim it off as best you can. If the mold dissipates and little bits are left remaining, remove most of it, as much as you can, and don't worry. After removing mold, evaluate the texture of the vegetables near the surface; if they have been softened by mold growth, remove and discard. Dig as deep as you have to. The longer you allow mold to grow on the surface of your ferment, the deeper its mycelia penetrate. Molds can lead to mushy vegetables and lowered acidity; eventually, the vegetables can come to taste like mold, a flavor I do not enjoy. If in doubt, trust your nose to be your guide. If you're still in doubt after that, taste just a little bit. Mix it with your saliva and swish it around your mouth like they do at wine tastings. Trust your taste buds. If it doesn't taste good, don't eat it.

The only cause for alarm is if other-colored molds start to grow, which I have never observed. If this should happen to you, discard the whole project, as certain bright molds can be extremely toxic.

Equipment and Ingredient Basics

The basic pieces of equipment required for most ferments are vessels to contain them. Gourds have been a traditional favorite for this, as have animal membranes, ceramic containers, wooden barrels, and glass jars. A wide-mouth vessel is easiest for kraut and many other fermentations, as it allows for a hand to comfortably fit inside. I like to use old-fashioned heavy ceramic crocks. Unfortunately, they are expensive, fragile, and can be hard to come by. Crocks come in various shapes and sizes. I typically use simple cylindrical ones without a tight-fitting top, and cover the top with a cloth. Some crocks are designed with water-lock channels that keep air out but allow pressure inside to release. Each design has pros and cons. Clever people accomplish this simple process in many different ways. No single vessel is the best, in my opinion.

If you find used crocks, check them carefully for cracks, and especially if the interior glaze is a bright color, use a lead-testing kit, available at hardware stores, to make sure it isn't lead-based. Maybe you'll luck out and find a new one in an old-timey local hardware store. Try to find crocks locally, or deals with free shipping, because they are heavy and expensive to ship. I ferment many things in wide-mouth glass jars, and occasionally in 55-gallon wooden barrels.

Food-grade plastic buckets and barrels work great and are widely available. Many of the vegetable fermentation businesses I have visited rely upon these as fermentation vessels. I personally do not see plastic as a desirable material to use, and can easily believe that chemicals from the plastic leach into the food, but we live in a

At Schumacher College in England with the late Frank Cook, a fellow fermentation enthusiast and plant educator.

plastic world and there really is no escaping exposure to those chemicals. Most food you buy is wrapped in the stuff. If you do use plastic, make sure it is food-grade. Do not use plastic buckets that once contained building materials, for example. And do not ferment in metallic containers, which can react with salt as well as the acids produced by fermentation.

Narrow-necked vessels (such as jugs or larger carboys) can be important for the later stages of fermenting alcoholic beverages. The narrow neck minimizes surface area and makes it easier to protect from oxygen. Generally the companion to the narrow neck is an air lock, a contraption that enables pressure to release from the carboy while protecting it from the flow of oxygen-rich air outside. More on these in Carboys and Air Locks, page 220.

A thermometer is a helpful tool for any of the many fermentation processes that require maintaining temperatures in a particular range, or cooling cooked ingredients to some moderate temperature before introducing cultures. While you can train yourself to recognize certain temperatures using your senses, as fermenters have done throughout the ages, a thermometer is very helpful.

Another piece of equipment that gives you a good deal of versatility when using grains and legumes in fermentation processes is a grain grinder. Grinding your own ensures that your ingredients are fresh, alive, and capable of germination until you are ready to use them, in contrast with pre-ground grains, which lose nutrients through oxidation and can become rancid. Grinding your own also gives you control over texture. Coarse is beautiful and delicious. The most basic inexpensive models are great for coarsely cracking grains and legumes; larger ones are better if you expect to be regularly grinding fine flour. Check Mexican markets for basic models; for a selection check out www.lehmans.com.

Masking tape and markers are indispensable kitchen tools for the fermentation revivalist. Label your ferments! Write what you are fermenting, the date, and the projected date of its completion. A journal for details and observations about your experiments is a wonderful resource too, but marking the vessels themselves is essential. Other equipment needs will be addressed as we go along.

The most common ingredient called for in the recipes in this book is water. Do not use water that is heavily chlorinated for fermentation projects. Chlorine is used in water precisely because it kills microorganisms. If you can smell or taste the chlorine in tap water, filter it, or leave it out in an open container overnight (or boil it) to evaporate the chlorine before using the water for fermenting. Or use unchlorinated water from another source.

Another frequent ingredient is salt. Salt inhibits certain organisms, but (up to a point) it is well tolerated by lactic acid bacteria, important in most food fermentation processes, and yeast. I like to use unrefined sea salts, but you can use any sea salt, pickling salt, or kosher salt. The reason most fermenters avoid standard table salt with added iodine is that iodine is antimicrobial, like chlorine, and could inhibit fermentation. That said, I've made kraut with iodized table salt and it worked fine. Be aware if you're using coarse salts that the same volume of salt will weigh a bit more, so you'll need a little less volume of it than with fine-ground salt the recipes in this book assume.

Other ingredients will be discussed as we come to them. In general, I would encourage anyone to use organic foods for your fermentation, first and foremost because of its lower impact on the Earth and the people working in the fields, and also because it is more nutritious and tastier—and, if it's local, also fresher. Local food is best for many important reasons, beyond fresh and delicious or even the environmental impact of food miles. Buying local food creates productive local jobs, expands the local skill base, and contributes toward greater regional self-sufficiency and food sovereignty. Best of all, grow your own. Then you know it's as fresh as could be, and you have the joy of participating in the miracle of plants (and other soil life). But don't fret too much over the source of the ingredients for your ferments. The microorganisms are not especially picky. They'll work fine with whatever you can get.

New Frontiers of Experience and Knowledge

As I first wrote this do-it-yourself guide in 2001, I was learning another new back-to-the-land skill. After years of enjoying the luscious, nutritious, fresh, raw milk of our herd of goats, without getting involved in their maintenance and care, I began learning to milk the goats, which taught me to relate to Sassy, Lydia, Lentil, Lynnie, Persephone, Luna, and Sylvia as individuals. Milking built my hand strength as I learned how to coax all the milk from the udders. Ultimately, the technique turned out to be about finding a rhythm.

Fermentation is not so very different. You get to know the microorganisms as you work with them, and find a rhythm with them. Until the relatively recent revolutions in refrigeration and food mass production, fermentation processes were all household, or at least local,

practices. They were considered sacred traditions, performed communally and often ritualistically. By reviving these fermentation practices in your home, you can bring not only extraordinary nutrition but also life and magic to the food you eat and share.

This is a process-oriented cookbook. That is, the techniques I describe are what is ultimately important. The specific ingredients are in a way arbitrary and meant to be varied. Many of the recipes for fermented delicacies from faraway places are re-created from written descriptions. Two sources that merit general acknowledgment are Bill Mollison's *Ferment and Human Nutrition* and Keith Steinkraus's *Handbook of Indigenous Fermented Foods*. Each of these authors has amassed a tremendous collection of practical information. I have also consulted many other books, websites, and people, and have credited them as appropriate. One problem with information is that it is often vague, and once you start to consult more than a single source, often it is conflicting. I cannot guarantee the authenticity of many of these culinary reconfigurations, only that they work, and that they taste delicious. Deviate from the recipes; investigate traditions of interest to you; incorporate your own favorite ingredients, or those most abundantly available to you, whether from your garden, a local farmer, an irresistible sale, or dumpster-diving resource recovery missions. Happy fermenting!

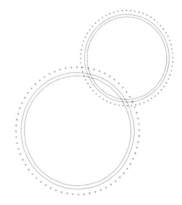

5: vegetable ferments

Fermenting vegetables is the ideal way to begin fermenting. It requires no special equipment; you can use a jar that you probably already have. There's no need for starter cultures, either; all the bacteria you need are already on the vegetables. Though some people recommend using whey, bacterial powders, or other starters in sauerkraut, this is unnecessary since lactic acid bacteria are present on all plants, and consistently dominate in the submerged environment. I'll say it again: Fermented vegetables are so safe, with no case history of problems, that the process of fermenting actually makes vegetables *safer* to eat than when consumed raw. Fermented vegetables are probiotic, improve digestion, and have been credited with wildly varied benefits, from preventing cancer to reducing social anxiety.

Fermented vegetables complement any meal. Their tangy flavors accent the rest of the food, stimulate digestion, and cleanse the palate. In many cuisines, they are routine elements. Koreans, for example, are so devoted to kimchi that most people eat it with every meal. I like to eat some fermented vegetables every day. It only takes 15 minutes of chopping or shredding to fill a jar that can ferment and feed you for weeks. Then nutritious and delicious fermented vegetables are available whenever you want them, with no additional work required. Keep a few jars of different styles going for variety. It's really easy.

The biggest difference between vegetables left to rot and those destined for delicious fermentation is whether they are submerged under liquid, or exposed to air. Molds will eventually develop on vegetables with exposure to air, and liquid protects them from air and molds. Usually this submerged fermentation environment is salty, but

not always, and the proportion of salt can vary considerably. Long-term or warm-climate fermentation needs more salt than shorter-term or cooler-climate fermentation.

sauerkraut

For me, it all started with sauerkraut. I'd always loved it as a kid in New York City, almost as much as I loved sour pickles. When my first year of gardening in Tennessee produced an abundance of cabbage, I made my first batch of sauerkraut. Sauerkraut is generally thought to have originated in China and spread westward via the Central Asian nomads. It is prepared in any number of regional styles. In Croatia and elsewhere in Southeastern Europe, cabbage is generally soured whole, in great barrels. A Russian variation uses apples or cranberries to sweeten the kraut. Germans are so strongly associated with sauerkraut that they are known, in derogatory slang, as Krauts, and when the United States was at war with Germany, sauerkraut was temporarily dubbed liberty cabbage.

The fermentation of cabbage into sauerkraut is not the work of a single microorganism. Sauerkraut, like most fermentations, involves a succession of several different organisms, not unlike the life of a forest, in which a series of different trees follow each other as the dominant species, each succeeding type altering conditions to favor the next. The fermentation involves a broad community of bacteria, with a succession of different dominant players, determined by the increasing acidity. Do not be deterred by the biological complexity of the transformation. That happens on its own once you create the simple conditions for it. Sauerkraut is very easy to make.

The sauerkraut method is also referred to as dry-salting, because typically no water is added and the juice under which the vegetables are submerged comes from the vegetables themselves. This is the simplest and most straightforward method, and results in the most concentrated vegetable flavor.

Timeframe: 3 days to 3 months
(and beyond)

Vessel: 1-quart/1-liter wide-mouth jar,
or a larger jar or crock

Ingredients (for 1 quart/1 liter):

2 pounds/1 kilogram of vegetables per
quart/liter, any varieties of cabbage
alone or in combination, or at least half
cabbage and the remainder any
combination of radishes, turnips, carrots,
beets, kohlrabi, Jerusalem artichokes,
onions, shallots, leeks, garlic, greens,
peppers, or other vegetables

Approximately 1 tablespoon salt (start with a
little less, add if needed after tasting)

Other seasonings as desired, such as
caraway seeds, juniper berries, dill, chili
peppers, ginger, turmeric, dried
cranberries, or whatever you can conjure
in your imagination

Other Ways to Keep Vegetables Submerged

If you don't want to have to manually release pressure by
loosening jar lids daily, there are
alternatives. One is to ferment in
a wide-mouth jar and use a
smaller jar that fits inside the
mouth, filled with water, to
weigh down the ferment. You
can even use a ziplock bag filled
with brine (in case it leaks) to
weigh down a ferment in a jar.
Innovate with materials close at
hand. Recycling centers can be
excellent sources of jars and
other fermentation vessels.

Process:

Prepare the vegetables. Remove the outer leaves of
the cabbage and reserve. Scrub the root vegetables
but do not peel. Chop or grate all vegetables into a
bowl. The purpose of this is to expose surface area
in order to pull water out of the vegetables, so that
they can be submerged under their own juices.
The finer the veggies are shredded, the easier it is
to get juices out, but fineness or coarseness can
vary with excellent results. (Fermenting whole
vegetables or large chunks requires a saltwater
brine; see Brining, page 59.)

Salt and season. Salt the vegetables lightly and add
seasonings as you chop. Sauerkraut does not
require heavy salting. Taste after the next step and
add more salt or seasonings, if desired. It is always
easier to add salt than to remove it. (If you must,
cover the veggies with dechlorinated water, let this
sit for 5 minutes, then pour off the excess water.)

Squeeze the salted vegetables with your hands for a
few minutes (or pound with a blunt tool). This
bruises the vegetables, breaking down cell walls
and enabling them to release their juices. Squeeze
until you can pick up a handful and when you
squeeze, juice releases (as from a wet sponge).

Pack the salted and squeezed vegetables into your
jar. Press the vegetables down with force, using
your fingers or a blunt tool, so that air pockets are
expelled and juice rises up and over the vegetables.
Fill the jar not quite all the way to the top, leaving a
little space for expansion. The vegetables have a
tendency to float to the top of the brine, so it's best to
keep them pressed down, using one of the cabbage's
outer leaves, folded to fit inside the jar, or a carved
chunk of a root vegetable, or a small glass or ceramic
insert. Screw the top on the jar; lactic acid bacteria
are anaerobic and do not need oxygen (though they
can function in the presence of oxygen). However,
be aware that fermentation produces carbon
dioxide, so pressure will build up in the jar and
needs to be released daily, especially the first few
days when fermentation will be most vigorous.

Wait. Be sure to loosen the top to relieve pressure
each day for the first few days. The rate of

fermentation will be faster in a warm environment, slower in a cool one. Some people prefer their krauts lightly fermented for just a few days; others prefer a stronger, more acidic flavor that develops over weeks or months. Taste after just a few days, then a few days later, and at regular intervals to discover what you prefer. Along with the flavor, the texture changes over time, beginning crunchy and gradually softening. Move to the refrigerator if you wish to stop (or rather slow) the fermentation. In a cool environment, kraut can continue fermenting slowly for months. In the summer or in a heated room, its life cycle is more rapid; eventually it can become soft and mushy.

Surface growth. The most common problem that people encounter in fermenting vegetables is surface growth of yeasts and/or molds, facilitated by oxygen. Many books refer to this as "scum," but I prefer to think of it as a bloom. It's a surface phenomenon, a result of contact with the air. If you should encounter surface growth, remove as much of it as you can, along with any discolored or soft kraut from the top layer, and discard. The fermented vegetables beneath will generally look, smell, and taste fine. The surface growth can break up as you remove it, making it impossible to remove all of it. Don't worry.

Enjoy your kraut! I start eating it when the kraut is young and enjoy its evolving flavor over the course of a few weeks (or months in a large batch). Be sure to try the sauerkraut juice that will be left after the kraut is eaten. Sauerkraut juice packs a strong flavor, and is unparalleled as a digestive tonic or hangover cure.

Develop a rhythm. Start a new batch before the previous one runs out. Get a few different flavors or styles going at once for variety. Experiment!

Variations: Add a little fresh vegetable juice or "pot likker" and dispense with the need to squeeze or pound. Incorporate mung bean sprouts . . . hydrated seaweed . . . shredded or quartered brussels sprouts . . . cooked potatoes (mashed, fried, and beyond, but always cooled!) . . . dried or fresh fruit . . . the possibilities are infinite . . .

crock method: information for larger vessels

The jar method is ideal for first learning and small batches, but if you have a garden and are using fermentation as a strategy for preservation for even a few cabbages at once, you'll want a larger vessel. Gallon-size/4-liter jars can be great, or ceramic crocks of various shapes and sizes, or wooden barrels, or plastic buckets or barrels. (See Equipment and Ingredient Basics, page 43, for a discussion of vessels.) Stay away from metallic containers (even stainless steel) because acids corrode them, which of course will negatively affect the ferments.

With a larger vessel, at any scale, the process is exactly the same, in terms of ingredients, proportions, preparation, and time. The only differences are in the vessel itself. In a crock or other larger vessel, it's more important to use a weight to keep the vegetables submerged. I typically use a cylindrical crock without an outer lid. I find a plate that fits inside the crock and let it sit on the vegetables. It's okay if there's a little space between the edge of the plate and the side of the crock. This plate that sits upon the fermenting vegetables is called a follower. You can find ceramic or wooden followers with crocks sometimes. If you custom-cut a hardwood follower, make sure you leave a margin for the wood to expand and for the possibility that the crock edges taper inward. For a weight, I usually use a 1-gallon/4-liter glass bottle filled with water; scrubbed and boiled round river rocks work well, too. Finally, I cover the whole thing with a cloth (generally a piece of an old sheet or towel) to keep flies away. If flies land on the aging kraut, maggots will likely develop. (If you catch them in the early stages, you can remove the top layer and the kraut below is fine to eat; as the maggots develop the brine becomes increasingly funky and eventually quite foul.)

Each time you scoop some kraut out of the crock, you have to repack it carefully. Make sure that the kraut is packed tight in the crock, the surface is level, and the cover and weight are clean. Sometimes water evaporates, so if the kraut is not submerged just add water as necessary. Some people further preserve kraut by canning and heat-processing it. This can be done, but so much of the power of sauerkraut is its aliveness that I wonder: Why kill it?

sauerrüben

A traditional German variant of sauerkraut is sauerrüben, made from turnips. The turnip is a much-maligned and underappreciated vegetable. In fact our local greengrocers, and maybe yours, are sometimes left with softening unsold turnips. I'm always glad to take aging produce off their hands. It is a valuable scavenger mission to rescue food that is past its glorious prime, but still edible and nutritious, before it gets relegated to the compost. Fermenting is a great way to make use of a sudden bounty like this.

I love the sharp, sweet flavor of turnips, and fermentation only intensifies their distinctive flavor. Sauerrüben can also be made from turnip's cousin rutabaga. You can also sour cabbage and turnips together, of course. Mix 'n' match is allowed.

Timeframe: 3 days to 3 months (and beyond)

Vessel: 1-quart/1-liter wide-mouth jar, or a larger jar or crock

Ingredients (for 1 quart/1 liter):

2 pounds/1 kilogram turnips and/or rutabagas
About 1 tablespoon salt (start with a little less, then add to taste)
Other seasonings as desired

Process:

Grate the turnips coarsely or finely, as you prefer.
Salt. Sprinkle the grated turnips with salt as you go. The process will work with more or less salt, so salt to taste.
Add any other vegetables, herbs, or spices you like. Or don't, and enjoy the strong flavor of the turnips unadulterated.
Squeeze or pound, pack into a jar, and get the vegetables submerged as for sauerkraut, page 52. Root vegetables contain more water than cabbage, so it does not take as much work to get them juicy.
Ferment. Release pressure daily and start tasting the sauerrüben after a few days. As time passes, the flavor will get stronger. Enjoy its evolving flavor over days, weeks, or months.

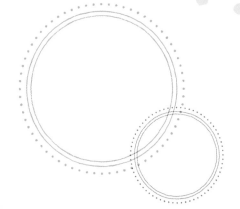

low-salt or salt-free sauerkrauts

Salt is not absolutely necessary for fermenting vegetables. Personally, I think ferments made with even just a tiny bit of salt taste much better and have a far superior texture than those with none; but if you wish to avoid all salt, you can still enjoy fermented vegetables. What salt does is to help establish a selective environment favorable to lactic acid bacteria by inhibiting other bacteria and molds, and slow the enzymes that make vegetables go soft. Even a tiny bit of salt, as little as ½ of 1 percent—1 teaspoon for 2 pounds/1 kilo of vegetables—can bring some of this benefit.

Without salt to provide these functions, salt-free ferments are typically fermented for much shorter periods of time; two or three days is plenty. Taste daily, and refrigerate when your ferment tastes ripe to you. Other mineral-rich ingredients can provide at least a portion of the beneficial functions of salt. Seaweed is an excellent source of minerals; soak seaweed in a little water to rehydrate. Press it under water and squeeze. Chop rehydrated seaweed and add to the ferment along with soaking water. Seeds such as caraway, celery, and dill are also mineral-rich. Celery juice is as well; the best salt-free kraut I have made incorporated celery juice. I juiced a few stalks of celery, diluted the thick juice with an equal quantity of water, and mixed this liquid with vegetables to ferment. In salt-free ferments, some people use the live cultures and acidity of whey, or the acidity of a small proportion of lemon or lime juice, as alternative means of creating selective environments.

Pulling water out of the vegetables—typically facilitated by salt—can be a challenge when fermenting without salt. Vegetables to be fermented without salt need more bruising, by pounding or squeezing, than salted vegetables. It can also help to expose more surface area, chopping vegetables more finely. With or without salt, the primary objective remains the same: to get vegetables submerged under liquid. Add whey or water as necessary. Or cover vegetables with fruit or vegetable juice, or wine for a wine-kraut.

brining

The dry-salting method used for sauerkraut works great when you shred or chop your vegetables, for only with lots of surface area exposed can the salt pull water out of the vegetables in order for them to ferment under their own juices. This results in the most concentrated vegetable flavor, but is impossible with whole vegetables, or large chunks. In this case, you need to cover the vegetables with a saltwater solution known as brine.

You want to mix the brine fairly strong, since it will be diluted by the vegetables that go into it. Although brining proportions vary, 5 percent is a good starting point, meaning 5 percent by weight or 1.6 ounces/50 grams per quart/liter. That translates to about 3 tablespoons of salt per quart/liter, a bit more with fine salt, a bit less with coarse. Stir well for several minutes until the salt is fully dissolved. While 5 percent salt would be extremely salty in sauerkraut, a 5 percent brine yields a much lower-salt product, because once the vegetables go into the brine, they absorb salt and release juices, thereby diluting the salt concentration by more than half.

Estimate required brine quantity as about half the volume of your vessel. Add as little brine as possible to the vegetables, packing them tightly and pressing down under brine. Salt in brine will pull water from the vegetables, and the amount of brine will increase. Salt will diffuse into vegetables gradually. Taste the brine after a day or two and adjust the salt by adding more, if necessary, or adding water if the brine is too salty. A general rule of thumb to consider in salting your ferments: more salt to slow microorganism action in summer heat; less salt in winter when microbial action slows.

Hands-on kraut-making with more than 200 people at Shelburne Farms in Vermont.

sour pickles

Growing up in New York City, experiencing my Jewish heritage largely through food, I developed a taste for sour pickles. These pickles were very different from most of what is sold in stores as pickles, and even what home canners pickle, which are preserved in vinegar. These too are pickles, which encompass anything preserved in an acidic medium, but my idea of a pickle is one fermented in a brine and preserved by lactic rather than acetic acid.

Pickle-making requires close attention. My first attempt at brine-pickling resulted in soft, mushy pickles that were unappealing, because I abandoned the project for a few days, and perhaps because the brine was not salty enough, and because of the heat of the Tennessee summer. And and and. "Our perfection lies in our imperfection." There are, inevitably, fermentation failures. We are dealing with fickle life forces, after all.

I persevered, though, compelled by a craving deep inside me for the yummy garlic-dill sour pickles of Guss's pickle stall on the Lower East Side of Manhattan and Zabar's on the Upper West Side. As it turns out, brine pickles are easy. You just need to keep the fermentation short in summer heat, when cucumbers are most abundant. In a cool (below roughly 65°F/18°C) place they can slowly ferment for weeks or even months. But in a very hot place, they may sour after just a few days and can start getting soft and mushy in less than a week.

One quality prized in a good pickle is crunchiness. It is enzymes activated by heat that break down the crunchiness. Salt slows them down, as do tannins, found on fresh grape leaves (and many others), frequently placed in the jar to help keep pickles crunchy. I recommend using them if you have access to grapevines. I've also had good results using horseradish leaves, sour cherry leaves, oak leaves, and tea bags!

One other variable in pickle-making is cucumber size. I prefer pickles from small to medium cucumbers; pickles from big ones can be tough and often hollow in the middle.

Timeframe: 4 days to 2 weeks, depending upon temperature

Vessel: 1-quart/1-liter jar (or for larger batches a larger jar or ceramic crock)

Ingredients (for 1 quart/1 liter):

1 pound/500 grams small unwaxed pickling cucumbers
1½ tablespoons sea salt
1 or 2 heads fresh flowering dill, or 1–2 tablespoons any form of dill (fresh or dried leaf or seeds)
1–2 heads garlic
1 small handful fresh grape, cherry, oak, and/or horseradish leaves (if available)
1 pinch whole black peppercorns

"Big Larry," the world's largest cucumber, transformed into the world's largest pickle, in Calgary, Alberta, Canada.

Process:

Prepare the cucumbers. Rinse the cucumbers, taking care to not bruise them, and making sure their blossoms are removed. Scrape off any remains at the blossom end. If you're using cucumbers that aren't fresh off the vine that day, soak them for a couple of hours in very cold water to freshen them.

Mix the brine. Dissolve the sea salt in 2 cups/500 milliliters of dechlorinated water to create a brine solution. Stir until the salt is thoroughly dissolved.

Fill the vessel. Clean the vessel, then place at the bottom of it dill, garlic, fresh grape leaves, and black peppercorns. Pack whole cucumbers in the vessel, tightly to help them remain submerged under the brine.

Add the brine. If the brine doesn't cover the cucumbers, add more brine mixed at the same ratio of ¾ tablespoon/12 grams salt to 1 cup/250 milliliters water. If the cucumbers are floating at the surface, an easy solution is to cut a chunk of a bigger cucumber to hold the others down, or to cut the top of a plastic food container a little bigger than the mouth of the jar, squeeze it through the mouth of the jar, and use it to hold the cucumbers submerged. If you're using a crock, use a plate to weigh down the cucumbers, and cover it with a cloth to keep out dust and flies. With a jar, loosely seal the jar with its lid.

Ferment. Leave the pickles until the color of the cucumbers changes from bright green to a duller olive green. Then taste every day or two. Sourness will develop over time, how fast depending primarily upon temperature. If any white surface scum appears, skim it from the surface, but don't worry if you can't get it all. Enjoy the pickles as they continue to ferment. Continue to check them regularly. If they start to get soft, or you don't want them to get any sourer, move them to the fridge.

mixed vegetable crock

The brining process described is not limited to cucumber pickles. Pretty much any vegetable you have in abundance, except for ripe tomatoes (which get soft and lose their form) can be fermented in this way. One memorable crock I made as the first frost was predicted, and we were scurrying to harvest the last of our summer garden, included small yellow summer squash, whole red chili peppers, baby eggplants, green tomatoes, and beans. I also used lots of basil, which gave the pickles and the brine a really unusual, sweet flavor. I especially enjoyed the pickled baby eggplants. They lost some of their dark color to the brine, and were left with a beautiful streaked appearance. Green tomatoes pickle well, especially the fleshy plum varieties.

brined garlic

I am a garlic fanatic. I believe that raw garlic is potent medicine, and I eat it often. As you get to the bottom of your pickle crocks, the garlic and other seasonings that you used will be left, either floating at the top or sunk to the bottom.

I like to collect the garlic pieces from the crock in a jar, cover them with a little of the brine, and keep them, either in the fridge or continuing to ferment on the kitchen counter. The garlic is still pungent, and flavored by all the other delicious vegetables and spices it's been fermenting with. I use this garlic for cooking (or eat it raw). I also like to use the brine, which quickly takes on a strong garlicky flavor, for salad dressings, or straight up in a small glass as a healthful digestive tonic. If this appeals to you, you could also skip the initial vegetable crock and simply brine garlic cloves.

brine as digestive tonic and soup stock

Brine serves not only to provide a salty, watery environment for vegetables to ferment, but also as a medium to meld the flavors of the various spices and vegetables you include in your pickles. The brine itself becomes full of complex flavor as it bubbles. It is also full of lactic acid bacteria, and an excellent digestive tonic.

Chances are, there is more brine left in your crock after you finish your pickles than you could consume raw. It is strong, salty stuff, and there is lots of it. Try using it as a soup stock. In Russian, brine is called *rassol*, and soup with rassol as its base is *rassol'nik*. Dilute brine with water to the level of saltiness you like, then add vegetables (including pickles) and a little tomato paste. Serve hot, with a dollop of sour cream. Pickle brine is also used in cold soups, such as okroshka (see page 165).

milkweed pod/nasturtium bud/radish pod "capers"

Capers are the flower buds of a Mediterranean shrub known as the caper bush (*Capparis spinosa*), which I have not personally encountered. But the delicious savory flavor of capers is largely due to the brining process, and certain other flower buds and seedpods.

My friend Lisa and I were eating capers and talking about how much we like them. In food as in fashion, the small accessories make all the difference. Lisa noticed that pods were just developing on the abundant milkweed plants and had the idea to try brining them. So we mixed up a batch and they were so good; better than capers from caper bushes, I daresay. You can't buy milkweed pods in a store, but it's a weed that's widespread in the United States. The seedpods you want appear in high summer, just after the big flowers fall away. The smaller the pods are when you pick them, the better. They are most suitable for this the first few days after they emerge. As they grow, they get tough and bitter.

Nasturtium flower buds are another great caper alternative, using this same process. Their flavor, like the nasturtium's leaves and flowers, is peppery and slightly hot. Radish seedpods that develop on unharvested radishes offer another "caper" alternative. Taste for tenderness first because they can become woody.

Timeframe: 4 days to several months

Vessel: 1-pint /500-milliliter jar

Ingredients (for 1 pint/ 500 milliliters):

1½ cups/120 grams small milkweed or radish seedpods or nasturtium buds
¾ tablespoon sea salt
1–2 heads garlic

Process:

Harvest the pods. Catch them when they are small and tender. Milkweed pods get very large, fibrous, and bitter. Radish pods get tough.

Mix the brine. Add salt to 1 cup /250 milliliters water. Stir well to dissolve.

Fill the jar. Use a pint/500 milliliter jar and fill it with seedpods and garlic. Pour the brine over them. If the brine doesn't quite cover the pods, add more brine mixed at the same ratio of ¾ tablespoon of salt to 1 cup/250 milliliters water. If the pods float, try holding them down with a small weight, or improvise with a plug from some larger vegetable, either a cabbage leaf or a chunk of cucumber or root. The important thing is to keep the pods, which want to float to the top, under the protection of the brine.

Ferment. Screw the top on the jar to keep flies out, and leave it on the kitchen counter. Remember to release pressure the first few days! Unscrew the top and press down to force any floating pods under the brine. After a few days, taste the "capers" daily. Enjoy them as they ferment, or move to the fridge at any time.

HEAT NO. **3**

GOOD FOOD CONFERENCE

KIMCHI CHALLENGE
OFFICIAL SCORE SHEET

JUDGING CRITERIA (rate on a scale of 1 to 5, 1 = lowest score, 5 = highest score)

CONTESTANT 1

	1	2	3	4	5
TASTE (circle one)	1	2	3	4	5
TEXTURE (circle one)	1	2	3	4	5
APPEARANCE (circle one)	1	2	3	4	5
ORIGINAL USE OF INGREDIENTS (circle one)	1	2	3	4	5

TOTAL SCORE _____

CONTESTANT 4

	1	2	3	4	5
TASTE (circle one)	1	2	3	4	5
TEXTURE (circle one)	1	2	3	4	5
APPEARANCE (circle one)	1	2	3	4	5
ORIGINAL USE OF INGREDIENTS (circle one)	1	2	3	4	5

TOTAL SCORE _____

CONTESTANT 2

	1	2	3	4	5
TASTE (circle one)	1	2	3	4	5
TEXTURE (circle one)	1	2	3	4	5
APPEARANCE (circle one)	1	2	3	4	5
ORIGINAL USE OF INGREDIENTS (circle one)	1	2	3	4	5

TOTAL SCORE _____

CONTESTANT 5

	1	2	3	4	5
TASTE (circle one)	1	2	3	4	5
TEXTURE (circle one)	1	2	3	4	5
APPEARANCE (circle one)	1	2	3	4	5
ORIGINAL USE OF INGREDIENTS (circle one)	1	2	3	4	5

TOTAL SCORE _____

CONTESTANT 3

	1	2	3	4	5
TASTE (circle one)	1	2	3	4	5
TEXTURE (circle one)	1	2	3	4	5
APPEARANCE (circle one)	1	2	3	4	5
ORIGINAL USE OF INGREDIENTS (circle one)	1	2	3	4	5

TOTAL SCORE _____

CONTESTANT 6

	1	2	3	4	5
TASTE (circle one)	1	2	3	4	5
TEXTURE (circle one)	1	2	3	4	5
APPEARANCE (circle one)	1	2	3	4	5
ORIGINAL USE OF INGREDIENTS (circle one)	1	2	3	4	5

TOTAL SCORE _____

kimchi

Kimchi is the Korean name for fermented vegetables, generally spicy, but not always, and made in nearly infinite variety. In certain respects, making kimchi is similar to making sauerkraut. The vegetables are submerged under brine in order to create an environment favorable to lactic acid bacteria present on the vegetables. But whereas in the sauerkraut dry-salting method the juice is pulled out of the vegetables, in kimchi generally the napa cabbage, radishes, and other vegetables are soaked in salty brine for several hours or days to leach bitterness and make them more flexible and thus easier to compress and submerge. Drained vegetables are then mixed with spices, often along with rice paste, sugar, fish sauce, fish, and/or crustaceans. Kimchi is most often spicy, with generous use of garlic, hot chili peppers, ginger, and shallots, scallions, leeks, or onions. Especially when rice paste or sugar is added, kimchi ferments fast, and is often fermented for a shorter time than sauerkraut.

Most Koreans eat kimchi with every meal, frequently several contrasting styles to complement a single meal. Though factory-manufactured kimchi is gaining in popularity (much of it imported from China), home production continues to be very important. It remains customary for employers to give their employees an annual "kimchi bonus" in the autumn so they can purchase the ingredients to make their annual supply. The United Nations Educational, Scientific, and Cultural Organization (UNESCO) has included the making and sharing of kimchi (Kimjang) on its list of the Intangible Cultural Heritage of Humanity.

bæchu (cabbage) kimchi

This is a basic kimchi to illustrate the process. Definitely feel free to experiment with different vegetables and proportions.

Timeframe: 3 days to weeks or months

Vessel: 1-quart/1-liter jar

Ingredients (for 1 quart/1 liter):

6 tablespoons/90 grams sea salt

2 pounds/1 kilogram napa cabbage
(½–1 head)

1 tablespoon rice flour (optional)

2–4 tablespoons (or more!) gochugaru,
Korean chili powder, and/or fresh or
dried chilies

1 bunch scallions or 1 onion or leek or
a few shallots (or more!)

3–4 cloves garlic (or more!)

2 tablespoons (or more!) fresh-grated
gingerroot

Process:

Coarsely chop the cabbage and place it in a bowl or pot, along with any other vegetables you might wish to include, but not the spices.

Mix a strong brine of about 4 cups/1 liter of water and salt. Stir well to thoroughly dissolve the salt. The brine should taste very salty. If you want to use taste as a guide, think seawater.

Pour the brine over the vegetables. Firmly press the vegetables down with your hands a few times to get them submerged. If it seems like there's not quite enough water to cover the vegetables, don't worry; the salt will pull more water out of the vegetables and there will be plenty. Cover the vegetables with a plate, place a full jar or other weight on it, and press firmly every few minutes until the vegetables are fully submerged. Leave the vegetables in their brine on the kitchen counter a few hours or overnight.

Make a paste. This step is optional. It gives kimchi a red pasty saucy quality, but you can make great kimchi without it if you want to keep it simple. In a small saucepan, mix the rice flour with ½ cup/125 milliliters of cold water. Stir thoroughly to dissolve the flour and break up clumps. Gently heat, stirring constantly to prevent burning. Keep stirring as the rice flour mix starts to cook and thicken. Cook for a few minutes until the mix achieves a gluey pastiness, but remains thin enough to pour. If it seems too thick, add a little hot water and stir well. Once it's cooled to body temperature (during which time it will further thicken), mix this with the chili powder into a bright red paste, and then incorporate the rest of the spices described below.

Prepare the spices. Grate the ginger; chop the garlic and onion; remove the seeds from the chilies and chop or crush, or throw them in whole. To make a Korean-style red pasty kimchi, use the Korean-style chili powder. Kimchi can absorb a lot of spice. Experiment with quantities and don't worry too much about them. Mix spices into a paste. If you wish, add a small amount of fish sauce to the spice paste.

Drain the water off the vegetables. Really let them drain, and even press them lightly to force water out. Taste the vegetables for saltiness. That initial salting mostly pulls water out of the vegetables, but not much of it absorbs into them. If you cannot taste salt, add 1–2 teaspoons salt to the spice paste. In the unlikely event that the vegetables are too salty, rinse them.

Mix the vegetables with the spice paste. Mix everything together well.

Pack the kimchi into a jar. Use a clean quart-size (liter) jar. Pack it tightly into the jar, pressing down until paste or liquid rises to cover the vegetables. Fill the jar almost all the way to the top, leaving a little space for expansion. If there is extra spiced vegetable mix, use it to fill a smaller jar. Press down repeatedly to get the vegetables fully submerged. Screw the top on the jar.

Ferment in a visible spot on the kitchen counter. Be sure to loosen the top to relieve pressure each day for the first few days. While you are there, use your (clean!) fingers to push the vegetables back under the brine, and after a few days taste the kimchi. Once it tastes ripe to you, move it to the refrigerator. Or if you have a cellar or other cool spot, ferment kimchi more slowly and for much longer. At the Flack Family Farm in northern Vermont, I enjoyed three-year-old kimchi that had been aging all that time in their cellar.

Crocks of fermenting kimchi in Seoul, South Korea.

Radish Dreaming

One root vegetable, the simple radish, changed my life with a mystical plant communication. It happened while I was briefly hospitalized during February 2000. Earlier that winter, one balmy sunny January day full of the promise of spring, I had decided to plant some radishes. Sowing seeds out of doors that early is largely a symbolic gesture, performed for the sheer life-affirming joy of seeing germination and growth in the winter, since any vegetables that might result are likely to be puny. Predictably enough, the weather turned cold and gray after this sunny day, and I didn't notice any seedlings emerge, so I gave up on the poor radishes and forgot about them. Meanwhile, I was feeling a bizarre internal sensation in my abdomen, and landed in the hospital.

Such a contrast to my life in the woods, outdoors most of the time, the hospital is a totally denatured environment. The windows are sealed shut, everything is white and antiseptic, the food is all ultra-processed, and they fed me chemicals through my mouth, my veins, and even my anus. I was feeling scared and just wanted to go home, when one night in my dreams the radishes came to comfort me and I woke up with a vivid image of the radishes I had planted germinating. It was very real. I felt like I had received a plant communication.

The day I was released from the hospital, I arrived home late in the afternoon and didn't make it out to the garden. I asked my garden co-conspirators whether they had noticed the radishes up, and they hadn't. Oh well, it was just a dream, I thought. The next morning, I made it out to the garden and, lo and behold, the radishes had germinated. Delicate, pert, tiny seedlings defied the elements to reach toward the sun with their potent life force. As I recuperated, radishes became one of my plant totems, and they continue so to this day: so easy to grow, sharp, tangy, in so many different colors and shapes. Radishes came to offer me hope at a frightening time, and to remind me how versatile plant allies can be.

radish and root kimchi

I have a strong affinity for roots. I am awed by their strength, growing deep into the earth. Some roots are gnarled, turning this way and that around rocks in their relentless search for water and nutrients in the soil. Others exhibit glamorous curves and showy colors. Their flavors are varied and in some cases extreme.

Korea has a tradition of radish (*moo*) kimchi. Turnips are also found in Korean recipes. Beyond tradition, I add others; you can make kimchi by fermenting any vegetables you like with the classic kimchi quartet of garlic, hot pepper, ginger, and onion (in any of its forms). In this kimchi, I add grated horseradish roots, which blend with and complement the traditional heating spices.

Some of the roots referenced in this recipe may be unfamiliar. Burdock (*Arctium lappa*) is a common weed, nutritious and delicious, with a flavor I think of as earthy; it's used widely in Japanese cuisine, where it is known as *gobo*. Burdock is also a powerful medicinal plant, stimulating lymphatic flows and tonifying the organs of elimination: skin, kidneys, and liver. "Burdock nourishes the most extreme, buried, and far-reaching aspects of ourselves," writes herbalist Susun S. Weed. "Burdock breaks the ground for deep transformation."[1]

Many health food stores sell fresh burdock roots. I harvest it from around my house, where I dispersed seeds just a couple of times, to get multiple generations going. Burdock is biennial. If you harvest your own, make sure you dig first-year roots, which is to say plants with the leaves all growing from the ground level. The second year, when it grows tall and develops the notorious burrs that cling to dogs and people, for which the plant is named, the roots become woody and tasteless.

Jerusalem artichokes, also called sunchokes (*Helianthus tuberosus*), are nothing like artichokes. They are knobby tubers in the sunflower family, native to the eastern United States, with a fresh, crunchy taste reminiscent of water chestnuts. Jerusalem artichokes are not widely available beyond farmers markets and organic shops. They are one of the easiest things you can grow. Once you plant them, they keep coming back year after year.

Meaghan Carpenter harvesting daikon radishes at Long Hungry Creek Farm in Red Boiling Springs, Tennessee.

Timeframe: 3 days to weeks or months

Vessel: 1-quart/1-liter jar

Ingredients (for 1 quart/1 liter):

Sea salt

2 pounds/1 kilogram root vegetables; at least half daikon or any variety of radishes, and/or any kind of turnips; which may be supplemented by carrots, Jerusalem artichokes, and burdock roots; of course cabbages, cucumbers, and other types of vegetables can be incorporated as well

1 tablespoon rice flour (optional)

2–4 tablespoons (or more!) gochugaru, Korean chili powder, and/or fresh or dried chilies

1 bunch scallions or 1 onion or leek or a few shallots (or more!)

3–4 cloves garlic (or more!)

2 tablespoons (or more!) fresh-grated gingerroot

1 small fresh horseradish root (or 1 tablespoon prepared horseradish, without preservatives)

Process:

Slice the roots. Scrub them well, but unless they're too tough, leave the skins on. Slice thin or chunky, as you like. Leave some smaller roots whole, even with their greens attached.

Continue with the basic kimchi process from the previous recipe (Bæchu Kimchi), soaking the vegetables in brine, mixing a spice mixture (add grated horseradish to the spice paste), packing it all into the jar, and fermenting.

fruit kimchi

A Tennessee neighbor of mine, Nancy Ramsay, spent many years living in Korea and told me about fruit kimchi. My method is improvisational, based on her description. The sweet fruit contrasts beautifully with the spicy and sour kimchi flavors, and makes for a surprising and bold taste sensation. If you ferment it for too long, the sweetness of the fruit all turns into acidity and you lose the dramatic contrast.

Timeframe: 3 to 5 days

Vessel: 1-quart/1-liter jar

Ingredients (for 1 quart/1 liter):

1 pound/500 grams napa cabbage, daikon radish, and/or other vegetables

Sea salt

1 tablespoon rice flour (optional)

2–4 tablespoons (or more!) gochugaru, Korean chili powder, and/or fresh or dried chilies

1 bunch scallions or 1 onion or leek or a few shallots (or more!)

3–4 cloves garlic (or more!)

2 tablespoons (or more!) fresh-grated gingerroot

Juice of 1 lemon

1 pound/500 grams fruit such as berries and/or plums, pears, grapes, pineapple

Process:

Coarsely chop the vegetables, but not the fruit or spices, and place in a bowl or pot.

Mix a brine of about 2 cups/500 milliliters water and 3 tablespoons salt. Stir well to thoroughly dissolve the salt.

Continue with the basic kimchi process from Bæchu Kimchi, page 68. Add lemon juice to the spice paste. Use any kind of fruit. Peel if the skin is inedible or tough. Chop larger fruit into bite-size pieces. Leave small berries whole. Add nuts if you wish. Mix everything together well and pack into a jar.

Ferment in a visible spot on the kitchen counter. Be sure to loosen the top to relieve pressure each day for the first few days.

Enjoy fruit kimchi young and refrigerate after a few days to enjoy the sweetness of the fruit before it ferments away.

Beyond types of vegetables, seasonings, and level of salinity, shape and color are important variables in fermented vegetables. These gorgeous beets were fermented by Happy Girl Kitchen Co. in California.

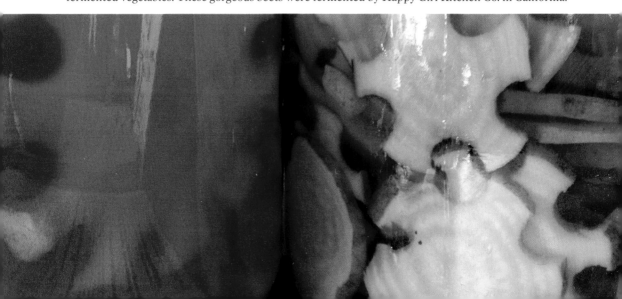

gundruk

Gundruk is a strong and delicious pickle made from vegetable greens traditional in the Himalayan mountains. What distinguishes this ferment is that its sole ingredient is the vegetable itself, greens. No salt or any other ingredient is used. The greens can be turnip greens, mustard greens, kale, collards, or any hardy green in the Brassica family. I originally learned about gundruk from books, and not until I was working on this revision in 2015 did I encounter it outside my own kitchen, when I tasted delicious gundruk made by Bhutanese gardeners who are part of the Tennessee Refugee Agricultural Partnership Program, and learned how they make it.

Timeframe: Weeks

Vessel: 1-quart/1-liter jar with screw top

Ingredients (for 1 quart/1 liter):

Greens, about 2½ pounds/1.25 kilograms

Process:

Wilt the greens in the sun. Start on a sunny day. Set the greens in the sun for at least a few hours so they wilt.

Chop the wilted greens. Then squeeze with your hands for a few minutes (or pound with a blunt tool). This bruises the greens, breaking down cell walls and enabling them to release their juices.

Pack into a jar. Stuff the juicy leaves into a jar. Use your fingers or a blunt tool to compress the greens in the jar and force more crushed greens in; this will force juice out of them. You may be surprised how great a volume of greens can be squeezed into a small jar. Keep stuffing greens in and pressing down with force until the jar is full and the greens are covered with liquid. The liquid is pungent Brassica juice.

Seal tightly in the jar. Don't worry if the liquid absorbs into the greens and they do not remain submerged.

Ferment in a warm sunny place for two weeks or longer. After a couple of weeks, open the jar and smell the greens. They should smell and taste sharp. Gundruk packs a lot of flavor!

Dry. Gundruk is generally dried for storage and use over the course of a long winter. Spread the fermented greens out on a rack, mat, or clean piece of cardboard, and set in the sun or in a warm dry spot. As the greens dry, mix them occasionally to expose different surfaces and make sure they all dry evenly. Once they are thoroughly dried, they may be stored in a jar or other airtight container.

How to use gundruk. Add gundruk to soups, as it is used throughout winter in the Himalayas. Try it as a chewy delicious probiotic snack, raw, too.

japanese nuka bran pickles

Nuka is a traditional Japanese pickle in which vegetables are buried in a paste of rice bran and water, along with salt, kombu seaweed, ginger, miso, and sometimes saké or beer, shiitake mushrooms, mustard, chili pepper, or other flavor embellishments. Each nuka pot is unique, but in this rich medium, the pickles develop deep complex flavors with hints of all these elements. In a mature nuka pot, vegetables can be pickled in mere hours.

Bran is the fibrous outer layer milled off grains to produce the white versions. Rice bran is traditional in Japan, but wheat bran works similarly as a pickling medium. The bran pickling medium takes a week or longer to get going. But once you develop a nuka bed, you can potentially keep adding and harvesting vegetables indefinitely.

This recipe is based on 1 pound/500 grams of bran, which will barely half fill a 1-gallon/4-liter vessel. It is important to leave lots of space in the vessel to make stirring easy, because frequent (at least daily) stirring is essential to the development and ongoing health and flavor of the nuka medium.

Timeframe: 1 week, then ongoing

Equipment:

Ceramic crock, wide squat jar, or food-grade plastic bucket of at least 1-gallon/ 4-liter capacity
Cloth cover for vessel

Ingredients (for a 1-gallon/ 4-liter vessel):

4 cups/500 grams rice (or wheat) bran
2 4-inch/10-centimeter strips kombu seaweed
1 dried or fresh shiitake mushroom (optional)
2 tablespoons sea salt
2 tablespoons miso
¼ cup/60 milliliters beer or saké (optional)
1 tablespoon powdered mustard
1-inch/2.5-centimeter/10-gram piece of gingerroot, cut into a few chunky pieces
Turnips, carrots, radishes, peas, green beans, cucumbers, or other seasonal vegetables

Process:

Dry-roast the bran in a cast-iron or other heavy skillet. Use a low flame and stir frequently to avoid burning. Roasting brings out the flavor of the bran, but it is not essential to the process. Roast until the bran feels hot and you can smell a pleasant toasted aroma. Allow to cool.

Hydrate the seaweed. Pour ½ cup/125 milliliters boiling water over the seaweed and dried shiitake (if using). Make sure they are fully submerged, and allow them to hydrate for about 30 minutes.

Mix the brine. Drain the seaweed-and-mushroom-soaking water into a measuring cup, putting aside the seaweed and mushroom. Mix in the salt. Stir well to completely dissolve the salt. Mix in the miso, smoothing any chunks. Add beer or saké if desired. Add a little water if needed to bring the total volume of liquid to 1 cup/250 milliliters.

Combine into a crock. Start with the toasted bran. Add the mustard powder and mix. Chop the mushroom into a few big pieces and add to the crock. Add the seaweed strips, ginger chunks, and brine and mix well with your hands, making sure the liquid is evenly distributed, without pockets of dry bran. The texture we are aiming for is a stiff paste that can be formed when squeezed but remains dry enough to be a little crumbly. This is the base of your nuka bed, ready for cultivation.

Develop the nuka bed. For the first week, each day bury one or two small whole vegetables (or chunks of larger ones) in the nuka bed and remove the vegetables from the day before. The bran medium is just developing, and fresh vegetables help build its microbial ecology. So do your hands! Use your clean bare hands to mix the bran well with each change of vegetables. Make sure the vegetables are not touching one another. The vegetables you remove at this early stage may taste good or not. Most recipes say to discard them, but I've enjoyed some. Taste them and see. Keep replacing the vegetables daily until they start to have a strong, pleasant, complex flavor. Then your nuka bed is ready to make nuka pickles.

Pickling in the nuka bed. Once mature, your nuka bed can pickle more than one or two vegetables at a time. The important thing is that they be packed loosely enough so that the vegetables do not touch. Depending on the vegetable, you might be able to bury about ½ pound/250 grams in a bed of this scale. Add more of everything if you want to scale up. Leave small vegetables whole; cut larger vegetables into chunks, but large enough that you will not lose them in the nuka paste. Before vegetables are buried in a nuka pot, they are generally salt-rubbed. With a little salt in the palm of one hand, roll the vegetable around in the salt for a moment, rubbing its skin with the abrasive salt. This little salt massage begins the breaking down of the skin of the vegetable and the release of fluids. If this causes any foamy white release from the vegetables

Judgment time: This plate of numbered pickles await tasting and evaluation while I judge a pickle contest at the Boston Fermentation Festival in 2014. (My problem is that almost all of them taste great to me!)

(for instance, cucumbers), rinse them before burying in the pickling medium. Pickle vegetables in the nuka for as little as a few hours (especially in hot weather) or for a day or several. Nuka is not typically a method for long-term preservation, and in fact the health of the nuka bed depends upon frequent stirring and fresh vegetables. When removing vegetables, brush as much bran as possible off the vegetables back into the crock. Then rinse or not (I prefer not), slice, and serve.

Nuka maintenance. Your nuka bran pickling medium can be used in perpetuity. It will stay healthiest if mixed by hand daily, or nearly so. If it gets too liquid as it absorbs water from fresh vegetables, or if the volume of bran seems to be reducing, add some more toasted bran. Salt migrates out with the vegetables, and needs to be replenished to maintain a pickle-friendly environment. Add more salt as you rub the vegetables, and add more if the flavor needs it. Enjoy the ginger and seaweed as pickles after a while. Add more ginger, seaweed, miso, mustard, beer, and saké, occasionally and in small amounts. If you go away, move the nuka bed to a plastic bag or other airtight container, store in a refrigerator, and pamper it when you return.

beet kvass (and other fermented vegetable infusions)

Beet kvass is a Ukrainian fermented infusion of beets in water, lightly salted. It and related fermented vegetable infusions represent the far end of a spectrum of vegetable:water ratios used in fermentation. At the other end is sauerkraut and the dry-salting method, where no water is added. In between are brined vegetables, where water is added, but as little as possible so as to minimize dilution of the flavor of the vegetables. In the case of these infusions, we use much more water than vegetables, and the liquid, flavored by the vegetables and lactic acid from fermentation, is the final product, while the vegetables end up being nearly tasteless. (Compost them, feed them to animals, or incorporate them into food.)

I usually make beet kvass in a quart/liter jar. Chop a large beet or several small ones into ½-inch/1-centimeter cubes, filling the jar just a quarter to a third of the way. Augment with horseradish root (yum!), ginger, garlic, turnips, or as you wish. Cover with water to mostly fill the jar. Add a pinch of salt. Some people add a little whey or sauerkraut juice as a starter, but the raw vegetables have all the necessary

bacteria. Ferment a few days; exactly how many days depends upon temperature, specific ingredients and ratios, microbial ecology, and flavor preferences. Taste daily. When it starts to develop a deep, dark color and a pleasing strength, strain out the beets. You can enjoy beet kvass just like that, as a beverage; use it as a base for borscht; or lightly carbonate it by transferring the liquid to a sealable vessel that can hold a little pressure, sealing, and leaving a day more at room temperature.

Another fermented vegetable infusion is known as cultured cabbage "juice."

To make it, fill a blender with chopped cabbage, then cover the cabbage with water, until the blender is about two-thirds full with water. Blend into a slurry and pour into a jar. Repeat a few times for a larger batch. Add a pinch of salt, cover, and ferment a few days, tasting daily. When it tastes ripe, strain out the cabbage. The liquid is cultured cabbage "juice."

Kaanji is a delicious spicy Punjabi beverage made by fermenting carrots and mustard seeds in water with salt. Recipes call for burgundy-colored carrots; if you don't have those, try adding a beet to your carrots. Slice vegetables into matchsticks. Use about ¼ pound/125 grams vegetables and 3 tablespoons mustard seeds (whole or ground), along with 1 tablespoon salt for a quart/liter. Ferment in a covered vessel in a warm spot for about a week, then strain and enjoy. *Salgam suyu* is yet another example, from Turkey, the sour and salty brine of fermented purple carrots and turnips.

How to Integrate Fermented Vegetables into Your Meals

For many people, the big challenge with fermented vegetables is less how to make them than how to use them. My own feeling is that sauerkraut, kimchi, pickles, and other fermented vegetables go with almost anything. They are a side accent that embellishes often plainer and more substantial foods. I generally think of them as condiments.

Start with breakfast. Fermented vegetables with butter or peanut butter(!) or alone on toast. With eggs. In oatmeal or congee (Chinese soupy rice) or fermented millet porridge, with other savories rather than sweets. On a grilled cheese sandwich or quesadilla. Or any kind of sandwich. On a burger or pizza or burrito or salad. Whatever your everyday food consists of, fermented vegetables can adorn and improve it.

I have emphasized eating fermented vegetables raw, because I believe that their most profound nutritional benefit is the live bacterial cultures in them, which are destroyed by cooking. Yet in the culinary traditions in which they evolved, fermented vegetables are frequently used in cooking as well, with delicious results. Some of the classics I have enjoyed are Polish bigos, meat marinated and cooked in sauerkraut; sizzling hot kimchi jjigae (stew); and sauerkraut pierogi. Eat most of your fermented vegetables raw, but don't be afraid to cook with them and experiment!

Sauerkraut, kimchi, pickles, and their juices can be easily incorporated into salad dressings, sauces, and spreads. Use finely minced fermented veggies and/or juice. Both have strong flavor, and sometimes just a very small amount is perfect.

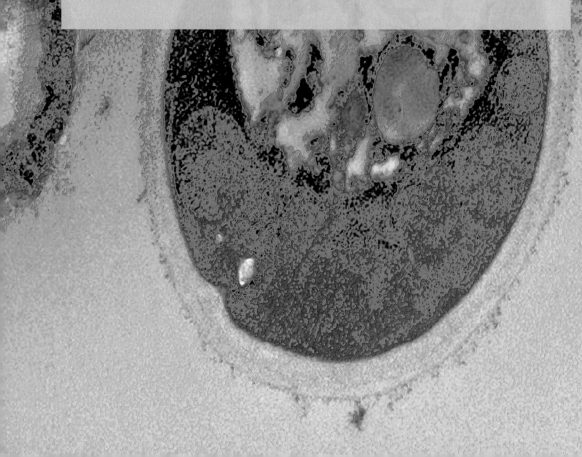

choucroute fromage roulades

These are a fun way to serve sauerkraut at a party, as finger food wrapped, with cheese, in soured whole cabbage leaves. I gave them this French name because I love the French word for "sauerkraut," *choucroute* (pronounced *shoo-kroot*), and because I first created them for my friend Jocelyn's annual Bastille Day party.

Make sauerkraut with the following modification: Peel the leaves off the cabbage until the central section that remains can fit through the mouth of your vessel. Shred the leaves you removed, and lightly salt. Use a knife to carefully remove the cylindrical core of the cabbage, so that juices will be able to penetrate to the center. Shred the core and mix with the salted leaves. Pack the vessel so that the head of cabbage is embedded in juicy shredded cabbage, all submerged, and ferment as for the basic kraut recipe, page 51.

After one to two weeks, remove the head(s) of cabbage. Carefully peel off individual cabbage leaves. In each leaf place a small portion of sauerkraut and some crumbled feta, chèvre, or other cheese, then roll the leaf and insert a toothpick to hold.

Further Reading

Centre Terre Vivante. *Preserving Food Without Freezing or Canning: Traditional Techniques Using Salt, Oil, Sugar, Alcohol, Vinegar, Drying, Cold Storage, and Lactic Fermentation.* White River Junction, VT: Chelsea Green Publishing, 2007.

Chun, Lauryn, with Olga Massov. *The Kimchi Cookbook.* Berkeley, CA: Ten Speed Press, 2012.

Feifer, Amanda. *Ferment Your Vegetables: A Fun and Flavorful Guide to Making Your Own Pickles, Kimchi, Kraut, and More.* Beverly, MA: Fair Winds Press, 2015.

Hachisu, Nancy Singleton. *Preserving the Japanese Way: Traditions of Salting, Fermenting, and Pickling for the Modern Kitchen.* Kansas City, MO: Andrews McMeel Publishing, 2015.

Hisamatsu, Ikuko. *Quick and Easy Tsukemono: Japanese Pickling Recipes.* Tokyo: Japan Publications, 2005.

Man-Jo, Kim, Lee Kyou-Tae, and Lee O-Young. *The Kimchee Cookbook: Fiery Flavors and Cultural History of Korea's National Dish.* Singapore: Periplus Editions, 1999.

O'Brien, Julie, and Richard J. Climenhage. *Fresh and Fermented: 85 Delicious Ways to Make Fermented Carrots, Kraut, and Kimchi Part of Every Meal.* Seattle, WA: Sasquatch Books, 2014.

Shockey, Kristen K., and Christopher Shockey. *Fermented Vegetables: Creative Recipes for Fermenting 64 Vegetables and Herbs in Krauts, Kimchis, Brined Pickles, Chutneys, Relishes and Pastes.* North Adams, MA: Storey Publishing, 2014.

Solomon, Karen. *Asian Pickles.* Berkeley, CA: Ten Speed Press, 2014.

Shimizu, Kay. *Tsukemono: Japanese Pickled Vegetables.* Tokyo: Shufunotomo, 1993.

6: lightly fermented beverages

Lightly fermented soft drinks can be made in nearly infinite variation. They are found in disparate traditional forms, and lend themselves to experimentation and creativity. Properly bottled to trap carbon dioxide, they are naturally carbonated, probiotic sodas, and they can be made in any flavor you could imagine, quite literally.

I have organized this chapter by different types of starters, then illustrate each starter with a recipe or two. You can largely mix and match starters and flavors. Experiment and find the approach that works best for you!

A note on alcohol: These lightly fermented beverages can have small amounts of alcohol, in most cases exceedingly small and insignificant, but sometimes stronger. None of them have enough alcohol to be considered alcoholic beverages, but if you wish to minimize alcohol content, ferment for as short a time as possible and/or in open vessels that allow for aerobic bacteria to metabolize alcohol into vinegar.

Kombucha fermenting in ceramic crocks at the Urban Farm Fermentory in Portland, Maine.

bottling and carbonation

These beverages may be carbonated, if desired. Carbonation is the release of trapped carbon dioxide. If you wish to carbonate these beverages, wait until fermentation is actively progressing (as evidenced by vigorous bubbling), then transfer and seal the beverage in bottles that can hold some pressure. Then let the bottles ferment, but only for a short time—in some cases measured in hours, depending upon temperature and level of fermentation activity. Refrigerate and enjoy.

Carbonating sweet beverages can be dangerous! It is imperative that you understand this. An active ferment, still sweet with lots of fermentable sugars, and trapped in a bottle, has the potential to explode. Bottling must be done with care and attention. Moderate carbonation enhances and enlivens these beverages. High-pressure carbonation can result in wasted beverages, a big mess, and dangerously explosive bottles.

It is difficult to gauge the pressure of glass bottles. One old way is to add a few raisins to each bottle you are seeking to carbonate; as the contents of the bottle carbonate, the raisins float to the top. My usual method is to bottle these still-sweet fermenting beverages mostly in plastic soda bottles. Even if I bottle most of them in glass, I bottle some in plastic. The benefit of plastic bottles is that you can feel how pressurized they have become by squeezing the bottle. If the plastic easily yields, it has not pressurized; if it is firm and resists pressing in, it has pressurized and should be refrigerated before more pressure builds, or enjoyed quickly.

Chill bottles before opening, and open them over a clean bowl in a sink so the bowl can catch at least some of the beverage if they spew. Begin by opening a bottle gradually, and if you see a large quantity of foam start to rise, screw the cap back down and wait a moment. Then begin to open again, and as foam rises tightly close. Repeat this process a few times, until the beverage is no longer so pressurized, and you can open without spewing.

starter: wild fermentation

The simplest starter for a lightly fermented beverage is wild fermentation, if you are using raw fruit or other microbe-rich raw ingredients. In this case there is no need to introduce a starter. As in fermenting raw vegetables, all the starter you need is on the fruit you are fermenting, and it will quickly permeate the mixture. My most important advice: Stir, stir, stir!

strawberry kvass

In the previous chapter we encountered beet kvass (page 78), a fermented infusion of beets in water. This is a fermented infusion of strawberries in water, with sugar. In a salty environment with vegetables, lactic acid bacteria dominate the fermentation, but in a sugary solution with fruit, yeasts thrive.

Strawberry kvass is fruity and delicious, great as a soft drink or as a cocktail mixer. Try varying it with cherries, raspberries, blueberries, mulberries, or other berries.

Timeframe: 3 to 5 days

Vessel: 1-gallon/4-liter (or larger) ceramic crock, bowl, wide-mouth jar, or food-grade plastic bucket with lid or cloth cover

Ingredients (for 2 quarts/ 2 liters):

2 pounds/1 kilogram (1 quart/1 liter) strawberries (or more if you have a great abundance!)

½ cup/125 grams sugar (any form)

Process:

Clean the strawberries. Gently rinse the berries and pick over them to remove any that are unripe or decomposing. Place the berries in your vessel.

Mix the sugar solution. Measure about 6 cups/1.5 liters of dechlorinated water. Add the sugar to the water and stir well to dissolve. Taste and add more sugar if you like it sweet.

Pour the sugar solution over the berries. The vessel should only be about half full, with plenty of room to stir vigorously.

Cover the vessel.

Ferment.

Stir—as often as you think of it, at least two to three times per day. Stir vigorously around the sides and try to form a vortex in the middle. A vortex aerates the water, and the stirring distributes activity and gets floating fruit submerged. Without stirring, the fruit may mold and fermentation will develop more slowly.

Observe. After a few days, you will begin to notice bubbles. Keep stirring and they will get more active. By the time bubbling is vigorous the color has changed, the berries have shrunk, and the liquid has a strong fruity flavor and aroma.

Enjoy strawberry kvass either strained, with still-flavorful fruit on the side, or with the berries still in.

starter: ginger bug

Ginger bug is a starter relying upon the yeasts and bacteria found in ginger. Be sure to use organic ginger (or homegrown!), since imported ginger is often irradiated, destroying its effectiveness as a starter, and organic standards prohibit irradiation. The ginger bug is simply water, sugar, and grated ginger, which starts actively fermenting within a couple of days.

Timeframe: 1 to 3 days

Vessel: 1-pint/500 ml jar or small bowl

Ingredients:

2 inches/5 centimeters/20 grams or more fresh organic gingerroot
¼ cup/60 grams sugar

Process:

Grate the ginger, skin and all. Start with 1 inch/2.5 centimeters/10 grams the first day and add the rest later.

Combine. Add the grated ginger and 2 tablespoons sugar to 1 cup/250 milliliters of water. Stir well. Cover with cloth to allow free circulation of air while keeping flies out.

Ferment in a warm spot.

Stir at least a few times a day or as often as you can, until the bug gets bubbly, in 2 to 4 days.

Feed the bug more ginger and sugar. Add another 1 inch/2.5 centimeters/10 grams gingerroot, grated, and another 2 tablespoons sugar, and stir. Feed bug every day or two until you are ready to make ginger beer.

Make ginger beer (see the next recipe) anytime after the bug becomes active. If you wait more than a couple of days, keep feeding the bug fresh ginger and sugar every 2 days to keep it healthy and vigorous. Ginger bug is a great starter for other types of root and bark beers, as well. A similar starter can be made using fresh turmeric roots.

ginger beer

Ginger beer is a soft drink, typically fermented just long enough to create carbonation but not enough to contribute any appreciable level of alcohol. It can range from spicy to mild, and if it is mild, many kids love it. Ginger beer could certainly be made entirely in the manner of the ginger bug, above. The most compelling reason to do a two-step process like this is that you get the fullest extraction of flavor from the ginger when you boil it, then add sweetener and cool it off before adding the already bubbly ginger bug.

Timeframe: 2 to 5 days after ginger bug is active

Equipment:

1-gallon/4-liter (or larger) ceramic crock, bowl, wide-mouth jar, or food-grade plastic bucket with lid or cloth cover
Plastic soda bottles or other sealable bottles for bottling

Ingredients (for 1 gallon/ 4 liters):

4 inches/10 centimeters/40 grams fresh gingerroot for a very mild ginger flavor (up to 12 inches/30 centimeters/120 grams or more for an intense ginger flavor)
1½ cups/375 grams sugar
2 lemons, juiced

Process:

Starter. Make sure the ginger bug is bubbly. Add 1 teaspoon of sugar and give it a good stir.

Boil 2 quarts/2 liters of water.

Grate the gingerroot and add it to the pot of boiling water. Reduce the heat.

Simmer for about 30 minutes.

Strain out the ginger, add the sugar, stir to dissolve, and add the lemon juice.

Add cold water to make 1 gallon/4 liters.

Add the strained ginger bug. (If you intend to make this process an ongoing rhythm, reserve a few tablespoons of the active bug as a starter and replenish it with additional water, grated ginger, and sugar.)

Ferment in a crock, jar, or bucket for about 24 hours, stirring frequently. If it doesn't seem bubbly after 24 hours, add a few slices of raw ginger and stir for another day or two until bubbly.

Bottle in sealable bottles.

Ferment in bottles in a warm spot for a day or a few depending upon temperature. The best way I know to monitor carbonation is bottling in plastic soda bottles, as described in Bottling and Carbonation, page 85.

Chill the bottles once they're pressurized.

starter: whey

Whey is the thin liquid that separates from curds when milk curdles or sours. Various factors can make milk form curds. Adding vinegar or lemon juice to hot milk makes it curdle. Rennet, a complex of enzymes used widely in cheesemaking, makes curds that can be manipulated in myriad ways. Yogurt is also a curd, and as it ages and further acidifies the yogurt releases more whey. Kefir, too, curdles as it acidifies.

The whey of yogurt, kefir, and raw milk cheeses is populated by elaborate microbial communities and can be used as a starter to get all sorts of other things to ferment, from mashed potatoes to ketchup. Sally Fallon's cookbook *Nourishing Traditions* has lots of great ideas for fermenting with whey (including Sweet Potato Fly, the next recipe). For carbonated beverages, the most vigorously active whey starter is from kefir (dairy), because the kefir community includes yeasts as well as lactic acid bacteria (see page 118). In the first day of fermentation, kefir typically does not curdle, but after 2 or 3 days it does, with milk fats and solids floating to the top; gently pour some off the whey that it's floating in. To get whey from yogurt, hang it as described for labneh, page 114, and collect the whey that drips from it.

Many regions of the world feature traditional, lightly fermented beverages. Here, a vendor at a St. Croix outdoor market is selling the beverage she brews—delicious, bittersweet mauby, popular on many Caribbean islands.

sweet potato fly

Sweet Potato Fly, from Guyana, is sweet, light, and fruity, with only a mild tartness. Eggshell is an ingredient that serves to neutralize the lactic acid produced by the fermentation. Sweet potato fly appeals to kids and other folks who mostly don't like fermented flavors.

Timeframe: 3 to 5 days

Vessel: 1-gallon/4-liter (or larger) ceramic crock, bowl, wide-mouth jar, or food-grade plastic bucket with lid or cloth cover

Ingredients (for ½ gallon/ 2 liters):

1 large sweet potato or 2 small ones (1 pound/500grams)
1 cup/250 grams sugar
¼ cup/60 milliliters whey
1 lemon
1 teaspoon powdered mace
Cinnamon
Nutmeg
1 eggshell

Process:

Grate the sweet potatoes.

Remove the starch. Cover the grated sweet potato with water; swirl it in the water for a moment; drain; and rinse. Repeat until the water runs clear.

Combine. In your fermentation vessel, combine the grated sweet potatoes, ½ gallon/2 liters of water, the sugar, the whey, the juice and zest of the lemon, the mace, and a pinch each of cinnamon and nutmeg. Crush the cleaned eggshell into the mixture. Stir and cover.

Ferment in a warm spot until bubbly, about 2 to 3 days.

Strain out the spent solids and discard or use in pancakes, bread, or other cooking.

Bottle in sealable bottles.

Ferment the bottles in a warm spot for a day or a few depending upon temperature. The best way I know to monitor carbonation is bottling in plastic soda bottles, as described in Bottling and Carbonation, page 85.

Chill before opening and serving.

KOMBUCHA

5/25, tea added 6/3

starter: kombucha

Kombucha is sugar-sweetened tea fermented into a delicious sour tonic beverage, sometimes compared to sparkling apple cider. Kombucha can be enjoyed like this or used as a starter for a secondary fermentation process with fruit juice or other flavorings. Kombucha is produced by a SCOBY, or symbiotic community of bacteria and yeast, also known as the *mother* of kombucha, that takes the form of a rubbery disk, which floats on the surface of the tea as it ferments.

No other ferment even approaches kombucha in terms of its sudden dramatic popularity (at least in the United States). I first tried kombucha around 1994, when my friend Spree, a fellow long-term AIDS survivor, who was dealing with a major health crisis at the time, got caught up in the kombucha craze for its promised immune-stimulating benefits. Soon she had more mother than she knew what to do with (it grows a new layer and thickens with each batch), and started getting everyone to try it and take home a mother. In those days, kombucha spread exclusively through such grassroots channels as enthusiasts grew more and more mothers and sought to share them.

The grassroots kombucha craze gave way to an industry, with US sales estimated around half a billion dollars in 2015. Along the way, there has been a lot of hype and unsubstantiated claims. We cannot expect foods to be panaceas. And yet, that they are not does not diminish their potential benefits. Like any ferment, kombucha contains unique metabolic by-products and living bacterial cultures. Try some, starting with small servings, and see how it tastes and feels to you.

If you like it, kombucha is easy and fun to make. The only tricky part is finding a mother. Ask around and look on the Internet. They are available from other users through several online exchanges, as well as for sale. (See the appendix.)

Kombucha is traditionally made with tea, meaning an infusion of the tea plant (*Camellia sinensis*), not the teas of other plants (such as chamomile or mint). You may use black, green, or other styles of tea, but in general stay away from heavily flavored or scented teas. That said, I have had fine kombucha brewed without any tea at all, made with a hibiscus infusion, or apple juice, or coffee. Definitely experiment: Your kombucha mother might have great adaptive potential. But it might not, so don't experiment with your only mother! Test with a layer of the mother, and consider adapting gradually, with half and half before a full switchover, or even more gradually. You may use tea bags

or loose tea, and brew the tea strong or weak, as you like. I typically brew a strong concentrate, then dilute and cool it by adding water, so I can add the SCOBY without having to wait for the tea to cool.

To sweeten the tea, add sugar. Sweeten to taste, bearing in mind that some of the sugar will ferment into acids and the mature kombucha will be considerably less sweet than the mixture you start with. Some people have reported excellent results making kombucha with honey, agave, maple syrup, barley malt, fruit juice, and other sweeteners; my friend Brett Love made kombucha from his favorite soft drink, Mountain Dew. Fermentation processes can be very versatile, but not always. I've heard many reports of people switching kombucha sweetener then having their SCOBYs sink and die. As with tea base, use just one layer of the SCOBY to experiment, while maintaining the other in the traditional sugar medium. Try for a few generations, to make sure the mother grows and continues to thrive.

Timeframe: About 7 to 10 days

Vessel: 1-gallon/4-liter (or larger) ceramic crock, bowl, wide-mouth jar, or food-grade plastic bucket with loose lid or cloth cover. It's best to use something broad and not fill it all the way; kombucha needs adequate surface area and works best if the diameter of the container is greater than the depth of the liquid.

Ingredients (for 2 quarts/ 2 liters):

½ cup/125 grams sugar

2 tablespoons loose black or green tea or 4 teabags

1 cup/250 milliliters mature kombucha

Kombucha mother

Process:

Boil 1 quart of water in a small cooking pot.

Steep the tea. Remove the water from heat, add the tea, cover, and steep about 5 minutes.

Strain the tea into your fermentation vessel.

Add the sugar and stir well to dissolve.

Add another quart/liter of water to cool and reach the target volume.

Taste and add more sugar if desired.

Cool. If it's not cooled to body temperature, give the sweet tea some time to cool to that temperature.

Add the mature acidic kombucha. When you obtain a culture, it will be stored in this liquid. Save a portion of subsequent batches for this purpose. In the absence of this add 2 tablespoons of vinegar to acidify the environment and keep the kombucha healthy.

Place the kombucha mother in the liquid, with the firm, opaque side up, and cover with a cloth.

Ferment in a warm spot, ideally above 70°F/21°C. The kombucha mother will float above the sweet tea as it ferments. Sometimes when you first place the mother in the tea, it sinks to the bottom. If the mother, or at least one edge of it, fails to float after about 24 hours, your mother probably is not viable and you need to find another.

Taste the kombucha after about a week, even sooner in a very hot place. It will probably still be sweet. The longer it sits, the more acidic it will become. The average fermentation time for kombucha is around 10 days, but when it's ready is a subjective call, depending upon the sweetness and acidity you like.

Remove the mother and 1 cup/250 milliliters of mature kombucha for the next batch.

Bottle the rest to drink as is, or use this kombucha as a starter in a secondary fermentation, as described below.

Start your next batch. Kombucha works best as a continuous rhythm. You now have another layer on your mother. Let the layers accumulate (for a while), or peel a layer off to experiment or share with a friend.

kombucha soda:
secondary fermentation

Kombucha can be a great starting point for any flavor of lightly fermented beverage. One commercial kombucha manufacturer is making it in all the classic soda flavors. The best I've had have been fruit-juice-and/or vegetable-juice-flavored. My friend Caeleb mixes it with pineapple juice and it's consistently great. The indefatigable experimentalists at the Cultured Pickle Shop in Berkeley introduced me to the clever idea of adding vegetable juices. You can use any kind of sweetened herbal infusion, decoction, or other flavoring. The requirements for the secondary fermentation are less exacting than for the first.

Timeframe: About 3 to 5 days

Vessels: 2 resealable quart/liter plastic soda bottles or other styles, including rubber gasket "bail-top" bottles; sealable juice jugs; or capped beer bottles, as described in Bottling Alcohol for Carbonation, page 226

Ingredients (for 2 quarts/ 2 liters):

6 cups/1.5 liters mature kombucha
2 cups any kind of fruit or vegetable juice; or an herbal infusion or decoction sweetened with about 2 tablespoons sugar or other sweetener

Process:

Mix the mature kombucha with fruit or vegetable juice, or sweetened herbal tea.
Bottle the mixture in sealable bottles.
Ferment the bottles in a warm spot for a day or a few depending upon temperature. The best way I know to monitor carbonation is bottling in plastic soda bottles, as described in Bottling and Carbonation, page 85.
Chill before opening (if possible).

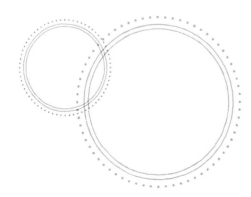

starter: water kefir

Water kefir is one of many names that describe a symbiotic community of bacteria and yeast (SCOBY) that manifests as small whitish translucent crystals. It is not directly related to kefir, the milk culture (see page 118), but because they are similar in form, people have perceived them as related phenomena. The culture is also known as *tibicos* or *tibis*, sugary water grains, Tibetan crystals, Japanese water crystals, and has many other names.

Water kefir is a versatile culture that can be used to ferment almost any carbohydrate-rich liquid. I usually use it to ferment sugar-, honey-, or sorghum-water with just a tiny bit of fruit in it for the primary fermentation, then mix that with more fruit or juice, herbs, or other flavorings for a secondary fermentation. I've also had pleasing results using it to ferment coconut water, and coconut, soy, almond, and rice milks.

Fermenting with water kefir is extremely simple, once you find water kefir grains, which are more readily available now than ever before (see the appendix). The only hard part is developing the rhythm to give water kefir the ongoing attention that it needs. The crystals are demanding pets, and if they go more than a few days without fresh nutrients, they can lose vibrancy, stop growing, shrivel, and eventually dematerialize.

If you feed them regularly, and start a new batch as you strain the grains out of the preceding batch, your kefir grains will likely multiply fast. Share them! If they fail to grow, the problem might be lack of minerals. Dominic Anfiteatro, an Australian fermentation enthusiast and the Internet's most comprehensive source of information about all things kefir, observes that mineral-rich "hard" water promotes water kefir SCOBY growth, while distilled water, or water purified using an activated carbon filter, can retard growth. A strategy for mineralizing water kefir is to add crushed eggshells, limestone, or ocean coral to the fermenting solution, in very small amounts, as too much may make it get slimy.

If you have need to temporarily suspend your water kefir rhythm, rinse the grains, pat them dry, and freeze them in a sealed plastic bag.

Timeframe: 1 to 3 days, then an ongoing rhythm

Equipment:

1-quart/1-liter jar
Cloth to cover it
Fine-mesh strainer or cheesecloth

Ingredients (for 1 quart/1 liter):

¼ cup/60 milliliters or more honey or less refined forms of sugar
1 unsulfured dried apricot or ½ lime
1 thin slice fresh ginger (optional)
1 tablespoon water kefir grains (see appendix for sources)

Process:

Mix the sugar solution. Add sweetener to just under 1 quart/1 liter of water. In addition to carbohydrates, the sugar needs to be a source of minerals, so use less refined sugars. If all you have is white sugar, add ½ teaspoon of molasses as a source of minerals. Sweeten to taste, and bear in mind that some of the sugar will metabolize into acids and after a day or two it will be less sweet. Start with ¼ cup sweetener and add more if desired.

Add the fruit and ginger, if desired. Water kefir can be sensitive, so don't add a lot of fruit or ginger. That can happen in the secondary fermentation. This one is primarily about keeping the crystals happy. It's tempting to add fresh berries and you certainly can, but remember that at some point you will find yourself trying to separate the crystals from the decomposing berries. These too I save for the secondary fermentation.

Add the water kefir grains. If you are reviving dried water kefir crystals, it might take a few feedings like this to get them plump and vigorous.

Cover the jar with cloth.

Ferment for 24 hours. Stir it a few times during this time.

Taste it. You'll probably want to give it another day or two, but if it appears to be bubbly and active and tastes ready to you, proceed to the next step. If you want to give it another day or two, just keep stirring and tasting until you judge it to be ready.

Remove the fruit (typically floating at the top).

Strain through a fine-mesh strainer or cheesecloth to remove the water kefir grains.

Enjoy as is, or use as a starter. The water kefir, now dense with the community of organisms from the crystals, may be used as a starter for a water kefir soda, as described in the following recipe.

Prepare a new sugar solution for the grains. They are like pets and require ongoing feeding. I generally reuse the fruit and ginger for a couple of batches.

grape water kefir soda

Freshly fermented water kefir is teeming with all the bacteria and yeast of the SCOBY, and can be mixed with fruit or vegetable juices, sweetened herbal infusions or decoctions, really any flavoring you could imagine. This recipe is for a grape-flavored soda. It's best with fresh juice squeezed from any kind of fresh grapes, but also works great with commercial grape juice.

Timeframe: 1 to 3 days

Vessels: 2 resealable quart/liter plastic bottles

Ingredients (for 2 quarts/ 2 liters):

2 cups/500 milliliters mature water kefir
1½ quarts/1.5 liters grape juice (or any fruit or vegetable juice; or an herbal infusion or decoction sweetened with about ½ cup/125 grams sugar or other sweetener)

Process:

Combine the mature water kefir with the juice.
Bottle the mixture in sealable bottles. Plastic soda bottles are the best way I know to monitor carbonation.
Ferment the bottles in a warm spot for a day or a few, depending upon temperature, until they become pressurized.
Chill before opening, if possible.

persimmon water kefir soda

Water kefir sodas can be made in infinite varieties. This is one made with my very favorite fruit, the small American persimmon (*Diospyros virginiana*), which is indigenous to this region. Every day from September through December I find these luscious fruits on the ground underneath the persimmon trees, and experience their sweet, sticky flesh as a healing ambrosia, nourishing my body and soul with all the rich goodness of the Earth. This seasonal pursuit has become an elaborate ritual of self-care, something I do for myself because it makes me feel so good. The sweet persimmon taste triggers a powerful visualization in my mind, in which I see the persimmon's concentrated vital energy permeating my being. One thing that I've learned about healing is that clearly visualizing it helps enable it to happen.

Sometimes there are so many persimmons on the ground that I can't stuff them all in my mouth, and need to find other ways to use them. A soda like this is a great way to enjoy persimmon's essence as a beverage. Unripe American persimmons have an awful astringent aftertaste, so be sure your persimmons are soft and fully ripe. Substitute any other fruit you like for persimmons.

Timeframe: 3 to 4 days

Equipment:

1-gallon/4-liter (or larger) bowl, crock, or jar
Cloth cover
2 resealable quart/liter plastic bottles

Ingredients (for 2 quarts/ 2 liters):

1 quart/1 liter mature water kefir
¼ cup/60 grams sugar
2 pounds/1 kilogram fresh ripe persimmons
    (about 1 quart/1 liter)

Process:

Combine. Mix the mature water kefir with the sugar and 2 cups of water in the vessel. Stir well to dissolve the sugar. Add the persimmons and cover with cloth.

Ferment in a prominent spot on your kitchen counter.

Stir frequently, at least three times a day. The water kefir should be bubbly and start taking on the color, aroma, and flavor of the persimmons.

Strain out the persimmons after about 2 days. If they still have much flavor, use them for another batch of water kefir, or eat them. Taste the water kefir soda and add sugar or water if necessary.

Bottle in sealable bottles. Plastic soda bottles are the best way I know to monitor carbonation, as described in Bottling and Carbonation, page 85.

Chill before opening, if possible.

starter: yeast

Finally, let's not forget about the most commonly used starter: yeast. My friend Lisa Klieger has made excellent yeast sodas for years. The following is her advice:

> Easy and quite expedient, yeast sodas are the instant gratification of the fermented beverage world. In my 70-degree kitchen a batch will fully carbonate in about 6 hours, so you can make it in the morning and serve it by supper. It makes a great last minute addition to a dinner party or a fun project with the kids. It is fun to experiment with different flavorings. Add a few peppercorns to a brew to bring a nice sharpness, leave in a slice of lime peel for a sophisticated bitter note, add fresh basil or other herbs for a bright, fresh soda. A bit of citrus makes a more vigorous boil and rounds out the yeasty flavor.
>
> Yeast can digest any carbohydrate sweetener and white sugar, honey, molasses, sorghum and fruit juices all yield nice results. Use caution as these sodas tend to build pressure quickly. Bleed pressure by gently and slowly opening the bottles several times a day. Also, if you want to avoid alcohol you must drink it young. When it has reached full carbonation it can be moved to the fridge to slow fermentation, but even there it begins to resemble session beer strength after just a few days. The following are two recipes that are favorites in my house.

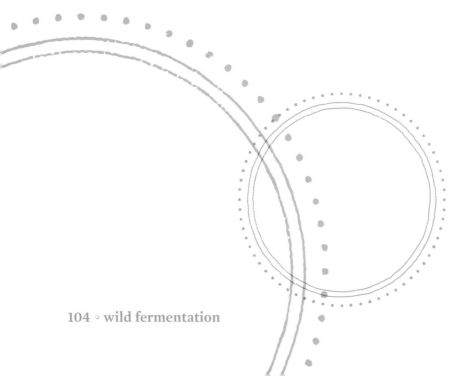

rosy raspberry soda

Timeframe: 6 to 8 hours

Vessels: 2 resealable quart/liter
plastic bottles

**Ingredients (for 2 quarts/
2 liters):**

½ cup/70 grams raspberries
Juice from ½ lemon
2–4 tablespoons honey
1 teaspoon rose water
Yeast

Process:

Combine and blend. Place all the ingredients except
the yeast in a bowl with a bit of water and mash
together with a fork, or put them all in the blender.

Divide between two 1-quart/1-liter bottles.

Top off with warm water.

Add yeast. Sprinkle about ¼ teaspoon bread or
champagne yeast into each bottle. Let it sit for a
few minutes, then shake the bottles to dissolve
and distribute the yeast.

Ferment on the counter. Check the carbonation after a
few hours. Bleed carbonation by gently and slowly
opening the bottles. Refrigerate when they seem
strongly carbonated, generally within 6 to 8 hours.

mock dry champagne

Timeframe: 6 to 8 hours

Vessels: 2 resealable quart/liter
plastic bottles

**Ingredients (for 2 quarts/
2 liters):**

½ cup dry damiana herb
Juice and whole rind from 1 lemon
¾ cup/185 grams sugar
Yeast

Process:

Boil water.

Combine the ingredients and steep. Place all the
ingredients except the yeast in a crock or non-metallic bowl. Cover with boiling water and let steep,
covered, until cool.

Strain the liquid and divide between two
1-quart/1-liter bottles.

Top off with warm water.

Add yeast. Sprinkle about ¼ teaspoon bread or
champagne yeast into each bottle. Let it sit for a
few minutes then shake the bottles to dissolve
and distribute the yeast.

Ferment on the counter. Check the carbonation
after a few hours. Bleed the carbonation by gently
and slowly opening the bottles. Refrigerate when
they seem strongly carbonated, generally within 6
to 8 hours. If you want an even more cham-
pagne-like experience, leave it in the fridge for 4
to 5 days, carefully bleeding several times a day to
release excess pressure.

Further Reading

Christensen, Emma. *True Brews: How to Craft Fermented Cider, Beer, Wine, Sake, Soda, Mead, Kefir, and Kombucha at Home.* Berkeley, CA: Ten Speed Press, 2013.

Crum, Hannah, and Alex LaGory. *The Big Book of Kombucha: Brewing, Flavoring, and Enjoying the Health Benefits of Fermented Tea.* North Adams, MA: Storey Publishing, 2016.

Frank, Günther W. *Kombucha: Healthy Beverage and Natural Remedy from the Far East, Its Correct Preparation and Use.* Steyr, Austria: Wilhelm Ennsthaler, 1995.

Lee, Stephen, and Ken Koopman. *Kombucha Revolution: 75 Recipes for Homemade Brews, Fixers, Elixirs, and Mixers.* Berkeley, CA: Ten Speed Press, 2014.

Mueller, Julia. *Delicious Probiotic Drinks: 75 Recipes for Kombucha, Kefir, Ginger Beer, and Other Naturally Fermented Drinks.* New York: Skyhorse Publishing, 2014.

7: dairy ferments
(and Vegan Alternatives)

It's 8 AM and my day to milk. I take the milking pail and a dish of warm water down to the barn. The goats are waiting for me. It's feeding time as well as milking time, and they look forward to it. Sassy's usually the first one in. She's the alpha goat, the queen of the herd. She often bullies the other goats, and eating first seems to be a way of asserting her dominance. I scoop some feed into a dish and give it to her. As she devours it, I milk. Her teats are nice and big, easy to grasp. I squeeze the teats firmly between my thumbs and the base of my index fingers, to prevent the milk from going back up into the udder, then use my remaining fingers against my palm to squirt the milk out. This action forces out a concentrated stream that froths in the pail. I relax my grip so the teat can fill with more milk, and repeat. With a teat in each hand, I rhythmically alternate.

I try to go fast, because as soon as Sassy is done with her food, she isn't so content to stay still. She squirms and tries to leave the milking platform. Worse than that, she lifts her hind legs to try to knock over or step into the pail of milk. Goats are quite intelligent and purposeful. From this point on, milking her is a battle of wills. I pour the milk I've gotten so far into a larger collecting pail, so if her sabotage efforts succeed, the loss will be minimal. I stroke her and whisper sweet nothings into her ear. "Sassy, you beautiful goat, you've been so good this morning. I'm sorry I'm so slow. Won't you please, please, please let me finish?" I negotiate, offering her more food if she'll cooperate. I milk with one hand, holding the pail with my other hand to protect it. As each squirt yields less milk, I knead her udder, trying to get all the milk out. When Sassy is done, there are three more still to go, and three who don't get milked but still need to be fed and tended.

Looking back on those days from my post-commune perspective, the goats are one of the things I miss most. On my own, even with a partner, I could never take on such a daily responsibility. It was only in the context of being part of a larger group effort that it was possible for me. Though I am no longer part of the regular milking rotation, I still enjoy when I get to drink their milk. These are not mass-bred animals treated as commodities and manipulated with growth hormones. These goats are fenced out of the garden areas, rather than into a small grazing range. They roam the mountainside, feasting on wild vegetation. Through their ruminant digestive tracts, the goats extract nutrition from leaves, barks, lichens, and more, which we get to share in via their milk. They even eat poison ivy; the milk with traces of poison ivy phytochemicals is said to help desensitize people to the effects of the plant.

Fresh milk, as we children of the 20th and 21st centuries grew up with, only really became possible with refrigeration. Prior to refrigeration, and in parts of the world where refrigeration is still not widespread, beyond the people milking the animals (who always get the freshest milk), the milk that has been practical is fermented milk. In every part of the world in which people domesticated animals for their milk, they developed distinctive styles of fermenting milk. In sharp contrast with fresh milk, fermented dairy products remain edible, even improve over time, without refrigeration.

Refrigeration has become the norm in American life. We have become accustomed to keeping a variety of prepared perishable foods on hand, to be available immediately, whenever we want them. Entering a big supermarket, you feel the chill of the open coolers and hear their constant hum. Though refrigeration renders the original preservation benefit of fermented milk less critical, supermarket coolers are full of fermented dairy products. Consumers are devoted to cheese, yogurt, sour cream, buttermilk, and other dairy ferments. We love cultured milk products for their flavors, their textures, and, in many cases, their health benefits.

Vegans and other non-milk-drinkers, do not despair. You do not need to forgo the benefits and pleasures of these fermentations. Many of the cultures used to ferment milk are versatile, adaptable to many substances besides mammalian milk. A special section at the end of this chapter addresses vegan adaptations of these fermentations. If you avoid milk because of a lactose intolerance, however, you might give cultured milks a chance. Lactic acid bacteria consume lactose in milk and transform it into lactic acid that may be easier for you to digest, and longer fermentations will generally result in more of the lactose being digested, along with a corresponding increase in acidity.

Broadside from Bread and Puppet Theater.

yogurt

No fermented food is better known or acknowledged for its health benefits than yogurt. "Substantial evidence currently exists to support a beneficial effect of yogurt consumption on gastrointestinal health," asserts the *American Journal of Clinical Nutrition*.[1] The fermentation results in improved calcium availability and confers many other benefits. "Yogurt is especially recommended for those at high risk of cancer, as it is superb at blocking cellular changes that initiate the cancer cascade," writes Susun S. Weed.[2]

Yogurt is creamy and delicious, too. In the United States, it is mostly consumed sweet, though my favorite ways to enjoy yogurt are savory. Savory flavors complement and accent its sourness rather than try to cover it up. (See the recipes following this for savory yogurt sauces.)

The word *yogurt* actually describes a range of distinctive regional cultured milk products. The yogurt-making process outlined below is for thermophilic cultures, which require temperatures above body temperature, around 110°F/43°C. Many contraptions are on the market to help you maintain that temperature range. If you have one, great; but it is easy to improvise with a preheated insulated cooler.

You need a starter culture to make yogurt. You can buy freeze-dried cultures for this, or use any commercial live-culture yogurt, or seek out a traditional heirloom culture. If you use a commercial yogurt as a starter, make sure it says "Contains live cultures" on the label to be sure it has not been pasteurized post-fermentation, killing the bacteria. Many commercial yogurt cultures will cease to be effective as starters after a couple of generations (see *The Art of Fermentation* for a discussion of the reasons for this). In contrast, heirloom cultures, given care and regular use, can keep on going indefinitely. Yonah Schimmel's Knishes on Houston Street in New York City makes delicious yogurt using the same starter culture the store's founders brought over from Eastern Europe more than 100 years ago. Sources for heirloom yogurt cultures are listed in the appendix.

Timeframe: 4 to 24 hours

Equipment:

2 1-quart/1-liter or 4 1-pint/500-milliliter jars
Insulated cooler that can fit the jars
Thermometer accurate in the range
    110°F/43°C–180°F/82°C

Ingredients (for 2 quarts/ 2 liters):

2 quarts/2 liters whole milk
2 teaspoons fresh live-culture plain yogurt
    for starter culture

Process:

Heat the milk to 180°F/82°C, or until bubbles begin to form. Use gentle heat, and stir frequently, to avoid burning the milk. A double boiler is a very easy way to accomplish this. This heating is not absolutely necessary, but it results in much thicker yogurt.

Add hot water to the insulated cooler to preheat it. This is what will enable the cooler to hold heat to keep the milk warm while it ferments. Heat water to a near boil and pour into the insulated cooler about 3–4 inches/8–10 cm deep. Close the cooler and check the temperature after 10 minutes. Add a little cold (or hot) water as necessary to adjust the temperature to about 115°F/46°C.

Cool the heated milk to about 115°F/46°C, or the point where it feels hot, but it is not hard to keep your (clean!) finger in it. You can speed the cooling process by setting the pot with the hot milk into a bowl or pot of cold water and stirring both warm milk and cooling water. Don't let the milk get too cool; the yogurt cultures are most active in the above-body-temperature range.

Introduce the starter. Mix a little warm milk into the starter, stir to dissolve the yogurt, then mix that into the milk. Use just 1 teaspoon per quart/liter. I used to use more starter, assuming that more is better, until I consulted my favorite all-around kitchen reference book, *The Joy of Cooking* (1964 edition), which I (and my fellow housemates through the ages) refer to affectionately as "Joy." "You may wonder why so little starter is used and think that a little more will produce a better result. It won't. The bacillus, if crowded, gives a sour, watery product. But if the culture has sufficient *lebensraum* [German for "room to live"], it will be rich, mild and creamy."[3] Mix the starter thoroughly into the milk.

Pour the mixture into jars. Cap the jars.

Make a final check on the insulated cooler. Be sure the water level isn't so high that jars will be floating. Remove some water if necessary. Check the temperature, aiming for 115°F/46°C (a few degrees will be absorbed by the jars, and the temperature will rapidly decline), and add a little hot water if necessary.

Place the jars in the insulated cooler, pre-heated and temperature-checked and adjusted if necessary. If much space remains in the cooler, fill it with bottles of hot water (not too hot to touch). Close the cooler and place it in a warm spot where it will not be disturbed. "Yogurt has the added idiosyncrasy that it doesn't care to be jostled while growing," notes Joy.

Check the temperature after an hour. If it has dipped below 110°F/43°C, add a little boiled water to raise the temperature.

Check the yogurt after 4 to 8 hours. Turn a jar sideways and observe its consistency. Ideally it should be solid enough to hold its form. If it isn't thick (hasn't "yoged"), remove some of the lukewarm water in the cooler and replace it with hot water to warm it back up to 110°F/43°C, and leave it 4 to 8 more hours. You can leave it to ferment longer if you wish. It will become sourer, as more of the milk's lactose is converted into lactic acid. A longer fermentation period can often make yogurt digestible even for lactose-intolerant individuals.

Enjoy plain, sweet, or savory, as you like it. Experiment! Yogurt has many varied uses. Yogurt can store in the refrigerator for months, though its flavor will become sourer over time. It stays fresh longest in full, unopened jars. Once there is air space and fresh air in a partially eaten jar, oxygen can lead to a yeasty flavor.

Save some of your yogurt to use as starter for the next batch.

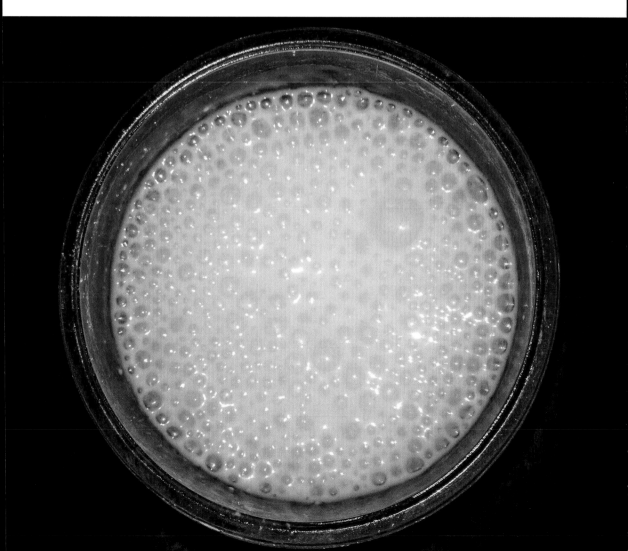

labneh (yogurt cheese)

In many of the cuisines where yogurt is most popular, it is often strained into thicker forms. The process is simple.

Line a colander with finely woven cloth or cheesecloth (a couple of layers if coarsely woven). Place the lined colander in a pot or bowl.

Gently pour yogurt into the lined colander. Lift the corners of the cloth out of the colander; then join the corners together and lift the yogurt-filled cloth out of the colander and remove the colander from the pot or bowl. Wrap the joined corners of cloth around the center of a long wooden spoon or other implement. Wrap it a few times so it holds on, or tie it, or secure with a rubber band, and hang it over the pot and bowl.

Let the yogurt drain, covered to keep flies away. It can drain for a short time, to result in a slightly thicker yogurt (what has become known as Greek yogurt), or for hours for a more solid yogurt cheese. The longer you drain it, the firmer it will become. Mix in salt and herbs after it drains for a beautiful dip, spread, or cheese.

The liquid that drains out is protein-rich whey. Use the whey for other fermentation adventures (see page 91), or in place of water in other cooking or baking.

savory yogurt sauces: raita and tsatsiki

Raita is a popular condiment in Indian cuisine. Tsatsiki is a similar though differently spiced condiment in Greek cuisine. They both mix yogurt with cucumber, salt, and garlic, then diverge just a little in other ingredients. If these sauces have a chance to sit, the flavors infuse and meld, so if you can, make them at least a few hours (or a day) in advance.

Timeframe: A few hours so flavors can infuse and meld

Ingredients (for about 2½ cups/625 milliliters):

1 large or 2 small cucumbers
1 tablespoon salt, or to taste
2 cups/500 milliliters yogurt
3–6 cloves garlic, crushed or finely chopped

For Raita:

1 teaspoon cumin, dry-roasted then ground (or pre-ground)
¼ cup/10 grams chopped fresh cilantro

For Tsatsiki:

2 tablespoons olive oil
1 tablespoon lemon juice
Ground white pepper
¼ cup/10 grams chopped fresh mint and/or parsley

Process:

Grate the cucumber into a colander, sprinkle generously with salt, mix well, and leave in a sink or over a bowl to drain the excess water (along with most of the salt) for about an hour.

Combine the other ingredients with the cucumber in a bowl. Try varying these standbys with other herbs (fresh dill, oregano, chives, thyme, bee balm, and other edible flower petals) or grated vegetables (kohlrabi, radishes, burdock).

Taste. Much of the salt will have dripped away with the water. If desired, add more salt as well as other seasonings.

Refrigerate until ready to serve.

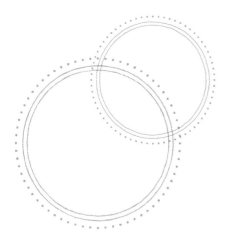

kishk

Kishk is a Lebanese ferment of yogurt and bulgur wheat. The two are mixed together into a dough and fermented for about 10 days. During its fermentation it can smell almost sweet, like coconut. But ultimately it develops the flavor of a strong, musky cheese. Kishk is dried after fermentation, then used to flavor and thicken soups and stews, and in other ways. The flavor of kishk is unique and distinctive, and I love it. It is also found in Iranian and other Middle Eastern cuisines. In Greece, it is known as *trahanas*.

Timeframe: About 10 days

Ingredients (for about 2 cups/ 500 milliliters):

1 cup/200 grams bulgur wheat
2½ cups/625 milliliters yogurt
2 teaspoons salt

Process:

Combine the yogurt and bulgur in a bowl, cover, and leave overnight.

Knead and add the salt. When you look in the morning, the bulgur will have absorbed most of the moisture of the yogurt. Knead, fold, and turn the mixture a few times with your hands. Add the salt and mix it in. If dough seems dry, as though it could absorb more moisture, add a little more yogurt and knead it in. Cover it and leave to ferment.

Mix the kishk daily. Check the kishk the next day. Fold and turn the mixture a few times with your hands. Continue to mix the bulgur-yogurt dough every day for about 9 days. This renews the surfaces and protects the developing kishk from surface molds.

Dry the kishk. Spread the kishk on a baking sheet to dry, and leave in a sunny spot, or in a dehydrator, or under a fan, or in a warm oven. As it dries, crumble it into smaller bits to create more surface area.

Crush into a powder. Once the kishk is completely dry, use a mortar and pestle or a food processor to crush it into powder and crumbs, and store at room temperature in a well-sealed jar. Kept dry, it should store indefinitely.

To use kishk in soups, fry the kishk in oil or butter with garlic, then add a little soup stock and cook to thicken, as in a flour-based gravy or sauce. Transfer the kishk gravy to the soup and cook altogether for several minutes. Kishk thickens as well as flavors soup. Use about 2 tablespoons of kishk (or more) per cup of soup.

Many other uses for kishk. According to the Lebanese Food Heritage Foundation: "Kishk can be prepared in different forms such as salads (Wild mint and kishk salad 'Meeykeh'); soups ('shorbet Kishk' and 'Kishkiyye'); fillings for turnovers or mana'eesh; hot dishes such as kebbeh with kishk ('kebbeh b kishk'), kishk with eggs ('kishk aala bayd'), cabbage with kishk ('malfouf aala kishk'), wheat-flour dough with kishk (maacaroon b kishk), meat raviolis with kishk ('shish barak b kishk'), etc."

doogh (persian yogurt soda)

Doogh is yogurt soda. I've enjoyed it for years whenever I found it in Middle Eastern markets. All the recipes I found called for mixing yogurt with carbonated water, which works fine, but I knew there had to be a more traditional method that relied upon fermentation. Finally, at the Boston Fermentation Festival I met chef Geoff Lukas, who learned Persian so he could study Persian cuisine in Iran, and he shared with me the deceptively simple method for carbonating yogurt soda: "Bloom bulgur and let it start to bubble a bit before adding it to yogurt, and use that as your source of yeast." By bloom he means add water, to awaken dormant yeasts and bacteria, and wait a few days for it to bubble. "The original version used the buttermilk from cultured butter-making so it was defatted. It was a secondary process. Modern versions use skim milk yogurt or goat milk." This bulgur bloom is another kind of starter that can also be used to start other kinds of lightly fermented soft drinks, as discussed in chapter 6.

Timeframe: 3 to 5 days

Vessel: Sealable quart/liter (or larger) bottle

Ingredients (to make 1 quart/ 1 liter):

2 tablespoons bulgur wheat
3½ cups/875 milliliters yogurt

Process:

Mix the bulgur wheat with water in a jar. Use about 1 cup/250 milliliters dechlorinated water. Cover with a light cloth and stir frequently.

The bulgur-water will begin to bubble after 2 to 3 days. Stir for another day as bubbling builds, then strain the bulgur from the bubbly water and pour the water into a ½-gallon/2-liter or larger mixing cup or bowl.

Mix the yogurt with the bubbly bulgur-water starter in the bowl. Beat them together to mix them and break the structure of the yogurt.

Transfer to a sealable bottle. Leave to ferment at room temperature for about 24 hours, then refrigerate. In a recycled plastic soda bottle, it's easy to gauge pressure by squeezing (see page 85).

Enjoy carbonated doogh refrigerated or at room temperature. It is delicious plain, or with a pinch of salt and/or a dash of pepper, or mint, or a spoonful of honey, maple, or sorghum. Or as a starter for other soda flavoring ideas, as discussed in chapter 6.

kefir

Kefir is a fermented milk beverage that originated in the Central Asian Caucasus mountains. As the milk ferments it thickens slightly, and depending upon how long it is fermented, the flavor can range from mild to extremely tart. If you get the timing right, it can be very bubbly. Rather than using a bit of the previous batch as a starter, as with yogurt and most other dairy ferments, the starter is a symbiotic community of bacteria and yeast (SCOBY), rubbery blobs known as kefir grains, which are strained out after fermentation, then used to start the next batch.

Kefir grains look something like plump little florets of cauliflower. Embodied in this rubbery mass is an elaborate community of at least 30 microorganisms, among them yeast (*Saccharomyces cerevisiae*), which gives kefir its bubbly effervescence, as well as a small alcohol content (about 1 percent). As you feed them milk, the kefir grains grow and multiply.

The kefir story is full of intrigue. The first kefir grains are said to have been a gift from Allah, delivered by his prophet Muhammad. The grains were treasured by the people who possessed them, passed down from generation to generation, and definitely not shared with strangers.

Early in the 20th century, the "All-Russian Physicians' Society" became interested in obtaining the mysterious source of this healthful drink. Since the keepers of the grains did not wish to share them, this required deception and cultural thievery. The scheme involved a young Russian woman named Irina Sakharova, whom the physicians hoped would be able to charm a Caucasus prince, Bek-Mirza Barchorov, into giving her some kefir grains. He refused, she tried to leave, he had her kidnapped, she was rescued, and he was arrested. For reparations, Sakharova was awarded the treasure she sought; the court ordered the prince to give her some of his cherished kefir grains. In 1908, she brought the first kefir grains to Moscow. Kefir became, and remains to this day, a popular drink in Russia.[4]

Compared with yogurt, kefir is very easy to make, because it requires no temperature control. The only tricky part is coming by the grains to get started; see the appendix for sources. Once you have kefir grains, they are like pets in that they require regular feeding. If you can maintain a rhythm they will thrive, produce delicious kefir, and grow rapidly, enabling you to share grains with others and spread the culture.

The most extraordinary kefir grains I have encountered,
Lou Preston's from Healdsburg, California.

Timeframe: 1 to 3 days

Vessel: 1-quart/1-liter jar

Ingredients (for 1 quart/1 liter):

1 quart/1 liter milk
1 tablespoon kefir grains

Process:

Fill the jar with milk. Add the kefir grains, and loosely cap.

Ferment at room temperature for about 24 hours, tightening the cap and agitating the jar periodically. The agitation is important, as it brings more of the milk into contact with the grains and distributes fermentation activity. Loosen the cap after agitation.

Strain out the grains with any straining implement. You may need to use a spoon or finger to stir and coax the thickened milk through the strainer.

Seal the strained kefir in a jar and leave it at room temperature for another 12 to 24 hours to carbonate (if desired). The fermentation continues even without the grains because all the organisms in them are now part of the kefir. (With so much more limited sugar content in milk, there is no need with kefir to worry about the jar exploding, as with sodas in chapter 6.)

Meanwhile, cover the kefir grains with fresh milk and start the next batch. Kefir works best as a continuous rhythm. Keep your batches small so you do not get overwhelmed.

Curdling. If you leave your kefir to ferment for a few days, it will curdle and separate. You can remix it by shaking, and enjoy sour kefir. Or, when the thick creamy kefir floats above the whey, you can gently scoop it out and enjoy it like sour cream. Use the whey for other fermentation adventures (see page 91), or in other cooking or baking.

Kefir grains grow and multiply in number over time. If you keep the scale of your production constant, it will ferment faster as the ratio of grains to milk increases. Eventually you will need to cull the extras. You only need a tablespoon or so of grains per quart/liter of milk. Share the extras, eat them, feed them to your pet, or toss them into the compost.

Hiatus. The best way to store kefir grains if you need to suspend production is to pat them dry, seal them in something airtight, and freeze them.

buttermilk

Classically, buttermilk is the by-product of making butter, what is left after cream is churned and agitated, causing the butterfat to separate out and form a solid mass of butter. The buttermilk widely available in supermarkets is not exactly this but rather a cultured milk, great for pancakes, biscuits, and other baking projects. It tastes delicious, and its acidity reacts with alkaline baking soda to make things rise. You can use kefir in place of buttermilk with fine results. You can also make your own buttermilk easily using commercial buttermilk as a starter. Add about ½ cup/125 milliliters of commercial live-culture buttermilk to 1 quart/1 liter of milk, then leave it at room temperature for about 24 hours; it will all become buttermilk, which can be stored in a refrigerator for months.

Nigde churning cream to make butter—using simple, clever technology—in a Himalayan village, Kalap, Uttarahkand, India.

cheesemaking

Cheesemaking involves many different variables. Milk can be transformed into a hard cheddar cheese, a runny Camembert, a moldy blue cheese, or, for that matter, Velveeta. Cheese exists in thousands of variations. Traditionally, it has been highly localized. A particular cheese is the product of the milk of particular animals grazing in particular pastures and host to particular microorganisms, subjected to particular temperatures and manipulations, then aged in a particular environment with its own particular microorganisms, which are generally selected by the application of a particular surface treatment, for a particular period of time.

An aging cheese is often host to a succession of different organisms, each influencing flavor and texture. Burkhard Bilger waxed poetic on the molds that age the cheese Saint-Nectaire, which he observed through a microscope: "Like a continent evolving in rapid motion, the ripening rind would be invaded by wave after wave of new species, turning from gold to gray to a mottled brown. The cat hairs [a type of mold] would sprout up like ancient ferns, then topple and turn to a velvet compost for their successors. The penicillium molds would arrive, their stalks too fine to be seen under a standard microscope, and put down pillowy patches of the palest gray. Then, at last, a faint-pink blush would spread across the surface like a sunset: *Trichothecium roseum*, the flower of the molds."[5] Microbiology has just in the 21st century developed the tools to study the complex microbial communities such as those found in cheese rinds.

It is somehow ironic that microbiology is coming to appreciate the complexity of the distinct microbial communities that develop in the rinds of different traditional cheeses. Earlier, microbiology isolated the pure strain cultures that enabled cheese to be mass-produced. The local particulars of traditional cheesemaking have largely been supplanted by uniformity. Mass production requires a standardized approach that contrasts starkly with the subjective rigors of artisan cheesemaking. "Human intervention has to be precisely right," observes French cheesemaker Michel Waroquier, quoted in the anthropology journal *Food and Foodways*, in an exploration of the cultural clash between traditional and industrial cheesemaking. "Experience, the nose, the glance of an eye are the only guides a cheesemaker has; his knack is his only measure. It is up to him to consider a multitude of variables that affect his craft: weather conditions, aspects of the milk, season of the year, amount of rennet required, time needed for optimal coagulation of the milk."[6]

My approach to cheesemaking has been very experimental, varying the various variables, and seeing what happens. In my experience, every homemade cheese is one-of-a-kind, and every homemade cheese is delicious. Here are a few different simple cheese recipes to get you started. Vary the process and participate in the creation of the incredible range of textures and flavors that cheese can embody.

Cheesemaking requires some special equipment, most of which can be improvised. The most basic thing you need for cheesemaking is a porous form that can contain the curds as the whey runs out. In certain cases this can be cheesecloth, often available more cheaply in fabric or painting supply stores than in supermarkets. If you don't have cheesecloth, you can use sheer woven cotton or other fabric.

In many cases, cheeses are drained and/or pressed into forms. These can easily be improvised by poking small drain holes (using an awl, ice pick, or drill) into yogurt and other hard plastic food containers. A second container of the same shape, filled with water, can function as a press for cheeses requiring pressing.

The ultimate specific requirement for cheesemaking is often the aging environment. This book keeps it simple with cheeses aged for a short time in which environmental requirements are not so specific. Certain aged cheeses call either for caves, cellars, or existing cool spots, or for simulating such conditions using temperature and humidity control. For anyone interested in going deeper with cheesemaking, there are great books listed in Further Reading, at the end of the chapter.

farmer cheese

This is the most basic process for making cheese. It involves heat and vinegar, and in this simplest manifestation, because it is cooked and not typically aged, it is not even a fermented food.

Timeframe: 20 minutes or longer

Equipment: Cheesecloth

Ingredients (for about ¾ pound/375 grams/ 2 cups cheese):

½ gallon/2 liters whole milk
¼ cup/60 milliliters vinegar

Process:

Heat the milk to a slow boil, stirring frequently to avoid burning. Remove from the heat.

Add the vinegar, a little at a time while stirring, until the milk curdles. Leave the curds to settle for about 10 minutes.

Strain the curdled milk through a cheesecloth-lined colander. Collect the curds in the cheesecloth into a ball by lifting the corners of the cheesecloth out of the colander; then join the corners together, and twist the cheesecloth to tighten the ball and force water out.

Hang the ball. Wrap the joined corners of cheesecloth around the center of a long wooden spoon or other implement. Wrap it a few times so it holds on, or tie it, or secure with a rubber band, and hang it over the pot and bowl. (See the photograph on page 131.) Once it drips and thickens a bit, this is farmer cheese, similar in consistency to ricotta, and great for lasagna or blintzes or Italian-style cheesecake.

paneer

Paneer is a simple fresh Indian cheese. Essentially it is a harder version of farmer cheese, made by pressing the curds to force more whey out. Recipes often call for cubing paneer, coating it with salt and spices, frying it, then adding it to other ingredients. Saag paneer is spiced and fried paneer cooked with spinach. Or you can enjoy this cheese on a plate with crackers.

Timeframe: 1 hour

Equipment: Cheesecloth

Ingredients (for just over ½ pound/250 grams/ about 1½ cups):

½ gallon/2 liters whole milk
¼ cup/60 milliliters vinegar

Process:

Make farmer cheese, as described above, but rather than hanging the ball after straining, press it as follows.

Use weight to force the whey out. Place the ball of cheese on a sloped surface (a cutting board propped up slightly under one end), then place a second flat surface on top of the curds, weighted by a big book or other moderately heavy object. After an hour (or more), the cheese will hold its form when you unwrap the cheesecloth.

rennet

Rennet is an enzymatic curdling agent, traditionally obtained from the stomach linings of infant ruminant animals. Today, "vegetable rennet" is also produced by fungi as well as by bacteria genetically modified to produce these enzymes (enzymes from GM bacteria are a hidden realm of genetic modification). Many different plants, including thistles and stinging nettles, can also be used to coagulate milk, though using different enzymes than rennet. I've enjoyed experimenting with varied coagulants, but most of my cheesemaking has relied upon rennet. Rennet is prized for the smooth, creamy texture of the curd it produces. The other great advantage of rennet is that it curdles milk at lower temperatures, so you can curdle raw or cultured milks into cheese without killing microbial cultures as boiling would, meaning that they can develop in the aging cheese.

Rennet may be found at certain very well-stocked retail stores, among them sometimes brewing supply shops, cheese shops, or other food shops. Various forms of rennet are also available online via cheesemaking suppliers, including cheesemaking.com and thecheesemaker.com.

Cheeses aging in the Cellars at Jasper Hill.

chèvre

Chèvre is the classic soft goat cheese, delicious plain or herbed.

Timeframe: 2 days or longer

Equipment: Cheesecloth

Ingredients (for a bit more than 1 pound/500 grams/ about 2 cups):

½ gallon/2 liters whole raw goat's milk
2 tablespoons kefir
¼ dose rennet (for the rennet I use, that means 3 drops at this scale)
2 teaspoons salt

Process:

Gently heat the milk to about 90°F/32°C. Stir frequently to prevent scorching.

Remove from the heat.

Add the kefir and stir.

Add the rennet. Dilute the rennet in 1 tablespoon of water, then stir gently into the warm cultured milk. Chèvre uses an exceedingly small amount of rennet and forms very soft curd very slowly. Cover.

Ferment for at least 24 hours (2 or 3 days is fine, too) at room temperature. Leave it be. Do not move it around or agitate, which could disrupt curd formation. The curd will form and sink to the bottom.

Line a colander with cheesecloth.

Drain the curd. Gently scoop the curd into cheesecloth to drain. Fold the cheesecloth over the curds to protect them from flies, and leave the curds to drain for a few hours.

Salt the curd. Add the salt, along with herbs and/or edible flowers, if desired, and mix in, then leave the salted curd to drain for another hour or more.

Enjoy chèvre fresh now, or it will last for weeks in the refrigerator.

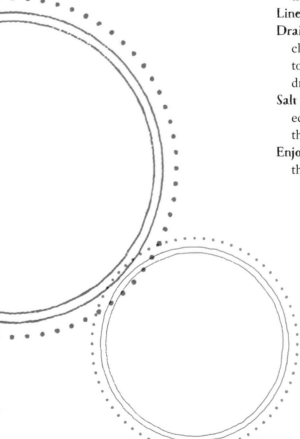

pinkie's basic rennet cheese

My first cheesemaking mentor was David J. Pinkerton, or Pinkie, who taught me his versatile rennet cheesemaking process, which I have adapted here.

Timeframe: Days–weeks–months

Equipment:

Cheesecloth

Plastic container(s) with drainage holes in bottom and sides (optional)

Ingredients:

1 gallon/4 liters whole milk, ideally raw and definitely not ultra-pasteurized

¼ cup/60 milliliters kefir (you can substitute yogurt but it generally has less microbial diversity than kefir)

5–20 drops rennet

4 teaspoons sea salt

Process:

Gently heat the milk to body temperature, around 100°F/38°C.

Add the kefir or yogurt. Stir well and keep warm for an hour or two, wrapped in a blanket or in a warm oven.

Rewarm the milk to around 100°F/38°C.

Add the rennet. The rennet I've mostly used comes in a small plastic vial with a dropper. Different rennet formulations have different concentrations; the one I use calls for between 10 and 20 drops per gallon/4 liters of milk. Ten drops will yield a softer cheese and 20 drops a harder cheese. Dilute the rennet in about 2 tablespoons of water before you add it, and stir the milk while you pour the rennet-water solution into it. Once you've added the rennet, stop stirring. It is important to leave the milk still while the rennet works its coagulating magic. Within half an hour or so, the milk will coagulate. The milk solids will draw together in a mass of curd, and you will notice it pull away from the sides of the pot.

Speaking at a Pickle Party at Grand Central Market in Los Angeles.

Cut the curd. Once the milk has coagulated, use a long knife or spatula to gently cut the curd. Reheat over a gentle heat to restore the temperature to 100°F/38°C as you do this. Cutting the curd creates more surface area on the curd exposed to the rennet. Each piece of curd will tighten and shrink. The curd is fragile and must be handled gently. Slice carefully with a sharp knife into pieces of roughly uniform size (I usually go for approximately 1-inch/ 2.5-centimeter cubes). As you cut the curds, keep them moving; gently agitate and stir to prevent them from sinking.

Keep it warm. For a soft cheese, maintain the just-above-body-heat temperature for about 10 minutes after cutting the curd. Keeping it warm longer, up to about 1 hour, will make the individual curds continue to tighten, resulting in a harder cheese. Increasing the temperature also hardens the cheese, but in order to maintain live cultures don't increase the temperature higher than 110°F/43°C. If you increase the temperature fast, you will end up with a more crumbly, grainier cheese. If you increase the temperature gradually, at a rate of no more than 1°F/0.5°C per minute, you will end up with a smoother, even-textured hardness. "Little wee nuances make a completely different product," explains Pinkie.

Drain the curd. Be gentle: The curds are still fragile. Line a colander with cheesecloth and place it in the sink, or a bowl. Use a slotted spoon to carefully scoop out the curds and place them in the colander. Fold the cheesecloth over the curds to protect them from flies, and leave the curds to drain for about half an hour.

Add the salt, herbs, edible flowers, or other flavorings, if desired, and mix in.

Scoop the curd into forms. Fill the forms all they way to the top, even slightly mounded up, as they will shrink as they drain. Fill another plastic container the same size with water and place on top of the curds in the form to press. Or do it Pinkie-style and simply collect the curds in the cheesecloth into a ball by lifting the corners of the cheesecloth out of the colander; then join the corners together and twist the cheesecloth to tighten the ball and force water out. Hang the ball and let it drip into a bowl, or press it.

Enjoy fresh once it's set, after about 24 hours, or age it.

Age the cheese in a cool, dry spot, and turn frequently. Often surfaces are rubbed daily with brine, whey, wine, vinegar, spices, or other rubs. Or age in brine, as in Feta Cheese, below.

feta cheese

Feta cheese is aged in salty brine, the simplest possible aging environment. Though it's traditionally made from sheep's or goat's milk, you can enjoy feta-style cheese from any milk.

Timeframe: 1 week or more

Equipment:

Cheesecloth
1½-quart/1.5-liter or larger wide-mouth jar
    for aging

Ingredients:

1 gallon/4 liters whole milk
¼ cup/60 milliliters kefir
Full dose rennet (for the rennet I use,
    that means 20 drops at this scale)
½ cup/125 grams sea salt

Process:

Follow the steps outlined in Pinkie's Basic Rennet Cheese, above, through cutting the curd. Use a full dose of rennet (20 drops per gallon/4 liters for the rennet I use).

Stir! Keep shrinking and firming up the curds in the warm whey for about an hour, gently stirring often to keep the curds from sinking.

Let the curds settle in the whey for a few minutes.

Pour 1 quart/1 liter of whey to mix the brine. Measure 3 tablespoons/45 grams of salt and dissolve it in the brine. Put aside in a jar until the cheese is ready for brining.

Drain the whey off the curds in a cheesecloth-lined colander.

Salt the curds. Sprinkle 2 tablespoons of salt onto the curds and gently mix by hand for a few minutes, as salt pulls more whey out.

Collect the curds in a ball. Lift the corners of the cheesecloth out of the colander; then join the corners together and twist the cheesecloth to tighten the ball and force water out.

Use weight to force the whey out. Place the ball of cheese on a sloped surface (a cutting board propped up slightly under one end), then place a second flat surface on top of the curds, weighted by a cooking pot, book, or other moderately heavy object. After an hour (or more), the cheese will hold its form when you unwrap the cheesecloth.

Cut the cheese into chunks that can fit into the jar.

Salt and air-dry. Sprinkle 2 tablespoons of salt onto the surfaces and air-dry on a rack at room temperature for a day or two, flipping a few times to make sure all surfaces get to dry.

Cover with brine. Fill the jar with cheeses and pour brine over them.

Age brined cheese in a cellar or refrigerator for at least 1 week.

ricotta cheese

Ricotta is Italian for "recooked," and ricotta cheese is simply the whey from other cheesemaking briefly fermented in order to acidify it, then cooked.

Timeframe: 24 hours or more

Equipment: Cheesecloth

Ingredients (for about ½ pound/250 grams/1 cup):

½ gallon/2 liters whey (left over from low-temperature raw milk or cultured cheesemaking)

Process:

Ferment the whey for 24 hours or longer to acidify it.

Boil the whey. No need to worry about burning but keep an eye on it because once it reaches a boil it foams and can easily boil over.

Remove from the heat as soon as it boils.

Settle. Allow the small curds that form to settle for about 10 minutes as whey begins to cool.

Strain through the cheesecloth and leave to drain until cool.

The Battle Over Raw Cheese Regulations

Traditionally, most cheeses have been prepared with methods like those just described, using raw milk and seeking to maintain the enzymes and live cultures present in the milk. Research on pasteurization in the cheesemaking process was first undertaken at the University of Wisconsin in 1907. By 1949, Congress passed a law requiring pasteurization of all milk and dairy products, including cheeses, unless the cheese is aged for at least 60 days.

This has been the status quo ever since. It has meant that many of the world's finest soft cheeses are unavailable (legally, at least) in the United States. The US Food and Drug Administration has repeatedly considered more stringent regulations on raw milk cheeses, always evoking vocal protests. "Tampering with fine aged raw-milk cheeses is like slashing an ancient painting by a master, or shredding the original score of a classic symphony," warned the American Society for Microbiology.[7] "Pasteurization . . . translates to a lowering of the flavor bar, eliminating the potential to produce a depth and complexity of flavor that can exist with unpasteurized milk cheese," explains Ruth Flore of the American Cheese Society. The threat to raw milk cheeses is not limited to the US. The European Alliance for Artisan and Traditional Raw Milk Cheese charges that traditional cheese "is now being insidiously undermined by the sterile hand of global hygiene controls."[8]

Do unpasteurized cheeses really pose a health threat? The US Centers for Disease Control (CDC) compiled a study titled "Cheese-Associated Outbreaks of Human Illness in the United States, 1973–1992." The CDC analysis found 58 deaths from contaminated cheeses, 48 of them from listeriosis traced to a single California factory producing queso fresco, a Mexican-style cheese made from milk that had been pasteurized. Food writer Jeffrey Steingarten investigated the CDC findings and reported that not a single death could be attributed to raw milk cheeses, only a single case of salmonella.[9]

If a single case of salmonella justified banning a food, we would have precious few foods to choose from. "If you can't stand a little risk . . . shoot the cow," quipped an anonymous microbiologist.[10] "There are no scientific reasons or health needs to compel the sacrifice of these cheeses on the altars of mass production and worldwide standardization," states Flore. Quirky local cheeses that cannot be easily reproduced do not hold much potential in the global marketplace. The homogenization of culture rears its ugly head in the regulatory arena.

vegan adaptations

Grains, legumes, seeds, and nuts can be rendered into milk and cheese form, and these milks and cheeses can be fermented. Many commercially available non-dairy cheeses succeed in obtaining cheese-like textures, but fail to incorporate the flavors or the cultures of fermentation. My personal experimentation in this realm is somewhat limited (primarily due to my love of dairy), but I have made and sampled many delicious fermented non-dairy milks and cheeses, and I encourage further experimentation.

While I was first experimenting for the original edition of this book, my friend and fellow communard River, who is vegan, used milk kefir grains to ferment a number of different milk alternatives, every single one of them delicious. My favorite was coconut milk kefir, bubbly and rich and sweet and sour. All he did was add about 1 tablespoon of kefir grains to a can's worth of coconut milk and leave it in a jar (not the can, since fermentation acids can react with metal) for a day or two at room temperature. Really you can do exactly the same with soy milk, hemp milk, almond milk, rice milk, or any seed, nut, or grain milk. (Read more about kefir on page 118.)

The catch is that the kefir grains cannot be sustained for long on non-dairy milks. They evolved on lactose, and without lactose they cannot thrive or reproduce. So every second or third batch they need some milk. Similarly, I've experimented with water kefir grains in various non-dairy milks, with delicious results, but with the same unsustainable limitation. The water kefir grains do not grow or thrive, and need to be returned to a sugar-water solution every couple of batches. I imagine that for most vegans regularly rotating in feeding the kefir sugar-water is more palatable than it would be for milk. (Read more about water kefir on page 98.)

pepita seed milk and kefir

River's favorite kefir is from pepita seed milk. Pepitas are pumpkin seeds, rich in flavor and nutrition; any edible seeds or nuts could be used. River's method is deceptively simple, much easier than soy milk, and tasty, too. One really great thing about finding an alternative to commercial non-dairy milk is that most of it has such wasteful packaging. Do-it-yourself seed milk just goes in a jar, no fancy multilayered disposable carcass required. Here's River's pepita milk process.

Timeframe: 20 minutes for milk; 1 to 2 days for kefir

Equipment: Blender

Ingredients (for about 1 quart/1 liter):

1 cup/160 grams pepita seeds (or substitute any seed or nut)

1 teaspoon lecithin (optional—serves as a binder)

Process:

Grind the seeds. Place in a blender and grind into a fine meal.

Add water. Start with ½ cup/125 milliliters water and blend into a paste. Add 3 cups/750 milliliters more water and the lecithin, if desired, and blend some more.

Strain through cheesecloth, pressing to squeeze moisture from the seed solids. Use the solid remains in bread or pancakes.

Add more water, a little at a time, and stir until you reach your desired consistency. Store in the refrigerator and stir before use.

To ferment pepita milk, add 1 tablespoon of water kefir or dairy kefir grains to 1 quart/1 liter of milk, and leave them together in a jar at room temperature for a day or two. Then strain out the grains and enjoy the tangy, bubbly, delicious treat.

non-dairy yogurt

Yogurt cultures seem most adaptable to coconut milk and soy milk. Proceed as for traditional dairy yogurt. Use a commercial coconut yogurt or soy yogurt as starter, or dairy yogurt. Heat milk to 180°F/82°C; cool it to 115°F/46°C; introduce a small proportion of starter (1 teaspoon per quart/liter); and incubate 8 hours at 110°F/43°C. See Yogurt, page 111, for more detailed instructions. Coconut yogurt and soy yogurt are thick, nearly solid, like milk yogurt. Some of my other experiments with non-dairy yogurts, such as rice milk, did not get thick, though they tasted fine.

sunflower sour cream

Seeds are very versatile and can be transformed into many different textures and consistencies (much like milk). This recipe came from the newsletter of our local food buying club. Inspiration comes from random places! My friend Orchid whipped up a batch, and I couldn't help myself from fermenting some of it with kefir grains. The delicious tart result was the most sour-creamy non-dairy concoction I've ever tried.

Timeframe: 2 days

Ingredients (for about 2½ cups/625 milliliters):

1 cup/150 grams raw sunflower seeds
2 tablespoons raw flaxseeds
¼ cup/50 grams cooked leftover grains
3 tablespoons olive oil
1 teaspoon honey (or other sweetener)
1 tablespoon finely chopped onion, scallion, or chives
¼ teaspoon celery seed
⅓ cup/80 milliliters lemon juice
1 tablespoon kefir grains
½ teaspoon salt

Process:

Soak the sunflower and flaxseeds in enough water to cover them, for about 8 hours.

Drain the seeds and reserve the water.

Purée the soaked seeds with the other ingredients (except the kefir grains and salt) in a blender or food processor. Add the reserved water, just a little at a time, until the mixture reaches a thick, creamy consistency.

Transfer the mixture to a jar or non-metal bowl.

Add the kefir grains.

Ferment 1 to 3 days, stirring a couple of times each day to distribute contact and activity.

Remove the kefir grains, if you can find them. If not, don't worry; they are edible and nutritious.

Add the salt and stir well before serving.

Enjoy sunflower sour cream on potatoes or as a spread or dip.

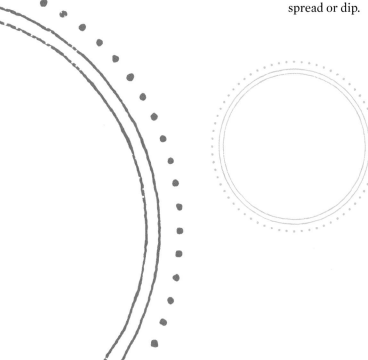

Further Reading

Asher, David. *The Art of Natural Cheesemaking*. White River Junction, VT: Chelsea Green Publishing, 2015.

Caldwell, Gianaclis. *Mastering Artisan Cheesemaking: The Ultimate Guide for Home-Scale and Market Producers*. White River Junction, VT: Chelsea Green Publishing, 2012.

———. *Mastering Basic Cheesemaking: The Fun and Fundamentals of Making Cheese at Home*. Gabriola Island, Canada: New Society Publishers, 2016.

Carroll, Ricki. *Home Cheese Making*. North Adams, MA: Storey Books, 2002.

Hill, Louella. *Kitchen Creamery: Making Yogurt, Butter & Cheese at Home*. San Francisco: Chronicle Books, 2015.

Karlin, Mary. *Artisan Cheese Making at Home: Techniques & Recipes for Mastering World-Class Cheeses*. Berkeley, CA: Ten Speed Press, 2011.

Kindstedt, Paul. *American Farmstead Cheese*. White River Junction, VT: Chelsea Green Publishing, 2005.

Lucero, Claudia. *One-Hour Cheese: Ricotta, Mozzarella, Chèvre, Paneer—Even Burrata. Fresh and Simple Cheeses You Can Make in an Hour or Less!* New York: Workman Publishing, 2011.

Rule, Cheryl Sternman. *Yogurt Culture: A Global Look at How to Make, Bake, Sip, and Chill the World's Creamiest, Healthiest Food*. New York: Houghton Mifflin Harcourt, 2015.

Schinner, Miyoko. *Artisan Vegan Cheese*. Summertown, TN: Book Publishing Co., 2012.

8: grain ferments
(Porridges, Soft Drinks, Soups, Flatbreads, and Breads)

The objective of grain fermentation is fundamentally different than with the fermentation of vegetables or milk, in which preservation is foremost. Grains (and legumes, covered in the next chapter) preserve best in their mature dried state, maintained in a cool, dry, and dark environment. It is their dryness that preserves them, for though they—like all the things that make up our food—are populated by elaborate communities of bacteria and yeast, these microbes remain dormant so long as they are deprived of water.

The same dense, dry quality that makes grains so stable for storage also makes them difficult to digest. They nourish us best with the pre-digestion of fermentation. Seeds have various biological strategies to fend off hungry critters (including us) that can be described as anti-nutrients—for instance, phytates and trypsin inhibitors, which prevent us from accessing nutrients within the seeds. These anti-nutrients are broken down by fermentation, improving the bioavailability of minerals and rendering the grains or legumes more nutritious and more digestible. Fermentation also makes grains and legumes more flavorful and contributes aeration and textural lightness.

There are many ways of fermenting grains. In Western culture, many think first of bread, synonymous with sustenance and representing much more than mere food. The elaborate process of growing and harvesting grain and making bread "symbolized civilization's mastery over nature," writes Michael Pollan in *The Botany of Desire*.[1] Bread, or

the lack thereof, has inspired revolutions; a rise in the price of bread was one of the sparks that ignited the French Revolution, for example. Bread is a staple food in many parts of the world. It is made in an extraordinary variety of styles, not all of them formed into loaves and baked.

There are many varied flatbreads, of course, cooked from doughs pressed or batters spread, and they are frequently first fermented. You can mill grains into flour (or more coarsely, such as bulgur, polenta, grits, or rolled oats), mix with water, and ferment that. Or you can soak whole grains, then grind them into a dough or batter, and ferment that. You can sprout the grains, first. You can make steam-breads, fry-breads, or crackers, or fermented grain-based porridges, soups, and beverages, among them beers (covered in chapter 11). The range of what grains mixed with water can become is nearly infinite, thanks to diverse grains and diverse traditional methods, all facilitated by the rich indigenous microbiota found on all grains, dormant until awakened by water.

Barley koji.

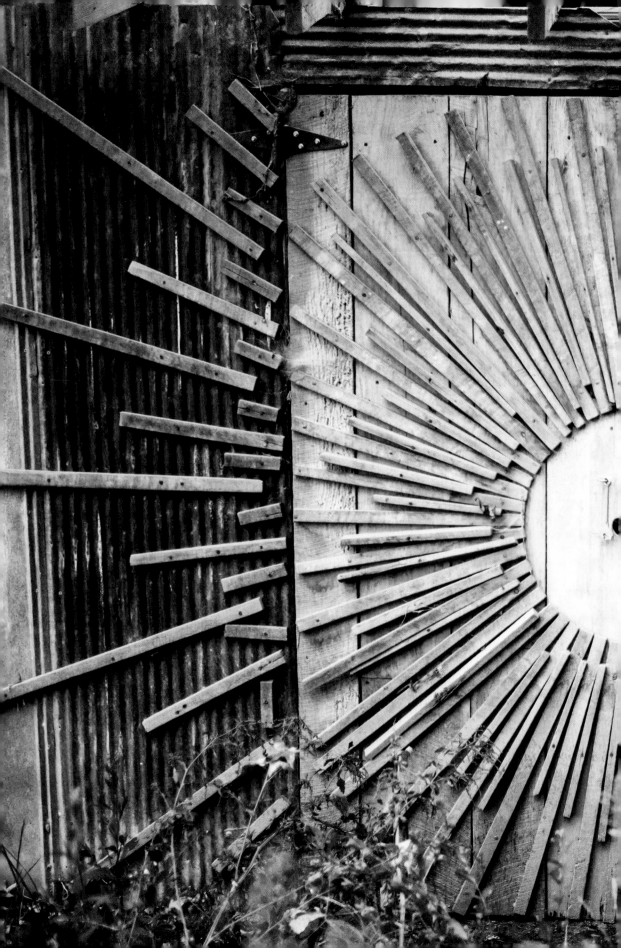

Seed Saving and Seed Freedom

Before getting into methods for fermenting grains, I must briefly address the simple fact that grains are seeds. Along with fermentation methods, language, and so much more, seeds are essential elements of the cultural legacy we have inherited from our ancestors. Through countless generations of selection and co-evolution, the seeds of our crops have been shaped to embody desirable traits ranging from flavor, yield, and ease of harvest to drought survival and pest resistance. Seeds, an integral and self-generating part of the plants that sustain us, are the first link in the food chain.

Like fermentation methods, seeds are manifestations of conditions in specific places. Yet over the course of the last century, and continuing today with greater intensity, farmers and gardeners have largely abandoned traditional locally evolved seeds in favor of buying supposedly improved varieties, initially created by hybridization, now also by genetic modification (GM). Whereas all traditional seeds were saved as part of the process of growing the plants, these new seeds require specialized propagation and cannot be easily perpetuated; and furthermore they are patented and so their genetics are legally property, thus breeding dependence and opening new avenues for corporate control of our food, as well as diminishing biodiversity of locally adapted varieties and hastening cultural homogenization. "What we are seeing is the emergence of food totalitarianism," writes Vandana Shiva in *Stolen Harvest: The Hijacking of the Global Food Supply*, "in which a handful of corporations control the entire food chain and destroy alternatives so that people do not have access to diverse, safe foods produced ecologically."[2]

Around the world, movements are emerging to preserve, propagate, and spread what survives of the heirloom seeds that are our heritage. Seed saving, an ancient practice at the core of agriculture, and indeed, culture, has become an act of resistance. In certain cases, where genes from patented GM crops have contaminated neighboring fields and turned up in saved seeds, farmers have been prosecuted for seed saving, and this foundational act of culture has literally become an act of civil disobedience. The struggle for seed freedom is very closely related to the fermentation revival in that both seek to give renewed relevance to ancient inherited cultural practices. Let us broaden the context of our thinking about fermentation beyond gustatory pleasure and personal health to encompass seed freedom and other struggles beyond for basic human rights.

soaking

The first step in fermenting grains is to soak them. Water is the source of all life, and the dry seed is able to persist intact precisely because, in the absence of water, the microbes inevitably present on it cannot function or grow. Yet they do remain, dormant until restored to life by water, much like the seed itself.

Grains benefit from soaking, even if you are not fermenting anything but just cooking them. Use dechlorinated water, in whatever proportion you wish, for cooking the grains. You can soak grains for just a few hours, if that's all you have; although pre-digestion will just be getting under way, it's better than not soaking at all. More pre-digestion will occur faster if you soak grains in warm (body-temperature) water and add some active live cultures—such as a little soaking liquid saved from a previous soak, whey, sourdough starter, buttermilk, or sauerkraut juice—or acids such as vinegar or lemon juice. If you can, soak 8 to 12 hours; or soak for a day or longer to allow for a fuller pre-digestion and to really develop flavor. The longer you allow grain fermentation to proceed (up to a point), the more acidic flavors will develop, thanks to the presence of lactic acid bacteria. Soaking is easy; it does not actually take any extra work, just a little planning.

Part of the seed library at Navdanya, Dr. Vandana Shiva's farm and school where I taught in India.

oat porridge

Oatmeal (or "oytmeal," as my father always calls it, in imitation of his Lithuanian-born grandmother) is the quintessential comfort food. It is soft and mushy, harking back to that long-ago time of infancy, when all our food was of such a consistency and lovingly spoon-fed to us. Fermenting oats before cooking them makes them creamier, richer in flavor, and more nutritious. I grew up eating oatmeal savory, with butter, milk, salt, and pepper. These days I doll it up with butter, peanut butter, and miso. Oatmeal is nothing if not versatile.

Timeframe: 8 hours or more

Ingredients (for 4–6 servings):

1 cup/125 grams oats, coarsely ground, steel-cut, or rolled
Sea salt

Process:

Soak the oats in about 3 cups/750 milliliters of water. Cover to keep dust and flies out.

Ferment overnight, or for several days. A short ferment begins pre-digestion but has a mild flavor not heavily influenced by fermentation. The distinctive flavors of fermentation emerge after 24 to 48 hours, depending upon temperature, and become more prominent the longer you let it ferment (up to a point).

Cook the oats. Add a pinch of salt and bring the oats and water to a boil. Lower the heat and cook until the oats absorb all the water, about 10 minutes. Add a little more water if you prefer a thinner, runnier texture; more oats if you prefer it firmer. Stir frequently, as the sticky, starchy oatmeal can burn easily.

Serve. However you like to eat your oatmeal, sweet or savory, you'll love the creaminess of this fermented version.

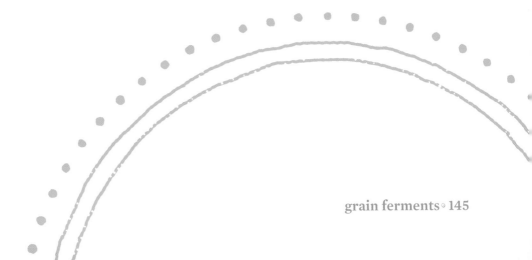

ogi (african millet porridge)

Porridge can be made from any grain or combination of grains. Millet porridge, which I first encountered in West Africa when I traveled there, is especially delicious. Millet's mild flavor is strengthened by fermentation, and the porridge can be further embellished with coconut oil, butter, miso, peanut butter, sweeteners, salt and pepper, garlic, kefir or yogurt, hot sauce, kraut, leftovers, or almost anything.

Timeframe: Flexible, from 1 to 4 days

Ingredients (for 4–6 servings):

1 cup/200 grams millet
Sea salt
1 tablespoon coconut oil or butter (optional)

Process:

Coarsely grind the millet using a grain mill or other grinding technology.

Soak the millet in about 1 quart/1 liter of water. Soaking time can range from about 8 hours to about 4 days; the taste will become progressively sourer as the days pass.

Cook the porridge. Add a pinch of salt and coconut oil or butter to the millet and water, and bring to a boil. Lower the heat and cook until the millet absorbs all the water, about 15 minutes, stirring frequently. Add more water as needed to reach your desired consistency.

Enjoy embellished as you like.

gv-no-he-nv
(cherokee sour corn drink)

This is a Cherokee sour corn drink. The *v* is pronounced like the *u* in *but*. Gv-no-he-nv is essentially a gruel, lightly fermented. In the early stages, this thick, milky drink has the sweet flavor of corn accented by mild hints of sourness. As it matures, gv-no-he-nv develops a strong, almost cheesy flavor.

I learned about gv-no-he-nv when I started to investigate southeastern native fermentation traditions. I strive to remain aware of the shameful history of genocide and land theft here where I live in

Tennessee, as throughout the United States. The indigenous inhabitants of these lush hills and hollows were forcibly removed and sent westward on the Trail of Tears nearly 200 years ago. I wanted to acknowledge them in this book and find out whether and how their food traditions, like those of most people in most places, incorporated fermentation. I was able to learn that at least some of the earlier inhabitants where I live practiced fermentation, as illustrated by this Cherokee beverage made by fermenting corn. "This was a customary drink to serve to friends who dropped by for a visit," according to one Cherokee source; it is also "enjoyed by those who worked in the field," notes another.[3] Gv-no-he-nv bears similarity in process to other corn-based fermented beverages, such as Mexican atole or South African mahewu.

Timeframe: A few days to 1 week (or more)

Ingredients (for about 2 quarts/2 liters):

2 cups/350 grams dry field corn, nixtamalized (see page 150)

Process:

Nixtamalize the corn, as described below. Though *nixtamal* is an Aztec word, the practice of processing corn with wood ash was widespread in the Americas, practiced by the Cherokee and many other North American tribes.

Crush the kernels, using a hand grinder, mortar and pestle, or food processor.

Cook the corn in 10 cups/2.5 liters of water for about 1 hour, stirring frequently to prevent burning, until the corn chunks are soft and the liquid is thick.

To sour, leave the liquid in a jar in a warm spot, stirring periodically. It starts out sweet and slowly develops its sourness. According to the recipe I learned from: "The drink may be kept for quite a while unless the weather is very hot."

Strain using a mesh strainer and pressing the solids against it; use the fermented corn chunks in pancakes, bread, corn bread, polenta, or in other cooking.

Enjoy! Drink strained gv-no-he-nv either plain as is (delicious!), or with a simple embellishment, such as salt, honey, chili, chocolate, ginger, or something more elaborate.

If gv-no-he-nv gets too strong to enjoy as a drink (and even if not), it also makes a great ingredient in cooking, especially to thicken soups.

corn and nixtamalization

People in the United States consume a lot of corn thanks to its importance in feeding animals for milk and meat, its prominence as a fragmented ingredient (such as high-fructose corn syrup or cornstarch) in food processing industries, and its use as a fuel. In its indigenous context, corn (*Zea mays*, also known as maize) has been used in very different ways, and historically was the main agricultural staple of the Americas, North and South, long before the arrival of Europeans. One of the myriad ways in which traditional usage of corn differs from how it has been adapted by most settlers and those who exported it is a process called nixtamalization. This is the anglicized version of an Aztec word. In the middle of the word you can find the word *tamale*. Tamales and most other Mexican corn products are prepared using this process. Flour of nixtamalized corn in Mexican markets is called masa. The corn so treated is known in English, especially the southeastern US, as hominy.

The process of nixtamalization is simple. The corn is briefly cooked with lime (the alkaline substance, not the citrus fruit) or its traditional source, wood ash, then rinsed. This alkalinizing process not only enables the tough outer skin of the corn to be removed, but also alters the color and flavor of corn and greatly enhances its nutritional quality. Specifically, it alters the availability of amino acids and vitamins, rendering nixtamalized corn a complete protein, and making niacin (vitamin B_3) available.[4] "So superior is nixtamalized maize to the unprocessed kind that it is tempting to see the rise of Mesoamerican civilization as a consequence of this invention," writes historian Sophie D. Coe.[5] Maize was exported around the world, but not the nixtamalization process, and maize-dependent cultures that developed outside the Americas consistently developed widespread niacin and protein deficiencies, rare where nixtamalization is practiced.

Nixtamalization is not itself a fermentation process. But many traditional corn fermentation processes (such as gv-no-he-nv, above) use nixtamalized corn, so I will briefly describe the process, which consists of gently cooking corn in water with wood ash or calcium hydroxide. The latter is available from Mexican markets as Cal, and from canning/pickling suppliers as hydrated lime; make sure it's food grade, as the same compound, less pure, is used in agriculture and construction.

Length of cooking varies, by local tradition, type of corn, and usage. In the first edition of this book I made the mistake of equating nixtamal with pozole (a particular type of corn with a distinctive alkaline treatment), and recommended soaking the corn first, then cooking with ash for 3 hours. Years later, after I met the great English-language interpreter of Mexican cuisine, Diana Kennedy, and she read the nixtamalization section, she wrote to me alarmed. "Who on earth told you that? You would end up with a sticky mess! Actually you are confusing two things here: 1. nixtamal, corn simmered, but not cooked, with lime, to be rinsed then ground for masa; and 2. preparing (dried) large corn kernels, usually cacahua zintle, for pozole . . . You only soak the pozole corn overnight, NEVER the ordinary corn for masa."

Indeed, I have had nixtamal become a sticky mess, with the corn completely dissolved into the ash-water. My learning curve continues. Thanks to Diana Kennedy, this is the improved process I now use to nixtamalize corn.

Timeframe: About 3 hours

Ingredients (for about 4 cups/ 1 liter nixtamal):

2 cups/350 grams whole-grain corn
1 cup/70 grams sifted wood ash,
   or 2 tablespoons Cal or hydrated lime
   (see above)

Process:

Cover the corn with a good amount of water in a pot and bring to a boil.

Add the ash or lime. Mix the sifted ash or hydrated lime with cold water, stir, and add the solution to the boiling water. If you use wood ash, be sure to use only the ash of untreated real wood—not plywood, particleboard, or other glued-together products, or pressure-treated lumber. The reason it is important to sift the ash first is that large chunks will not dissolve and are difficult to rinse out.

Gently simmer. The corn will turn bright orange immediately. Cook for about 15 minutes, or until the skins begin to loosen from the kernels. To test for doneness, rub a kernel of corn between your palms to see if the skin is loose. If so, remove from the heat; if not, continue cooking. (If you cook too long, the skins, and eventually the entire kernels, will dissolve.) Once the skins are separating from the kernels, remove the pot from the heat, cover, and leave the corn to sit in the hot alkaline solution until cool.

Rinse and knead. After the lime-cooked corn cools, rinse well to remove the lime solution, kneading and rubbing the corn kernels between the palms of your hands to loosen and remove the skins. Rinse until the water is clear. If the skins are still attached to the corn, continue rubbing kernels between your palms to remove them.

Nixtamal is now ready for grinding into masa, or for fermentation projects.

injera
(ethiopian sponge bread)

One special fermented flatbread that I love is injera, the spongy bread that is a staple in Ethiopian cuisine. In Ethiopian restaurants, food is served on trays lined with injera, and you eat by ripping off pieces of injera and scooping food into it. Enjoy with Groundnut Sweet Potato Stew (recipe follows), or any saucy dish; an Internet search will yield many other more traditional Ethiopian recipes. Injera is also a great vehicle for wraps of pretty much anything. Injera typically is made without a starter, but you can certainly speed up the process by adding a little bubbly sourdough starter (see page 158). Injera is generally cooked in advance and served at room temperature.

Timeframe: 1 to 3 days, depending upon temperature

Ingredients (for 12–16 injera):

4 cups/500 grams flour, all teff (a grain grown and used in Ethiopia), or half teff and half whole wheat

½ teaspoon salt

½ teaspoon baking soda or baking powder (optional)

Vegetable oil

Process:

Mix the batter. In a large jar or bowl, combine the flour with 3 cups/750 milliliters lukewarm water. Stir well until smooth. The mixture should have the consistency of thin pancake batter. Add a little more water or flour if necessary. Cover to keep flies out.

Ferment in a warm place, stirring as often as you think of it. It is ready to use when bubbly, about 24 hours in a warm environment, 2 to 3 days in a cool environment.

Add the salt when you are ready to cook the injera.

Heat a well-seasoned crepe pan or skillet over medium heat. Lightly oil the pan.

Pour the batter onto the hot skillet, taking care to spread it as thinly as possible. If the batter won't spread thinly, thin it with a little more water. Get the pan hot enough to sizzle when you pour the batter on, but cook the pancakes gently over medium heat.

Cover the pan as the injera cooks. Cook until holes appear all over and the top is dry. Cook on one side only; do not flip. Remove from the pan onto a towel to cool. Once cooled, injera may be stacked.

Where are the bubbles? If you find that your injera is not as bubbly as you desire, add baking soda to the batter and stir well. Baking soda leavens because it's alkaline and reacts with the acidity of the souring dough, thereby neutralizing some of the sour flavor. Alternatively, you can leaven with baking powder, which contains baking soda as well as acid compounds that react with the soda when wet, so it produces comparable bubbling with less of a neutralizing effect on the acid flavor.

With Dr. Vandana Shiva at Navdanya,
her farm and school where I taught in India.

groundnut (peanut) sweet potato stew

My friend MaxZine has encouraged my fermentation explorations from the start, in many ways. In the early years of my obsession he would organize big feasts around fermented goodies, including a few Ethiopian nights. I made injera and t'ej, Ethiopian-style mead (see page 216), and he made the rest. This easy and delectable dish is one he made for an Ethiopian feast, inspired by the cookbook *Sundays at Moosewood Restaurant*.

Groundnut is what the peanut (*Arachis hypogaea*) is called in English-speaking regions of Africa.

Timeframe: 30 to 40 minutes

Ingredients (for 6–8 servings):

2 tablespoons coconut or other vegetable oil
2–3 onions, chopped
About 1 pound/500 grams sweet potatoes, cubed to about 4 cups/1 liter
4 cloves garlic, chopped
1 teaspoon cayenne
2 teaspoons ginger, fresh or powdered
1 teaspoon cumin
1 tablespoon paprika
1 teaspoon fenugreek
1 teaspoon salt
Dash each cinnamon and clove
4 cups/1 liter fresh or canned tomatoes
1 cup/250 milliliters apple juice, or 1 cup/250 milliliters water plus 1 tablespoon honey
¾ cup/185 milliliters peanut butter
4 cups/350 grams chopped cabbage or other dark leafy greens

Process:

Heat the oil in a good-size, deep cooking pot.

Sauté the onions in the oil until translucent, about 5 minutes.

Add the sweet potatoes, garlic, and cayenne; sauté, covered, for 5 minutes.

Add the other ingredients, except the peanut butter and greens. Bring to a boil, reduce the heat, and simmer about 10 minutes.

Add the peanut butter near the end of cooking, to avoid burning. Remove about 1 cup/250 milliliters of the hot liquid from the pot, and combine it with the peanut butter into a creamy paste. Return this to the pot and mix in.

Add the greens last and simmer about 5 more minutes, stirring frequently to prevent burning on the bottom. Add more water if the stew is too thick, and adjust the seasonings to taste.

Serve with injera and/or over millet.

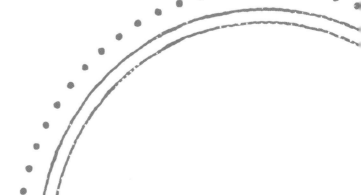

infinite buckwheat bread (and pancakes)

This is the best gluten-free bread I have eaten and the easiest I have made, with rich flavor, moistness, and great texture. I first tried it when I was teaching in Nova Scotia, in eastern Canada. At a post-workshop potluck, Anke and Roberto of Conscious Catering shared it. They told me how they made it, and I've been making it and sharing the method ever since. Their recipe, along with their great tips, troubleshooting, and variations, is posted on their website at http://consciouscatering.ca/nama-bread.

Timeframe: About 36 hours

Ingredients (for 1 loaf):

3 cups/600 grams whole raw buckwheat (not roasted)
2 teaspoons sea salt
Coconut or other oil (for greasing pan)
¼ cup/40 grams sesame or poppy seeds

Process:

Soak. Rinse the buckwheat, cover with plenty of water, and soak for 8 to 12 hours.

Drain. After soaking, drain the buckwheat through a sieve. The water will be a little slimy. Leave the grains in the sieve for a minute in order to drain fully.

Blend. Combine the buckwheat with ¾ cup/185 milliliters of fresh water and salt and blend for at least 1 to 2 full minutes or until there are no more visible pieces of buckwheat. The batter should be of pancake batter consistency. If necessary add just a little more water.

Ferment in a non-metallic bowl, covered with a clean cloth, at room temperature for approximately 24 hours (less in a hot environment, more in a cool environment).

Grease a loaf pan and sprinkle the bottom and sides generously with seeds (or line with parchment paper). Pour the batter into the pan.

Let the batter rise in the pan for 1 to 3 hours.

Preheat the oven to 400°F/205°C.

Bake. Place the loaf in a heated oven and reduce the heat to 350°F/175°C. Bake for an hour. Remove the loaf from the oven and allow the bread to rest in the pan for about 15 minutes. (These loaves can be fragile until they cool briefly; but if you leave them cooling in the pan too long, they can get soggy.)

Remove the loaf from the pan and allow to fully cool before slicing and eating.

Make pancakes using the same batter, adding water, just a little at a time, and stirring, until your desirable consistency is achieved.

Variation: Replace up to half the buckwheat with millet, quinoa, and/or other whole grains.

yeast and natural leavening

We generally think about the fermentation of bread primarily in terms of yeast, used in bread-making to make dough rise. In our time, yeast is available in every grocery store as an isolated microorganism, a fungus called *Saccharomyces cerevisiae*: The word *saccharo* means "sugar," *myces* means "fungus," and *cerevisiae* might seem more familiar when you think about the Spanish word for "beer," *cerveza*. The same yeast that makes most beer makes most bread. They are made from grains, just with different processes. In both, the yeast does the same thing: It consumes carbohydrates and transforms them into alcohol and carbon dioxide. In bread, the carbon dioxide is the more important product. Its bubbles are what rise the bread, giving it texture and lightness. The alcohol evaporates as the bread is cooked.

Though yeast as a particular type of organism was not isolated until the mid-19th century, the word *yeast* is ancient and comes from the Greek *zestos*, meaning "boil" (like the word *fermentation* itself, from the Latin *fervere*). Prior to the science of microbiology, yeast referred to the visible action of fermentation, the rising of a dough, or the frothing of a batter or a beer, and to the various clever methods that people developed to perpetuate that bubbling transformative power. Yeast is the lifting action, the bubbles, the leavening. Until Louis Pasteur isolated a particular fungus and named it yeast, neither yeast nor any other microorganism ever existed in isolation. French historian Bruno Latour, in his book *The Pasteurization of France*, observes of Pasteur's isolation of pure microbial strains: "For the first time—for them as well as for us—they were to form homogenous aggregates . . . which none of their ancestors ever knew."[6]

The yeasts you find in nature are never pure. They travel in motley company. They are always found with other microorganisms. They embody biodiversity. They have distinctive flavors. And they are everywhere. All earlier "yeast" consisted of biodiverse microbial communities including the type of fungus we know as yeast but also lactic acid bacteria and others. Such biodiverse microbial communities exist in abundance on our grains, as well as in (non-chlorinated) water and air, always ready to stop and feast.

In bread-making, the perceived advantage of working with pure yeast is that the huge concentration of yeast works fast and that makes the process of making bread easier and more predictable. Natural leavening with wild fermentation is slower. The bacteria in the mixed culture get a chance to break down hard-to-digest gluten, liberate minerals, and add B vitamins. The lactic acid and other metabolic by-products of fermenting organisms contribute complex sour flavors and enable the bread to keep longer. With pure yeast breads, nutrition, digestibility, flavor, and preservation potential are sacrificed for speed and ease.

Prior to the widespread availability of commercial yeast, people used any one of a number of methods to propagate their yeasts. Most often bread makers reserve a bit of their yeasty batter or dough as a "starter." A starter can be maintained for a lifetime and passed on for generations. It often accompanied immigrants (dried on a cloth) on their journey to new unknown lands. Starter is mostly referred to nowadays as sourdough or natural leaven. In recipe books and on supermarket shelves, sourdough is widely included as a gourmet novelty. But I like to remember that until relatively recently, all bread was made this way. Any kind of bread you like, except perhaps the totally bland, squishy kinds that fill supermarket shelves, can be made with natural leavening. Sourdough breads don't even have to be especially sour!

starting and maintaining a sourdough starter

Starting a sourdough is as easy as mixing flour and water in a bowl and leaving it on the kitchen counter for a few days, stirring periodically. The yeast is there, along with lactic acid bacteria and many others, and they will all reveal themselves. The work is in building the vigor of the starter, then maintaining it and keeping it alive and fresh. A sourdough starter requires regular feeding and attention, not unlike a small pet.

Timeframe: About 1 week

Ingredients:

4 cups/640 grams flour (any kind)

Process:

Combine. In a small jar or bowl, mix ¼ cup/40 grams of the flour and ¼ cup/60 milliliters dechlorinated room temperature water. The reason to start with such a small amount is that with each subsequent feeding you will add three times as much fresh flour and water, so it will get big fast! I have generally used rye flour because it gets bubbly faster, and I love rye bread, but the flour of any grain will do.

Stir frequently. This speeds the process by distributing microbial activity and also by aerating, which stimulates rapid yeast growth. Stirring also protects the developing ferment by keeping the surface fresh. All you need to do is keep stirring a couple of times a day. If you are impatient, drop a few pieces of whole small fruits into it. Often on grapes and berries you can actually see the chalky film of yeast ("the bloom") that is drawn to their sweetness. These and other fruits with edible skins (not bananas or citrus) are great for getting sourdoughs bubbling. If you do this, use local or organic fruit; who knows what antimicrobial compounds could lurk on the skins of the fruits of chemical agriculture?

Cover with a cloth that will keep out flies but allow for free circulation of air.

Ferment. A warm place (70–80°F/21–27°C) with good air circulation is ideal, but work with what you have. Stir vigorously at least a couple of times each day. After a few days you will notice tiny bubbles releasing at the surface of the batter. Note that the action of stirring the batter may create some bubbles. Do not confuse these with the bubbles the batter produces when you are not actively introducing air into the mixture. The number of days it will take for yeast to become active in your batter will depend upon temperature, your flour, your water, and environmental factors. If you do not find bubbles forming after 3 or 4 days, try to find a warmer spot.

Feed the starter. Once bubbling is evident, the starter is alive and needs to be fed. In a larger bowl, mix together ¾ cup/120 grams flour and ¾ cup/185 milliliters water. Add the bubbly starter (with any fruit removed) to that and stir vigorously. It is important to feed the developing starter a high proportion of fresh flour and water rather than feeding it a small amount of fresh flour, because this dilutes and decreases the acidity, which makes for a more hospitable environment for yeast activity to build vigor.

Stir a couple of times a day.

Observe that the starter will get bubbly, and then the vigor will recede.

Feed it again. When the bubbling slows, feed it a high proportion of fresh flour again. In a larger bowl mix together 3 cups/480 grams flour and 3 cups/750 milliliters water. Add the bubbly starter to that and stir vigorously. Once this gets bubbly, your starter is ready to use.

Always save starter. Use sourdough starter as directed in the recipes that follow, or in other ways. Each time you use it, be sure to save some of the starter. All you need to save is a little. I keep mine in a jar (1-pint/500-milliliter size) and replenish the starter with what remains on the edges of the jar. To replenish the starter, I add about ¾ cup/120 grams flour and ¾ cup/185 milliliters dechlorinated water, stir well, and leave it in a warm place to bubble.

Ongoing maintenance. Generally, the more frequently a sourdough is used and fed, the more vigorous it will be. If you use the starter only sporadically, refrigerate it a day after feeding to slow microbial metabolism. A day or two before you plan to use it, move the starter from the fridge to a warm location and feed it a larger volume of flour and water, to get it active again. If you neglect your sourdough, it may get very acidic, then eventually become putrid. Even if they become putrid, starters can generally be revived. Pour off any liquid that has risen to the top and discard the entire top half of the sourdough starter. Take a teaspoonful from the bottom of the jar and place it in a fresh jar. Add 1 cup/160 grams flour and 1 cup/250 milliliters water to this and stir well. This high-proportion feeding will dilute the putrid flavor and reawaken the dormant yeasts and lactic acid bacteria. Pamper it: Stir daily, keep it warm, and feed it every day or two. Sourdoughs are very resilient and can come back from even extreme neglect.

savory vegetable sourdough pancakes

I have found that the way I use my sourdough most frequently—and thereby keep it fresh and vigorous—is by making pancakes. You can make sourdough pancakes sweet, if you like (as in Alaskan Frontier Sourdough Hotcakes, below), but the pancakes I typically make are savory pancakes, incorporating vegetables, leftover grains, cheese, eggs, or even meat. I make a batter like this a couple of times a week, and throw in whatever there's a lot of. Every batch is different. But here is a basic recipe to guide you on proportions.

Timeframe: 12 to 24 hours for initial fermentation, up to several days

Ingredients (for 12–16 4-inch/10-centimeter pancakes):

½ cup/125 milliliters bubbly sourdough starter

1 cup/160 grams whole wheat flour (experiment with combining or substituting other flours and coarser grinds)

2 cups/200 grams (or more) vegetables, which can include any of the following, alone or in combination: grated raw (or cooked) radish, turnip, carrot, parsnip, sweet potato, potato, and/or other root vegetables; mashed cooked squash, pumpkin, or sweet potato; sautéed onions, leeks, scallions, ramps, garlic, celery, peppers, okra, mushrooms, any kind of greens or cabbage; sprouts; anything!

1 cup/200 grams (or more) leftover cooked grains (optional)

2 ounces/50 grams cheese or more (optional)

1 teaspoon salt

1 egg (optional)

Butter or oil for greasing pan

Process:

Combine. In a bowl, mix the bubbly sourdough starter with 1 cup/150 grams flour and 1 cup/250 milliliters dechlorinated water. I generally use whole wheat flour or that mixed with rye, oats, or any leftover grains, but experiment with other grains you like, or totally gluten-free variations. Mix well and break up any clumps, so you have a smooth batter. Add a little more water if it seems too dense, or flour if it seems too thin, then mix again.

Don't forget to replenish your sourdough starter!

Add vegetables to the batter and stir. Any vegetable you like, cooked or raw, as elaborated above.

Add cheese if you like, any kind. Personally, I like to cube it so the pancakes have little puddles of melted cheese in them, but it depends on the cheese; you can also grate or crumble.

Add cooked grains if you have them: rice, oatmeal, polenta or grits, whole wheat or rye berries, or partially spent grains from other fermentation projects.

Add any other random ingredients you might want to incorporate, like leftover bite-size pieces of meat, pesto, or anything that strikes your fancy.

Stir well to combine all ingredients. Cover with a cloth.

Ferment 12 to 24 hours or longer. Once the batter is bubbly it can be used, though it develops more pronounced flavor after another day or two.

Add salt when you are ready to first use the batter.

Add an egg, if desired. I think it lightens the pancakes, but it is certainly not necessary.

Mix well. Evaluate the batter consistency. It needs to be liquid enough to be pourable and spreadable, but substantial enough to hold a form. If the mixture seems too thick, add water, just a little at a time; if it seems too thin, add flour, just a little at a time. Stir well and repeat if necessary.

Preheat a griddle or cast-iron pan. I use a crepe pan with low edges so it's easy to get under the pancakes to flip them. I like to get the pan hot, then reduce to a moderate heat.

Grease the pan with butter or oil.

Pour or scoop the batter into pancakes. I generally make three or four small pancakes, each with just 3 to 4 tablespoons of batter. As the pancakes cook, they bubble and their color shifts. Use a spatula to gently pry under the edges and loosen the pancakes, and peek at the color of the cooking side. When a pancake is golden brown, flip it and cook it on the other side. Add butter if the pan appears dry.

Enjoy! I serve my pancakes with yogurt-based condiments. Yogurt hot sauce—simply yogurt mixed with any of various hot sauces or pastes—is my everyday go-to. Another favorite is horseradish yogurt. In summer I love yogurt pesto. In lieu of sweet syrup, pancakes can be embellished and moistened by any number of creamy, savory condiments.

If you have leftover batter, or you want to wait longer, your batter can continue to ferment and slowly acidify for several days. I often like the pancakes better after 3 days than after 1. Eventually, after 4 or more days, it might start to develop less pleasing smells and flavors. Active batter can be preserved for weeks in the fridge.

alaskan frontier sourdough hotcakes

Sourdough was an important and mythological food along the American frontier; pioneers valued sourdough for its hardiness and reliability. San Francisco's signature sourdough is a memento of the California gold rush. And in Alaska, the frontiersmen themselves were known as sourdoughs, so dearly did they cherish this staple provision. "A real Alaskan Sourdough would as soon spend a year in the hills without his rifle, as to tough it through without his bubbling sourdough pot."

This quote is from Ruth Allman's longhand volume *Alaska Sourdough: The Real Stuff by a Real Alaskan*.[7] Allman recounts fantastic stories about the popularity of sourdough. "Somehow, word got around that baking powder, like saltpeter, was an anaphrodisiac. The he-man of the North was justly proud of his virility . . . [and] took no chances of his libido being impaired. The old-time Alaskan would not include baking powder biscuits in his regular diet. Thus was born the fame and popularity of sourdough."

The Arctic cold presented challenges to sourdough. "There is a serious problem when the thermometer skids down to –50 degrees," Allman writes. "Many a winter traveler has wrapped his sourdough pot in a canvas tarp and taken it to bed to keep it from freezing—to make sure he would have his sourdough for food tomorrow. While mushing on the trail with the temperature flirting below zero, Jack [her husband] would put some sourdough in an old Prince Albert tobacco can. This he tucked inside the pocket of his wool shirt to make certain it would not freeze. It takes very little sourdough to start the old sourdough pot a-bubbling again."

Allman recommends using baking soda in sourdough pancakes to neutralize sourness. "Sourdoughs never need to have the strong sour taste—only a fresh yeasty flavor," she writes; repeatedly reminding: "Remember soda sweetens." Sometimes sour isn't what you want.

Timeframe: 8 to 12 hours (mix batter the night before for breakfast pancakes)

Ingredients (for 12–16 4-inch/ 10-centimeter pancakes):

½ cup/125 milliliters bubbly sourdough starter
2 cups/275 grams whole wheat pastry flour (and/or white flour)
1 tablespoon sugar (or other sweetener)
1 egg
1 tablespoon vegetable oil
½ teaspoon salt
½ teaspoon baking soda

Process:

Combine. In a large bowl, mix the sourdough starter with 2 cups/500 milliliters lukewarm water, the flour, and the sugar. Stir until smooth. (Don't forget to replenish your starter.)

Ferment in a warm spot, covered, for 8 to 12 hours.

Add the final ingredients. When you are ready to make pancakes, beat the egg and add it to the batter, along with the oil and salt. Stir until the texture is smooth and even.

Mix the baking soda with 1 tablespoon of warm water and fold it gently into the sourdough mixture.

Heat a griddle or cast-iron pan, and lightly oil.

Ladle the batter into pancakes. When many bubbles have formed on the surface, flip and cook the other side. Cook well, to a medium brown.

Serve the pancakes as they are cooked, or place them in a warm oven until they are all cooked. Enjoy with yogurt and maple syrup or preserved fruit.

kvass

Kvass is a lovely, refreshing, effervescent sour beverage usually made from old, dry bread, refermented. It is traditional in Russia, Ukraine, Lithuania, and other regions of Eastern Europe, where mobile kvass wagons can still be found, especially in summer. Kvass is so iconic in this region that other types of sour beverages are also called kvass—beet kvass (see page 78), for instance, or tea kvass, a name for kombucha (see page 93).

Kvass is nutritious and energizing. This recipe is for fairly sour kvass, as I imagine it was traditionally enjoyed in rural Russia, with little access to sweeteners. I think it is delicious but some people wince at its sour flavor. The bottled kvass I found in the Brighton Beach neighborhood of Brooklyn was much sweeter, like molasses-flavored soda.

Timeframe: 2 to 4 days

Ingredients (for ½ gallon/ 2 liters):

1½ pounds/750 grams stale bread (traditionally hearty Russian black bread, made of coarsely ground whole-grain rye and/or barley, but any bread will do, and it doesn't have to be stale)

3 tablespoons/5 grams crushed dried mint

¼ cup/60 grams sugar or honey

1 lemon, juiced

Pinch of sea salt

¼ cup/60 milliliters bubbly sourdough starter (or 1 package yeast)

A few raisins

Process:

Cube and dry the bread. Cut the bread into cubes, and toast in an oven preheated to 300°F/150°C for about 15 minutes, until dry.

Cover with water. Place the bread cubes in a crock or pot with the mint and 12 cups/3 liters boiling water. Stir, cover, and leave for 8 hours (or longer).

Strain out the solids, pressing out as much liquid as possible. The soggy bread will retain some water, so you will end up with less volume of liquid than you started with.

Combine. Add the sugar or honey, lemon juice, salt, and bubbly sourdough starter or yeast to the strained liquid. Mix well, cover, and leave at room temperature.

Ferment 1 or 2 days, stirring periodically, until bubbly.

Bottle and seal. Transfer the kvass to quart/liter bottles. Add a few raisins to each bottle and seal. Leave the bottles at room temperature for a day or two, until the raisins float to the top. Kvass is then ready to drink, and may be stored in the refrigerator for a few weeks.

okroshka (kvass-based soup)

This is a refreshing Russian summer soup, served chilled. It uses not only kvass but also pickle brine or sauerkraut juice, and it doesn't cook them, so it's a live culture soup! I adapted this recipe from *The Food and Cookery of Russia* by Lesley Chamberlain.

Timeframe: 2 hours

Ingredients (for 4–6 servings):

2 potatoes

1 carrot

1 turnip

½ pound/250 grams mushrooms

3 eggs (optional)

4 spring onions

1 apple

1 cucumber

1 quart/1 liter kvass

½ cup/125 milliliters pickle brine or sauerkraut juice

2 teaspoons ground mustard

1 tablespoon fresh or dried dill

1 tablespoon fresh parsley

Salt and pepper to taste

Process:

Cut and cook the vegetables. Cut the potatoes, carrot, turnip, and mushrooms into spoon-size pieces and steam for 5 to 10 minutes, until soft.

Hard-boil the eggs in a separate pot for about 10 minutes, if you wish to include them.

Chop the raw ingredients—spring onions, apple, and cucumber—into spoon-size pieces.

Combine. Mix the kvass, pickle brine or sauerkraut juice, mustard, dill, parsley, and vegetables. Stir well and refrigerate for at least 1 hour.

Peel and chop the cooled eggs.

Before serving add the salt, pepper, and eggs.

Serve in a bowl with an ice cube, accompanied by yogurt, kefir, or sour cream.

zur

Sourdough can be used not only in a cold soup like okroshka (see the previous recipe), but as a base and thickener for hot soups, as well. Polish cuisine features a delicious soup called zur (or zurek), the base of which is sourdough rye, cooked into what could be described as thin rye porridge, typically with Polish sausage and vegetables.

Timeframe: 3 to 5 days

Ingredients (for 4–6 servings):

½ cup/125 milliliters sourdough starter

1 cup/100 grams rye flour

4 cloves garlic, divided

4 bay leaves, divided

4 allspice berries, divided

2 large onions, divided

3–4 large carrots, divided

1–2 parsnips, divided

2–3 celery stalks, divided

3 potatoes

Butter or oil for sautéing

1 pound/500 grams kielbasa (optional; most recipes specify white or fresh as opposed to smoked)

1 tablespoon dried marjoram

6 black peppercorns

¼ cup/60 milliliters grated white horseradish (fresh or jarred in vinegar)

Salt and pepper

1 cup/250 milliliters sour cream or yogurt

Crusty rye bread for serving (optional)

Process:

Prepare the zakvas, or sour rye starter. In a quart/liter jar or bowl, combine the sourdough starter, 2 cups dechlorinated water, and the rye flour. Stir well to break up any clumps of flour. Add 2 of the garlic cloves, crushed and chopped, 2 of the bay leaves, and 2 of the allspice berries. Cover with a cloth and leave for 3 to 5 days, stirring once or twice a day. Bubbling will build and then slow, and the zakvas will develop a sour aroma. Once the zakvas is sour, you can make the zur.

Make a vegetable stock. Fill a pot with 6 cups of water, and add to it one of the onions (quartered with skin) along with half the carrots, parsnips, and celery stalks. Bring to a boil, lower the heat, and simmer about 45 minutes. Strain the broth and discard the vegetables. (Or use a chicken or meat stock.)

Cook the potatoes. While the stock is cooking, cover the potatoes with water, bring to a boil, lower the heat, and simmer about 15 minutes. Drain, and when the potatoes are cool enough to handle, chop them into bite-size pieces.

Assemble the soup. In a soup pot, heat the butter or oil and sauté in it the remaining onion and 2 cloves of garlic, coarsely chopped. Add the kielbasa, cut into bite-size pieces. Sauté over medium heat until browned. Add the vegetable stock, the zakvas, the rest of the carrots, chopped into bite-size pieces, 2 bay leaves, 2 allspice berries, the marjoram, peppercorns, and horseradish. Bring to a boil, reduce the heat, and simmer for 20 minutes. Add salt and pepper to taste. Add the cooked potato.

Serve. Remove the hot soup from the heat, remove the bay leaves, and serve with a generous dollop of sour cream or yogurt in each bowl and crusty rye bread on the side.

baking bread

Baking bread takes the humblest of ingredients, flour and water, and turns them into a daily staple that is one of the cornerstones of Western civilization. The fundamentals of baking bread are simple. Mix flour, water, starter, and salt into a dough; work the dough a bit as it ferments and rises; form loaves and give them a final rise; then bake, cool, and enjoy. Anyone can do it, and I aim to walk you through a few simple naturally leavened loaves.

Bread is made in many varied styles, and there is no single way to do it. Any of them can be made using natural leavening. I love baking bread and I've been doing it for more than 25 years. I'm generally pretty improvisational with it, and experimental. Many excellent books have been published on the subject (some are listed at the end of this chapter), with far more nuanced techniques. I've been humbled by observing some masters who have devoted long careers to this fine art, and who practically dance through the rhythmic and repetitive tasks of mixing, fermenting, kneading, forming, and finally baking hundreds of gorgeous loaves of bread.

Many bakers I have known feel that bread-making is a spiritual exercise that connects them with life forces. I quite agree: Like any ferment, bread requires the harnessing and gentle cultivation of microbial communities. This, in the form of a vigorous starter, is the most important single ingredient for baking sourdough bread. Your starter need not have an ancient pedigree, but it must be vigorous, meaning that it must be actively kinetic, visibly bubbling and rising.

Do not build your dough with a flat or barely active starter. Feed and stir your starter frequently, as described previously, until you have a vigorous starter that froths at the surface and rises the thick starter batter. Only then is it primed to rise the denser bread dough.

Natural leavening can sometimes take a while, especially in a cool environment. Be patient. Fermentation takes time. Enjoy the smells of the sourdough, and the anticipation of how good the bread will taste.

recycled grain bread

My fanaticism about recycling food and not letting it go to waste leads me to make most of my breads out of leftover grains. Bread can incorporate a great variety of leftovers, not only grains but also vegetables, soups, and more. My friend Amy, a champion dumpster diver from way back, is guided by a goddess she calls Refusa. Refusa says: Be creative and daring in your food recycling.

This lays out the basic process. From here, using your sourdough starter, the possibilities are endless.

Timeframe: Feed starter the night before, then 5 to 12 hours or more, depending upon temperature. (Be patient!)

Equipment:

Large mixing bowl

2 loaf pans roughly 5x9 inches/ 13x23 centimeters

Ingredients (for 2 loaves):

½ cup/125 milliliters bubbly sourdough starter

2 cups/400 grams leftover cooked grains (rice, oatmeal, millet, buckwheat, or any grain)

7 cups/1.1 kilograms flour (at least two-thirds wheat), plus extra to dust surface for forming loaves

2 tablespoons sea salt

Oil for greasing loaf pans

Process:

Prepare the starter. The night before baking day, give your already bubbly starter a high-proportion feeding. In a jar of at least 1-pint/500-milliliter capacity, mix ½ cup/125 milliliters lukewarm water, ½ cup/80 grams flour, and 2 tablespoons bubbly starter. Stir well, then leave in a warm spot to ferment overnight. It will get very bubbly and rise; when you see this, it is ready to use.

Mix the dough. Start with a large mixing bowl. Add 4 cups/1 liter lukewarm water, about 90°F/32°C. Add the bubbly sourdough starter. Make sure it's vigorous, and use the recommended proportion; in this case more is not better. (Replenish your starter!) Break up the leftover grains and add them. Add the flour. Use at least two-thirds wheat or spelt, but augment that with some of whatever other flours you have: Buckwheat, rye, rolled oats, and cornmeal are all good. Stir the dough well. It will be somewhat stiff, but still wet and sticky, not dry. Cover by placing the whole bowl inside a plastic shopping bag and loosely tying it, to maintain moisture.

Rest the dough in a warm spot, so the flour can fully absorb the water, for at least half an hour and up to an hour.

Add the salt, then to distribute it, fold the dough over itself, turn, and fold from another edge, and then another, a few times.

Ferment in a warm place, covered, for 3 to 6 hours. Every half hour or so, spend a minute or two folding the dough over itself, then turning and folding from another edge, and then another, a few times. This action helps develop the gluten in the dough. By doing this throughout the fermentation, you can also see and feel the dough transform. Every half hour is a rough guideline; don't stress about it if you go longer. After a few hours, the dough will start to feel light and well aerated. If not, continue to ferment, folding every half hour or so until it does. In a cool space it can take a while.

Form loaves. First, oil two loaf pans. I like to form loaves directly on the counter. Scoop about ¼ cup/40 grams flour onto your working surface and spread it with the palm of your hands around an area about 1 foot/30 centimeters in diameter. Divide the dough roughly in half, cutting with a knife and pulling the mass apart. Place one half on the floured working area; leave the other in the bowl. Work your fingers under the soft dough mass, so the floured edge rests in one hand. Lift it up, redistribute the flour on your working surface with your other hand, and flip the dough mass over, so the wet side lands down in the flour. Then fold the edge into the center, turn the mass a quarter rotation, fold another edge into the center, turn, and repeat until you have gone around and the mass is a bit drier around the edges and easier to handle. Flatten the dough mass into an oval, and roll it into a log. Gently pick it up with both hands and place it seam-side down in an oiled pan. Spread a little more flour (if needed) on the working surface and repeat with the other loaf.

Final rise. Place the loaves in their pans in a plastic shopping bag and loosely close it to keep them from drying. Leave in a warm spot to rise. For lightest and most flavorful loaves, let them rise for a couple of hours. But if time is short, an hour is plenty, and in some cases as little as half an hour may suffice. You always want to see rising action before baking, but it need not be extreme.

Preheat the oven to 400°F (205°C).

Bake. Place loaves in the heated oven and reduce the temperature to 350°F (175°C).

Check the loaves after about 40 minutes. Most likely they will require a little more time than this—maybe 45 or 50 minutes, maybe an hour or even longer. The way to test the doneness of bread is to remove it, upside down, from the loaf pan. Tap the bottom of the loaf. When it is done it will sound hollow, like a drum. If it's not done, return it to the oven quickly and continue baking.

Cool. When the bread is done, remove it from the hot pan and cool it on a rack or cool surface. The bread continues to cook and set as it cools. It's hard to be patient when it smells so good, but try to wait at least an hour before cutting and it'll taste that much better.

all-rye bread

The flavor of rye is rich and sweet. Most contemporary US rye breads are mostly wheat with a little rye for flavor. These breads have the texture of wheat, which can be great, but I love the very different bread that is all rye. Historically, this was a bread of cold and damp northern regions. Rye bread is hearty sustenance for people in harsh climates. "I come from a stretch of land where bread meant bread, not the pretext for a hot-dog nor a sponge to clean up sauces with," recounts renowned baker and puppeteer Peter Schumann, from Silesia in eastern Germany, "but an honest hunk of grainy, nutty food which had its own strong taste and required a healthy amount of chewing."[8]

Working with rye dough is very different from working with wheat. For one, rye simply is not as cohesive and easy to handle. It does not develop the elasticity characteristic of wheat doughs. Rather than working the dough with dry floured hands, rye works best if you keep your hands wet while handling it.

Peter Schumann, founder of Bread and Puppet Theater, baking rye bread in his wood-fired oven.

Timeframe: 16 hours or more

Equipment:

Large mixing bowl
Loaf pans

Ingredients (for 2 loaves):

1 cup/250 milliliters bubbly sourdough starter
1 cup/200 grams whole rye berries, chops, or
    coarsely milled rye
8 cups/800 grams rye flour, sifted if it is at
    all clumpy
4 teaspoons salt
Oil for greasing loaf pans
¼ cup/45 grams coarsely milled rye, or corn
    grits, or sesame seeds

Process:

Mix a sponge. Start sponge the day before you plan to bake. Combine 3 cups lukewarm water, about 90°F/32°C, with the bubbly sourdough, rye berries, chops, or coarsely milled rye, and 4½ cups/450 grams of the rye flour. (Don't forget to replenish your starter.) Stir well, until evenly mixed and smooth like pudding, then leave in a warm spot to ferment overnight.

Ferment at least 12 hours and up to about 24 hours. The sponge will get very bubbly and light.

Mix the sponge into the dough. Add the salt and the remaining 3½ cups/350 grams rye flour. Mix well into a sticky dough and stir for a few minutes.

Divide into loaves. First, oil two loaf pans. For extra protection against sticking, sprinkle the bottom of the loaf pan with coarsely milled rye, corn grits, or sesame seeds. Use wet hands to divide the dough into two masses, shape them into logs, and place them in the loaf pans. Use wet hands to smooth the surface of the loaves. Place the loaves in their pans in a plastic shopping bag and loosely close it to keep them from drying.

Ferment in a warm spot for another 2 to 3 hours, until the loaves have risen, even if only a small amount.

Preheat the oven to 350°F/175°C.

Bake. Check the loaves after 1½ hours. It will probably take 2 hours, or even longer, but check earlier. Test doneness by removing a loaf from its pan and tapping the bottom. When it is done it will sound hollow. If it's not done, return it to the oven quickly and continue baking.

Cool the bread on racks. Let it cool all the way and even let it sit for a day before eating. In sharp contrast with yeasted wheat breads, which are best eaten fresh and dry out quickly, sourdough rye bread retains its moisture and improves with age, for several weeks. If the crust gets hard and dry, slice through it with a sharp serrated knife to find soft, moist, delicious, sour bread. Dense breads like this are best in thin slices.

Variations: Add sautéed onions to the dough . . . add caraway seeds . . . add whole rye berries, soaked and cooked, or even just soaked.

sonnenblumenkernbrot (german sunflower seed bread)

France and Italy are the nations most often acclaimed for their bread, perhaps because their loaves are so light and airy. But the country whose bread most excites me is Germany. I particularly love the dense moist sour sonnenblumenkernbrot.

Timeframe: 2 to 3 days

Ingredients (for 2 loaves):

3 cups/500 grams sunflower seeds (hulled)
1 cup/250 milliliters bubbly sourdough starter
4 cups/640 grams wheat flour (white and/or whole wheat), plus extra to dust surface for forming loaves
1 cup/100 grams rye flour
4 teaspoons salt

Process:

Soak the sunflower seeds in water for 24 hours or longer before preparing the dough.

Prepare the starter. The night before baking day, give your already bubbly starter a high-proportion feeding. In a jar of at least a quart/liter capacity, mix ¾ cup/185 milliliters lukewarm water, ¾ cup/120 grams flour, and ¼ cup/60 milliliters bubbly starter. Stir well, then leave in a warm spot to ferment overnight. It will get very bubbly and rise; when you see this, it is ready to use.

Mix the dough. Drain the seeds and discard the soaking water. Into a large mixing bowl, add 2 cups/500 milliliters lukewarm water, 1 cup of bubbly starter, the soaked and well-drained seeds, and the flour. Stir well into a doughy mass, stiff but still wet and sticky. Add a little more flour if necessary. Fold the dough over itself from one side, then turn and fold it from another edge, and then another, a few times. You will repeat this folding-and-turning action through the process. Cover by placing the whole bowl inside a plastic shopping bag and loosely tying it, to maintain moisture.

Allow the dough to rest in a warm spot, so the flour can fully absorb the water, for at least half an hour and up to an hour.

Add the salt and repeatedly fold and turn to distribute it.

Ferment in a warm place, covered, for 3 to 6 hours. Every half hour or so, spend a minute or two folding and turning. This is a rough guideline; don't stress about it if you go longer. After a few hours, the dough will start to feel light and well aerated. If not, continue to ferment, folding every half hour or so until it does. In a cool space it can take a while.

Form loaves. First, oil two loaf pans. Scoop about ¼ cup/40 grams flour onto your working surface and spread it with the palms of your hands around an area about 1 foot/30 centimeters in diameter. Divide the dough roughly in half, cutting with a knife and pulling the mass apart. Place one half on the floured working area; leave the other in the bowl. Work your fingers under the soft dough mass, so the floured edge rests in one hand. Lift it up, redistribute the flour on your working surface with your other hand, and flip the dough mass over, so the wet side lands down in the flour. Then fold the edge into the center, turn the mass a quarter rotation, fold another edge into the center, turn, and repeat until you have gone around and the mass is a bit drier around the edges and easier to handle. Flatten the dough mass into an oval and roll it into a log. Gently pick it up with both hands and place it seam-side down in

an oiled pan. Spread a little more flour (if needed) on the working surface and repeat with the other loaf.

Final rise. Place the loaves in their pans in a plastic shopping bag and loosely close it to keep them from drying. Leave in a warm spot to rise. For the lightest and most flavorful loaves, leave them to rise for a couple of hours. But if time is short, an hour is plenty, and in some cases as little as half an hour may suffice. You want to see some rising action before baking.

Preheat the oven to 400°F/205°C. Place the loaves in the heated oven, reduce the temperature to 350°F/175°C, and bake.

Check the loaves after about 40 minutes. Most likely they will require a little more time than this—maybe 45 or 50 minutes, maybe an hour or even longer. The way to test doneness of bread is to remove it, upside down, from the loaf pan. Tap the bottom of the loaf. When it is done it will sound hollow, like a drum. If it's not done, return it to the oven quickly and continue baking.

Cool and enjoy.

Etain Addey baking bread on her farm, Pratale, in Umbria, Italy.

challah

Sourdough bread-making is most definitely not limited to dense whole-grain loaves like the ones covered so far. The traditional bread of the Jewish Shabbat (Sabbath) ritual is challah, a light, eggy, braided loaf. In my family, we didn't observe much religious tradition, but we sure loved challah.

My uncle Len's mother Tobye Hollander was famous for the challah she made for her Shabbat observance every Friday. She was born in the 19th century; when I was a child, she and her husband, Herman, were the most ancient people in my universe. Tobye's challah-making was acclaimed enough that her recipe was deemed "fit to print" in *The New York Times*. Tobye's recipe (like every challah recipe I've seen) calls for commercial yeast, but I've adapted it to illustrate the versatility of wild yeast sourdough.

Timeframe: Feed starter the night before, then 5 to 8 hours

Ingredients (for 1 large loaf):

5½ cups/700 grams white flour, plus extra to use while working the dough
½ cup/125 milliliters bubbly sourdough starter
1 tablespoon sugar
2 teaspoons sea salt
3 tablespoons vegetable oil
3 eggs, beaten

Process:

Prepare the starter. The night before baking day, give your already bubbly starter a high-proportion feeding. In a jar of at least a pint/500 milliliters capacity, mix ½ cup/60 milliliters lukewarm water, ½ cup/60 grams flour, and 2 tablespoons bubbly starter. Stir well, then leave in a warm spot to ferment overnight. It will get very bubbly and rise; when you see this, it is ready to use.

Sift the flour into a large mixing bowl. Make a well in the center of the flour.

Pour the bubbly sourdough into the well and dust it with flour. (Don't forget to replenish your starter.)

Combine the sugar, salt, oil, and 1½ cups/375 milliliters of water in a heat-resistant measuring cup or small metal bowl. Heat it by setting the cup or bowl in a saucepan of warm water over a low flame. When the mixture is lukewarm, add the beaten eggs, reserving about 1 tablespoon of the eggs for brushing on the finished loaf. Continue to gently heat the pan of water while whisking or stirring the mixture, until it is smooth and custard-like. Do not allow this mixture to heat to the point where it stings your finger; keep it under 115°F/46°C.

Mix into a dough. Add the warm egg mixture to the bubbly starter in the well of the flour. Mix liquids and flour into a dough. Once it forms a soft, cohesive ball, Tobye told *The New York Times*, "then comes the revolution."

Knead. Tobye recommends kneading directly in the bowl, easier to clean up than using a countertop. Knead for at least 10 minutes. "Knead away for dear life," instructs Tobye, "up and around, down and outwards. Pat it gently and say a prayer." This part is very important: Put clear intentions into your loaf.

Ferment. Lightly oil the surface of the ball of kneaded dough and place it in the bowl. Cover by placing the whole bowl inside a plastic shopping bag and loosely tying it, to maintain moisture. Set the bowl in a warm place and leave it to ferment for about 3 hours, until the dough has doubled in bulk.

Braid the dough. Punch down the risen dough, knead for a few moments, and then divide it into three equal parts. Shape the braided loaf by rolling and squeezing each ball into a rope about 18 inches/45 centimeters long. Line the three ropes up side by side, join them together at one end, and braid them, lifting a rope from one side into the middle, then from the other, and so on. When you reach the end of your ropes (as it were), join them together and tuck them under the end of the braid.

Final rise. Lightly oil a cookie sheet, and gently lift the braided loaf onto it. Leave the loaf in a warm spot to rise for 1 or 2 hours, until it has roughly doubled.

Preheat the oven to 400°F /250°C.

Brush the top of the loaf gently with the reserved egg.

Bake 30 to 45 minutes, until lightly browned. Cool on a rack near an open window to increase crustiness.

Enjoy challah fresh. If it dries out, it makes outstanding French toast.

afghan bread

I was first embarking upon this book on September 11, 2001, and felt powerless as the tragic events of that day and their immediate repercussions unfolded. Because the first military retaliation was against Afghanistan, I decided to honor the culture of that place by learning something about its cuisine. Of course, like every cuisine, it contains fermentation traditions. Once I read about Afghan bread, *noni afghani*, I remembered eating it as a kid in New York, one of the many exotic foods my adventurous mother brought home.

Afghan bread is a delicious flatbread, spiced with black cumin seeds (*Nigella sativa*), a Middle Eastern spice very different from the larger cumin seeds more commonly found.

Timeframe: Feed starter the night before, then 4 to 8 hours

Ingredients (for 1 large flatbread, enough for 6–8 servings):

½ cup/125 milliliters bubbly sourdough starter

2 cups/320 grams whole wheat flour

2 cups/240 grams) unbleached white flour

2 teaspoons sea salt

¼ cup/60 milliliters vegetable oil

1 egg yolk

1 tablespoon black cumin seeds
(*Nigella sativa*)

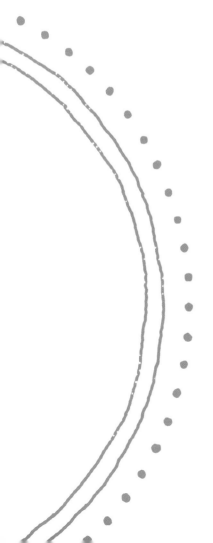

Process:

Prepare the starter. The night before baking day, give your already bubbly starter a high-proportion feeding. In a jar at least 1 pint/500 milliliters in capacity, mix ½ cup/125 milliliters lukewarm water, ½ cup/80 grams wheat flour, and 2 tablespoons bubbly starter. Stir well, then leave in a warm spot to ferment overnight. It will get very bubbly and rise; when you see this, it is ready to use. (Don't forget to replenish your starter.)

Mix the dough. Mix the flours and salt in a mixing bowl and create a well in the center. Pour the bubbly sourdough starter and oil into the well in the flour and mix into a dough. Add up to about ¾ cup/185 milliliters additional lukewarm water, just a little at a time, until all the flour blends into a cohesive ball.

Knead the dough in the bowl or on a lightly floured surface for about 5 minutes. Return the dough to the bowl and cover the bowl by placing it inside a plastic shopping bag and loosely tying it, to maintain moisture.

Ferment in a warm place for about 3 hours, until the dough has doubled in bulk. In a cooler environment, this can take longer.

Preheat the oven to 350°F/175°C.

Roll out the dough. On a floured surface, roll the dough into a sheet less than 1 inch/2.5 centimeters thick. Roll from the center out toward the sides, trying to maintain uniform thickness. Flip the sheet of dough over and work on the other side. You could aim for a rectangle or an oval, or let it assume an amorphous amoeba-like form. Place the sheet of dough onto an ungreased cookie sheet.

Final coating. Mix the egg yolk with 1 tablespoon of water. Spread the egg-and-water mixture onto the surface of the dough, then sprinkle black cumin seeds over it.

Bake for 20 to 25 minutes, until the top is golden. It may puff up like a giant pita bread.

buckwheat rye
sourdough crackers

Crackers are easy to make, especially delicious from sourdough, and gorgeously irregular when handmade.

Timeframe: 26 hours (or more)

Ingredients (for about 36 crackers):

½ cup/100 grams kasha (toasted buckwheat), dry
1 medium onion
4 cloves garlic
2 tablespoons oil or butter for sautéing onion
2 tablespoons oil for batter
2 teaspoons salt
2 teaspoons caraway seeds
2 teaspoons cumin (*Nigella sativa*) seeds
½ cup/125 milliliters bubbly sourdough starter
1 cup/160 grams whole wheat flour (pastry flour if available)
1 cup/100 grams rye flour
2 tablespoons oil for baking

Process:

Toast the buckwheat (unless you purchase kasha, already toasted). Heat a dry cast-iron skillet and gently toast the buckwheat, stirring frequently to prevent burning. Toast until the buckwheat begins to darken and get fragrant.

Cook the kasha. In a small pot with a lid, combine the kasha with 1 cup/250 milliliters water. Bring to a boil, reduce to a simmer, and cook for about 5 minutes, then remove from the heat but leave the pot covered for 10 more minutes. Then remove the cover and allow the kasha to cool.

Sauté the onion and garlic. Peel and finely dice the onion and garlic, and sauté in the oil or butter

Outdoor kitchen with ovens at Embercombe in England.

until they begin to brown, stirring frequently to prevent burning. Remove from the heat to cool.

Mix a sponge. In a bowl combine the kasha, sautéed onion and garlic, oil, salt, and ¼ cup/60 milliliters water. Coarsely grind the caraway and black cumin using a mortar and pestle or electric grinder, and add them. Test the temperature and make sure it is below body temperature before adding the bubbly sourdough starter. Finally, add half the whole wheat flour and half the rye flour, and stir it all into a thick homogeneous batter.

Ferment for a minimum of 24 hours or several days.

Mix the dough. Add the salt and mix it in. Then gradually add the remaining rye and wheat flours, a little at a time, and mix in until the batter thickens into a cohesive dough.

Ferment the dough. Cover by placing the whole bowl inside a plastic shopping bag and loosely tying it, to maintain moisture. Set the bowl in a warm place and leave it to ferment for at least 2 hours, or as long as 24 hours.

Divide the dough into a few small balls when you are ready to make crackers.

Preheat the oven to 350°F/177°C.

Oil a cookie sheet.

Form the crackers. On a floured surface, roll out each ball of dough like a pizza. Roll from the center to the edges in different directions. Flip it a few times as you roll it out. Roll to a thickness of about ⅛ inch/3 millimeters, or as thin as you can. Use a pizza cutter or sharp knife to cut rolled-out dough into individual crackers. I like diamonds, triangles, and mixed trapezoid shapes, but cut them however you like. Prick crackers with a fork to increase surface area and help them crisp during baking. Place them on the cookie sheet and brush with oil.

Bake 15 to 20 minutes, until the crackers are dry and crispy.

Cool fully before stacking or storing.

amazaké

Amazaké is a rich, sweet Japanese pudding or drink that is one of the most dramatic fermentations. Plain rice (or any other grain) is made intensely sweet in a matter of hours by the action of koji, grain grown with *Aspergillus oryzae*, a fungus with a plethora of useful enzymes, some of which rapidly digest complex carbohydrates into simple sugars. It is astounding that a grain can be so sweet without any added sweetener. Koji is also used to make saké, miso, soy sauce, and other ferments, and similar fungi are used in varied fermentation processes throughout Asia. (More on koji in chapter 9.) For sources of koji, see the appendix; see my book *The Art of Fermentation* for detailed information on how to make your own.

Traditionally amazaké is made with sweet rice, though it can be made from any grain.

Timeframe: 8 to 24 hours

Equipment:

2 1-quart/1-liter jars
Insulated cooler, big enough for jars to fit inside, but as small as possible to contain heat

Ingredients (for about 1½ quarts/1.5 liters):

2 cups/500 grams sweet rice (or any other grain)
2 cups/330 grams koji

Process:

Cook the grain in about 6 cups/1.5 liters of water. Use a pressure cooker if you have one. This high proportion of water (3:1) will result in somewhat softer-than-usual grain.

Preheat the insulated cooler and jars by adding a few inches of hot water to each.

Cool the cooked grain to 140°F/60°C. Remove from the heat, uncover the pot, and stir from the bottom to release heat. Don't let it get too cool. Koji can tolerate heat as high as 140°F/60°C. Cool to this temperature or, if you are without a thermometer, until you can hold a finger to it for a moment but it is still steaming hot.

Add the koji to the cooked grain and stir well.

Pack into jars. Pour warming water out of the jars and fill with the warm grain-koji mix. Pack it in tightly so it all fits in the two jars. Screw the lids on the jars.

Ferment in the preheated insulated cooler. Check the temperature after a few minutes and add additional hot water to help maintain the heat. Shut the cooler and place it in a warm place.

Check after 8 to 12 hours. Amazaké takes about 8 to 12 hours at 140°F/60°C, or 20 to 24 hours at

90°F/32°C. If the amazaké is very sweet, it's ready. If not, heat it up by adding hot water to surround the jars of amazaké. Leave to ferment for a few more hours.

Boil. Once your amazaké is sweet, gently bring it to a boil to stop fermentation. Be careful not to burn the amazaké when you boil it. The way I do this is to first boil about ½ cup/125 milliliters of water in a pot, then slowly add the amazaké, stirring frequently to avoid burning the bottom.

Serve the amazaké as a pudding, thick and with the grains intact, or thin it with more water and run it through a food processor to break down the grains into a liquid consistency. Amazaké is delicious either hot or cold. Plain amazaké has a very distinctive sweetness, or you can season it. Amazaké seasoned with a little nutmeg (and perhaps even rum) makes a nice eggnog alternative. Vanilla extract, grated ginger, slivered toasted almonds, and espresso are other flavorings I've enjoyed in amazaké. Amazaké can also be used as a sweetener in baking. Amazaké can be stored for a few weeks in a refrigerator.

rejuvelac

My friend and long-ago neighbor Mat Defiler introduced me to rejuvelac, which she was using as part of an anti-candida regime. Rejuvelac is fermented from sprouted grains.

Popularized by early raw-foods guru Ann Wigmore, rejuvelac is extremely simple to make. At its best it can be a pleasant and refreshing tonic; gone too far it can become quite putrid.

Timeframe: About 4 to 6 days (including sprouting time)

Ingredients (for about 1 quart/ 1 liter):

1 cup/200 grams of any whole grain

Process:

Sprout the grains in a 2-quart/2-liter or larger jar, as described on page 246.

Soak the sprouts. Once the grains have sprouted, rinse them for a last time and cover with 1 quart/1 liter water.

Ferment in the jar, covered to keep flies and dust out, for about 2 days at room temperature.

Decant. Pour the rejuvelac off the grains. Enjoy it fresh, or store in the refrigerator.

Second pressing. A second batch of rejuvelac may be made from the same sprouts. Simply refill the jar with the sprouts with fresh water and ferment, this time for only 24 hours.

other grain fermentations

Also see Kishk in chapter 7, Dosas and Idlis, Miso, and Black-Eyed Pea and Oat Tempeh in chapter 9, and Beers in chapter 11.

Subsistence farmers milling their grain in a water-powered mill in a Himalayan village, Kalap, Uttarahkand, India.

Further Reading

Alford, Jeffrey, and Naomi Duguid. *Flatbreads and Flavors: A Baker's Atlas*. New York: William Morrow, 1995.

Bertinet, Richard. *Crust: From Sourdough, Spelt, and Rye Bread to Ciabatta, Bagels, and Brioche*. London: Kyle Books, 2007.

Brown, Edward Espe. *The Tassajara Bread Book*. Boston: Shambhala Publications, 2011.

Buehler, Emily. *Bread Science: The Chemistry and Craft of Making Bread*. Hillsborough, NC: Two Blue Books, 2006.

Forkish, Ken. *Flour Water Salt Yeast: The Fundamentals of Artisan Bread and Pizza*. Berkeley, CA: Ten Speed Press, 2012.

Hamelman, Jeffrey. *Bread: A Baker's Book of Techniques and Recipes, 2nd Edition*. Hoboken, NJ: Wiley, 2013.

Leader, Daniel, and Judith Blahnik. B*read Alone: Bold Fresh Loaves from Your Own Hands*. New York: William Morrow, 1993.

Mardewi, Yoke. *Wild Sourdough: The Natural Way to Bake*. Sydney: New Holland Publishers, 2009.

Mason, Jane. *Homemade Sourdough: Mastering the Art and Science of Baking with Starters and Wild Yeast*. McGregor, MN: Voyageur Press, 2015.

Rayner, Lisa. *Wild Bread: Handbaked Sourdough Artisan Breads in Your Own Kitchen*. Flagstaff, AZ: Lifeweaver, 2009.

Reinhart, Peter. *The Bread Baker's Apprentice: Mastering the Art of Extraordinary Bread*. Berkeley, CA: Ten Speed Press, 2001.

Risgaard, Hanne. *Home Baked: Nordic Recipes and Techniques for Organic Bread and Pastry*. White River Junction, VT: Chelsea Green Publishing, 2012.

Robertson, Chad. *Tartine Book No. 3: Modern Ancient Classic Whole*. San Francisco: Chronicle Books, 2013.

Robertson, Laurel, Carol Flinders, and Bronwen Godfrey. *Laurel's Kitchen Bread Book: A Guide to Whole-Grain Breadmaking*. New York: Random House, 1985.

Whitley, Andrew. *Bread Matters: The State of Modern Bread and a Definitive Guide to Baking Your Own*. Kansas City, MO: Andrews McMeel Publishing, 2009.

———. *Do Sourdough: Slow Bread for Busy Lives*. London: Do Books, 2014.

9: bean ferments

Like grains, beans preserve best in their mature dried state, maintained in a cool, dry, and dark environment. The objective of bean fermentation is less to preserve them than to make them more digestible, unlock their nutrient potential, and give them compelling flavors as well as pleasing textures. Soybeans, renowned for their protein richness, are mostly indigestible by our human digestive tracts (when simply cooked and not fermented), so not only do we not access their protein, but they also contain toxic compounds associated with a host of problems. Fermentation, however, pre-digests the beans, breaking down proteins into amino acids that we can more easily absorb, while simultaneously breaking down toxic and nutrient-blocking compounds. Fermentation is the most effective way to realize the powerful nutritive potential of especially soybeans but really any legumes. In addition, when beans are fermented together with grains, as they frequently are, the ferment is a complete protein, containing all the amino acids essential to human nutrition.

Documentation of bean fermentation goes back thousands of years. Ancient Chinese texts refer to jiangs, condiments fermented from beans as well as fish, meat, grains, and vegetables. Jiangs were (and are) made in elaborate variety, and imbued with meaning. The Analects of Confucius (circa 500 BC) direct that "Foods not accompanied by the appropriate variety of jiang should not be served. Rather than using only one to season all foods, you should provide many to ensure harmony with each of the basic food types."[1]

Most bean ferments start just as most grain ferments do: by simply adding water to bring the seed back to life, swelling and awakening dormant microbial and enzymatic activity.

dosas and idlis

Dosas and idlis are South Indian ferments. Dosas are thin pancakes, and idlis are steam-breads, both made from batters born of the same rice-and-lentil fermentation of just a day or two. They share a wonderful flavor, with very different textures. I saw idlis compared with matzo balls in one cookbook, but I think they have a distinctive spongy texture all their own. Dosas and idlis are the easiest, fastest, and most straightforward of the bean ferments included in this book.

Timeframe: 1 to 2 days

Equipment:

Dosas require only a well-seasoned griddle or crepe pan.

Idlis need forms in which to steam. These are available in Indian shops and via the Internet. I have used a four-tier model that steams 16 idlis at a time and a six-tier model that steams 24. To steam, I place them in a pot, large enough for them to fit entirely inside, covered by a tight-fitting lid.

Ingredients (for approximately 32 small dosas or idlis):

2 cups/400 grams rice (I generally use white rice though I've tried it with brown rice and liked it fine, and many Indian recipes suggest using parboiled rice)

½ cup/120 grams lentils (most recipes call for urad daal, white lentils, available in Indian groceries; I've most often used red lentils, which yield a gorgeous pink batter, and had great results experimenting with a variety of beans)

1 teaspoon fenugreek seeds

1 teaspoon salt

Coconut or other vegetable oil

Process:

Soak the rice. Rinse the rice until the water runs clear, then cover with water and soak for at least 8 hours (longer is fine).

Soak the lentils and fenugreek. Rinse the lentils, add the fenugreek, and cover with water, at least twice the volume of the lentils, as they will double in size. Soak for at least 8 hours.

Grind the lentils and fenugreek into a batter in a blender or other grinding tool. Add soaking water as needed, but as little as possible. Grind it for a few minutes, until it is smooth and fluffy. Scoop out of the blender and into a mixing bowl.

Grind the rice, in a couple of small batches if necessary. Add soaking water but again, as little as needed. Grind into a smooth paste and add it to the bowl with the lentils and fenugreek.

Mix the batter. Add the salt and beat the two batters together into one.

Ferment the batter in a bowl or jar with plenty of room for it to expand, for 8 to 24 hours, or even longer in a cool environment, until it has roughly doubled. Once it rises, make dosas and/or idlis, or refrigerate for later use.

For Dosas:

Add water to thin the batter by adding just a little bit of water at a time and stirring it in until you reach a pourable, spreadable consistency.

Heat a well-seasoned griddle or pan. It should be medium hot, hot enough for the batter to sizzle, but not too hot. Do not oil it, unless you find you need to, and then very, very lightly oil it. This is a case where less is more.

Fry the dosas. Use a ladle or spoon to pour batter into the center of the pan, then use the bottom of the spoon to spiral the batter from the center out toward the edges of the pan. Cook as a pancake, flipping after bubbles appear on the surface. Dosas should be thin, with crispy edges. If necessary, thin the batter by adding a little more water.

Enjoy dosas while they are hot. Eat them plain, with coconut chutney (recipe to follow), with a little yogurt or kefir, or stuffed with savory vegetable fillings.

For Idlis:

Lightly oil idli forms.

Spoon batter into them and gently stack. Leave room for batter to expand during steaming.

Steam. Add water to the steaming pot, about ½ inch/1 centimeter deep, but not so deep that the bottom layer of idlis will be touching it. Gently lift the filled idli form into the pot, cover, and then steam the idlis 15 to 20 minutes, until they are firm.

Remove the idlis from the forms using a spoon. Clean and oil the molds between batches.

Serve idlis with coconut or other chutney, or sambar, a delicious spicy vegetable dal, recipes follow.

Tasting a variety of experimental miso flavors at the Momofuku test kitchen in New York City.

coconut chutney

Chutneys are condiments in Indian food, made in infinite variety. This coconut chutney, from southern India, is an excellent accompaniment to idlis or dosas. It is sweet and sour simultaneously, and can be eaten fresh or fermented for a few days. This recipe is inspired by Shanta Nimbark Sacharoff's *Flavors of India: Vegetarian Indian Cooking*.

Timeframe: 20 minutes to 4 days

Ingredients (for about 2 cups/ 500 milliliters):

1 cup/80 grams shredded coconut, fresh or dried

3 tablespoons chana dal (an Indian split pea, optional)

2 tablespoons coconut or other oil

2 tablespoons tamarind paste or juice of 1 lemon

1 teaspoon salt

1 teaspoon cumin

1 teaspoon coriander seed

1 tablespoon honey

½ teaspoon mustard seeds

Pinch of asafetida powder (also called hing)

¾ cup/185 milliliters kefir or yogurt

Process:

Soak the coconut in ½ cup/125 milliliters warm water.

Fry the chana dal, if using, in the oil for just a moment, until it begins to darken (but don't let it burn).

Combine and purée. In a food processor or blender, combine the fried chana daal with the tamarind paste or lemon juice, salt, cumin, coriander seed, honey, and soaked coconut. Process until well blended and puréed.

Fry the mustard seeds in 1 tablespoon oil, briefly. When they start popping, add the asafetida and half of the yogurt or kefir, and stir to combine as the mixture sizzles. Remove from the heat.

Combine and purée. Add the yogurt mixture to the coconut-spice mixture in the food processor or blender, and blend until well combined. Finally, add the remaining uncooked yogurt or kefir, bacteria still alive.

Enjoy the chutney fresh, or ferment it for a sour accent and more developed live cultures. To ferment, transfer it to a jar and leave it in a warm spot, loosely covered, for a few days. After that, store in the refrigerator.

sambar

Sambar is a vegetable dal I for love its rich flavors and its incredible versatility, in that it can incorporate almost any vegetables that might be available. I was first introduced to sambar by my departed and much-missed friend and teaching partner Frank Cook, who traveled extensively in southern India. We would always serve idlis in our workshops, along with sambar.

Timeframe: ½ hour prepping; then at least 1 hour of cooking, but a few hours is better

Ingredients (for 6–8 servings):

¾ cup/180 grams red lentils (or other dal)

3 tablespoons shredded coconut, dried or fresh (optional)

3 tablespoons ghee, butter, or oil, divided

Pinch of asafetida

1 tablespoon coriander, whole or ground

1 tablespoon cumin, whole or ground

¼ teaspoon ground clove

1 tablespoon cayenne or other flaked or ground chili pepper

1 tablespoon mustard seeds

1 large or 2 small onions, peeled and chopped

3 cloves garlic (or more!), peeled and chopped

2–3 fresh tomatoes or a small can (14 ounces) of tomatoes, diced

1 tablespoon turmeric

2 inches/5 centimeters/20 grams ginger, peeled and coarsely chopped

A few whole dried or fresh chili peppers

1 tablespoon honey

2 tablespoons tamarind paste, lemon juice, or kimchi or sauerkraut juice

1 medium potato, finely diced

2–3 cups/500 grams (or more) diced veggies including any of these or others: carrot, cauliflower, eggplant, okra, radish, turnip

Salt and pepper to taste

Process:

Cook the lentils in about 3 cups of water. Bring to a boil then lower to a simmer for about 30 minutes, stirring periodically, until lentils begin to fall apart.

Roast the coconut, if available, in a dry skillet over medium heat. Stir frequently until fragrant and just beginning to brown. Remove from the heat and put aside to add later.

Heat 2 tablespoons of the ghee, butter, or oil in a stew or soup pot large enough to hold and stir the sambar: 6 quarts/6 liters in size or larger.

Fry the spices over medium heat. Start with a pinch of asafetida, and add to it the coriander, cumin, cloves, and chili pepper. Stir to prevent burning. Move the spices toward the edges to clear the center of the pan. Add the remaining 1 tablespoon of ghee, butter, or oil, and once it heats, add the mustard seeds and fry until they begin to pop. Stir the spices all together.

Add the onion and garlic and cook with the spices about 5 minutes.

Add the lentils with their cooking water, the coconut, and all of the remaining ingredients to the pot, along with a little water, if necessary. Bring to a simmer, stirring to prevent burning, at least until the vegetables are tender, about half an hour. As it cooks, add water as necessary to maintain a soupy consistency. A few hours of cooking, or even letting it sit and cool, and then reheating, will meld the flavors more and improve the sambar.

Taste and add seasonings as desired before serving. Sambar is great reheated; add a little water each time you reheat.

Koji room at South River Miso in Massachusetts.

miso

Miso is Japanese fermented soybean paste, made in a wide range of styles. Varieties of miso may be fermented in as little as a couple of weeks, or for many years. Miso is rich in flavor and can be quite salty. It is most famous as a soup, but also used as a marinade, rub, pickling agent, and flavoring in dressings, sauces, spreads, and condiments. In Japan, miso is an iconic food, long associated with good health and longevity.

The first homemade miso I tried was made by my late friend Dr. Crazy Owl, a quirky practitioner of Chinese medicine who extolled the healing powers of miso. The first time I tried Owl's homemade miso I fell in love with it, so chunky and flavorful. Its aliveness inspired me to learn how to make miso, and I have made crocks of it every winter since. Of all the foods I have fermented, this is the one that has met with the greatest appreciation over time. So few people make their own miso, and the people who use miso at all are very passionate about it. Making your own miso to share with the people you love is a way to nourish them deeply.

Though miso is classically made with soybeans, it can be made with any legume or combination of legumes. The distinctive color and flavor of

Miso-maker Connor Eller of Ionia in Kasilof, Alaska, with his barrels and crocks full of miso.

each bean carries over into the miso it produces. Use what is abundantly available to you, and be bold in your fermentation experimentation!

The process of actually making miso is quite simple. The only thing hard about it is making or finding koji, a critical ingredient in miso. Koji is grain or beans with the mold *Aspergillus oryzae* grown on it, used as a starter for miso as well as saké, soy sauce, amazaké, and other fermentations. Making koji is beyond the scope of this book, though it can certainly be done, and you can find extensive information on the process in my book *The Art of Fermentation*, and even more in Shurtleff and Aoyagi's *The Book of Miso*. To buy koji (or koji starter for making your own), see the sources listed in the appendix.

Miso is made in many different styles, with huge regional variation. One way of conceptualizing two broad categories is sweet misos, which ferment for less time, require less salt, and use more koji, all of which makes them sweet; and salty misos, which ferment much longer, using roughly twice as much salt and half as much koji. I would recommend trying the long-fermenting salty misos only if you have a cellar or other unheated winter space. Even a garage or shed is fine. In a heated space miso can dry into a dense brick, a stark contrast with its typical soft, spreadable, and pasty consistency. Sweet misos are incredibly delicious and can be fermented pretty much anywhere, and for only one to four weeks, making them more accessible.

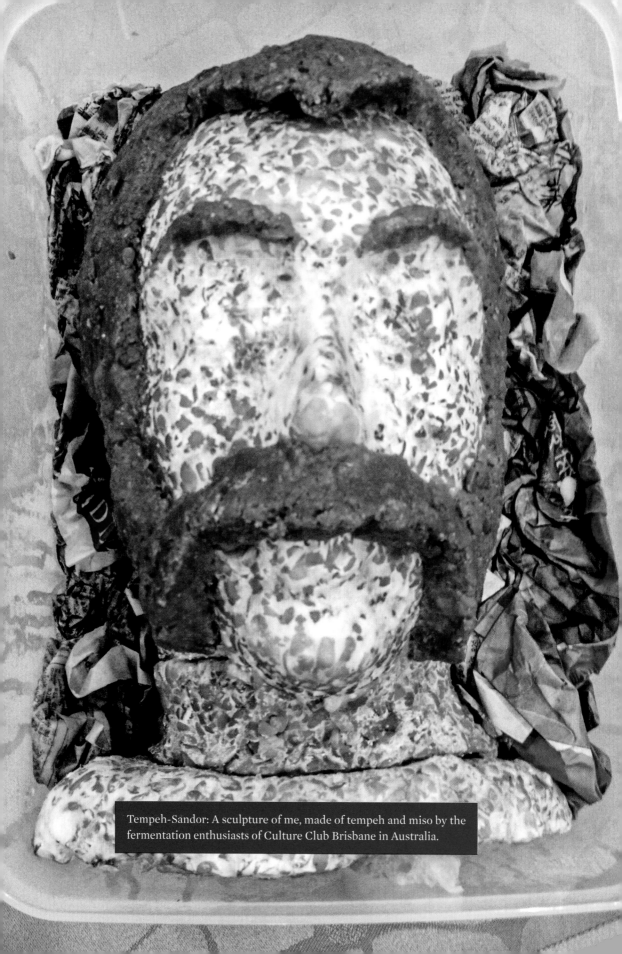

Tempeh-Sandor: A sculpture of me, made of tempeh and miso by the fermentation enthusiasts of Culture Club Brisbane in Australia.

sweet miso

Sweet miso is almost like a chutney, something that can stand on its own as a condiment and isn't so strong that it must be diluted, like its saltier cousin. I like the flavor and textural variation of incorporating other ingredients beyond beans and koji. One of my favorite classic styles is finger-lickin' miso, which incorporates vegetables. Another favorite is natto-miso, in which beans are left whole, and seaweed and a sweetener are added. This sweet miso is a hybrid, incorporating elements of both of these styles. This miso is ready to taste in as little as a week, producing a rich and complex flavor that will evolve with passing time.

Timeframe: 1 to 4 weeks

Equipment:

Ceramic crock or food-grade plastic bucket, 1-gallon/4-liter capacity
Lid that fits snugly inside (plate or hardwood disk)
Heavy weight (a jug filled with water or a scrubbed and boiled river rock)
Cloth (to cover the crock and keep dust and flies out)

Ingredients (for ½ gallon/2 liters):

3 cups/500 grams koji
2 cups/500 grams adzuki or other dried beans
6 tablespoons/90 grams sea salt
2–3 cups/500 grams shredded vegetables, any combination of cabbage, radish, turnip, peppers (sweet and/or hot), eggplant, onion, garlic, seaweed, or . . .
½ cup/125 milliliters honey, sorghum, maple, rice syrup, barley malt, sugar, or other sweetener

Process:

Make or obtain koji before you start.

Soak the beans overnight with plenty of water so that even if they double in size they will remain covered.

Drain the soaking water and place the beans in a cooking pot. Cover with fresh water, just enough to submerge the beans, no more.

Bring the beans to a boil and gently simmer until soft. Length of time can vary with beans, from half an hour to several hours, and can be shortened significantly with a pressure cooker.

Drain the cooked beans, reserving a cup of cooking liquid. Allow the beans to cool.

Dissolve the salt in the still-hot cup of bean cooking liquid.

Chop or grate a mix of vegetables, a small amount of each. If you incorporate seaweed, soak it in a little hot water to rehydrate, and chop into small pieces.

Add everything to the beans and mix. While the beans are still cooling, as soon as they reach 140°F/60°C, cool enough to touch for a couple of seconds, then add the koji. It can tolerate the heat; its enzymes even optimize at this temperature. Add the salt dissolved in bean water, and the sweetener. Once the mix cools to body temperature, add the vegetables. Mix everything well.

Pack into a vessel, pressing the miso down to force out air pockets. Weight to keep the miso pressed, and cover to keep flies away.

Stir every few days, taste to monitor the developing flavor, clean the edges as necessary, level the miso surface, weight, and cover.

Enjoy the miso as its flavor evolves. Transfer to jars and refrigerate when you are ready to slow fermentation.

red miso

This miso is strong and salty. It requires most of a year of fermentation, or longer. The shortest it would typically ferment would be through spring, summer, and fall, and in a heated space, this would be your best bet, as fermenting miso through a winter or more in a heated space dries the miso into a dense brick. In a cellar or other unheated space, this miso gets even better if you can wait a few years. Red miso is traditionally made with soybeans, though its color can vary, especially using different beans. I like to make miso with chickpeas, pinto beans, and field peas, among others. I've experimented widely and can honestly say that every bean I've ever tried has made miso that has tasted delicious.

Timeframe: 1 year or more

Equipment:

Ceramic crock or food-grade plastic bucket, at least 1-gallon/4-liter capacity

Lid that fits snugly inside (plate or hardwood disk)

Heavy weight (a jug filled with water or a scrubbed and boiled rock)

Cloth (to cover the crock and keep dust and flies out)

Ingredients (for 1 gallon/ 4 liters):

3 cups/500 grams koji

4 cups/1 kilogram dried beans

¾ cup/185 grams sea salt, plus ¼ cup/60 grams more for the crock

2 tablespoons live unpasteurized mature miso

Process:

Make or obtain koji before you start.

Soak the beans overnight with plenty of water so that even if they double in size they will remain covered. Drain the beans after soaking.

Cook the beans in fresh water. Bring to a boil, remove any sludge that collects on the surface, then gently simmer until soft. Length of time can vary with beans, from half an hour to several hours, and can be shortened significantly with a pressure cooker.

Drain the cooked beans, reserving the cooking liquid, some of which will be mixed back in. Allow the beans to cool.

Mix the brine. Dissolve the salt in about 2 cups/500 milliliters of the bean cooking liquid (or boiling water). Stir for a few minutes in order to dissolve as much salt as possible. Set the brine aside to cool.

Mash the beans to your desired smoothness, using whatever tools are available. I generally use a potato masher and leave the beans fairly chunky.

Mix it all together. First, check the temperature of the brine. Look for under 110°F/43°C—comfortable to the touch, like a hot bath. Mash the mature miso into the brine, then mash it all into the beans. Next add the koji and mix until the texture is uniform. It should be a bit chunky and dry, firm enough to form into a shape. Add a little more bean cooking liquid (or water) if necessary, but not too much; the fermentation will release water and everything will get juicier. This mixture is what will become your miso; the remaining steps involve packaging it for its long fermentation.

Salt the bottom and side surfaces of your vessel. Rinse to wet the surfaces, then lightly sprinkle with fine-ground salt. The idea is to have higher salt content at the edges to protect the miso.

Pack the miso into the vessel, taking care to expel air pockets. Smooth the top and sprinkle a layer of salt over it. Don't be timid about salting the top.

Cover the miso with a lid, weight, and outer cloth (as explained in Crock Method: Information for Larger Vessels, page 54). Label clearly with indelible markers. Labeling is especially important once you have multiple batches going from different years. Store in a cellar, barn, or other unheated environment.

Wait. Try some after the first year of fermentation. Repack it carefully, salting the new top layer. Then try it a year later, even a year after that. The flavor of miso will mellow and develop over time. I've tried nine-year-old miso, and it was sublime, like a well-aged wine.

A note on decanting: When you open a crock of miso that has been fermenting for a couple of years, the top layer may be quite ugly and off-putting, with a diverse abundance of oxygen-loving organisms. Skim off that ugly layer, throw it in the compost, and trust that below the surface the miso will be gorgeous and smell and taste great. I usually dig out a whole batch of miso at once. I pack the miso into thoroughly clean glass jars. If the tops are metal, I use a layer of waxed paper between the jar and the lid, as miso causes metal to corrode. I store the jars in the cellar. Since fermentation continues, the jars build up pressure, which needs to be periodically released by opening them. Occasionally, mold will form on the surface of a jar of miso. As with the crock, scrape it away, and enjoy what remains beneath it. To avoid these inconveniences, you can store miso in the fridge.

Miso fermenting in huge barrels at South River Miso in Massachusetts.

miso soup

The classic way to enjoy miso is in the form of miso soup. No food I know is more soothing.

When you make miso soup, miso is the last thing you add. In its simplest form, miso soup is just hot water with miso, about 1 table-spoon of miso per cup/250 milliliters of water. Add the hot water to the miso and blend it thoroughly. Avoid boiling miso; gentler heat helps preserve its aliveness.

On the other hand, miso soup can be as elaborate as you want. Adding seaweed is generally where I start. Seaweeds have deep, complex flavors. Some people think it makes them sound more appealing to call them sea vegetables. But I like to honor their wildness by calling them weeds. They carry the essence of the sea. They are mineral-rich and nourish the cardiovascular system, improve digestion, help regu-late metabolism and glandular and hormonal flows, and calm the nervous system.[2] One of their specific benefits is a compound called alginic acid, which binds with heavy metals, such as lead and mercury, and radioactive elements like strontium 90, and carries them out of your body. I love to incorporate a little of it into pretty much anything I cook. Miso soup is almost always prepared with seaweed. Japanese recipes for dashi, or soup stock, traditionally call for kombu, a Pacific Ocean seaweed. I have frequently bought seaweed from small-scale harvesters in Maine, where kombu is not found. The North Atlantic equivalent is called *Laminaria digitata*. Digitata is a thick and hardy variety of kelp. Each stalk's growth splits off into several digits of wavy green-brown flesh, hence the name digitata.

I had a memorable experience harvesting digitata, helping my seaweed harvester friends Matt and Raivo, off the Schoodic Peninsula in "Downeast" Maine. We woke up at 4 AM, squeezed ourselves into skintight wet suits, and drove down to the harbor. We got into a wooden boat that Matt had built himself, and towed a smaller wooden boat, which he had also built. Do-it-yourself has no limits. We glided through the calm bay waters into the foggy dawn for a long time. I wondered how my guides could possibly navigate in the dense gray-ness where the sea, sky, and land all blended into one. We saw seagulls and seals. The water got choppier. We were headed beyond the harbor to the turbulent ocean waters where digitata thrives.

We arrived at our destination just as the tide was getting low enough to give us access. Seaweed harvesting is ruled by the tides, as the plants are most accessible when the tides are at their lowest. We anchored the big boat and got into the smaller boat, then aimed for a large stand of digitata growing from an underwater rock ledge. When we got near the digitata, we jumped out of the boat into the cold, choppy water. Matt and Raivo took turns staying in the boat to keep it from drifting away, continually rowing back to near where we were, so we could toss the digitata that we harvested into the boat.

There I was in the ocean, with a sharp knife in my hand. The idea was to stand on the rock ledge from which the digitata was growing and cut the stalk to harvest it. Sounds straightforward enough. And it would have been, had the waves been kind enough to stop. But every time a wave came rolling rhythmically in, suddenly the water over the rock ledge I was standing on was about 5 feet deep instead of 2 feet. Reaching down to the digitata stalk in the deeper water involved dunking my entire body, head included, into the ocean. And half the time the wave would knock me right off the rock ledge.

I spent a lot of that morning flailing around, knife in one hand, seaweed in the other, feeling like Lucy Ricardo in another madcap misadventure. When I'd actually get a handful of digitata, the goal was to throw it into the rowboat, another challenge intensified by the rough water. It was crazy, and incredibly fun, regardless of how little I managed to harvest. As my body was pushed around by the waves, I identified with the seaweeds, whose lives are a continual push and pull of tidal influences. Several small rowboat loads later, the tide was rising too high for us to continue, so we boated back in the mid-morning sun to the South Gouldsboro harbor, nestled in a bed of slippery digitata.

Most of the seaweed available in the United States is imported from Japan, where it is a popular food and is farmed intensively, with unknown radiation impact from the Fukushima nuclear disaster. I want to make a plug for seaweed bioregionalism. Edible seaweeds are abundant in many cooler coastal areas; in general they are rarely harvested. If you live in such an area, try to find clean and accessible spots to harvest. Take only what you need and limit your impact. Or try to find and support small seaweed harvesters in nearby coastal regions.

We were making miso soup. Here's how I do it:

Start with water. One quart/1 liter of water makes soup for two to four people. Quantities of the other ingredients are in proportion to a quart of water. Start heating the water to a boil while you add other ingredients; once it boils, lower the heat and simmer.

Add the seaweed first. As it cooks, its flavors and qualities melt into the broth. I use scissors to cut up dried seaweed into small pieces, easier to fit in a spoon. Cut up a 2- to 3-inch/5- to 8-centimeter strip of digitata, kombu, or another variety of seaweed, or more than one type. Add the small pieces of seaweed to the water. Once this simmers for a little while, you have a traditional Japanese dashi, or stock.

Add the miso and seasonings. Remove the stock from the heat. Take a cup of the stock and mash about 3 tablespoons of miso into it. Add a little grated ginger and/or garlic. Once well blended, add it to the pot of stock and stir. Taste the soup. Add more miso or seasonings, as needed, using the same technique.

Garnish the soup with chopped scallions, wild onions, or chives.

Reheating. Heat leftover soup gently, trying not to boil the miso.

Variations: Make miso soup simple like this, or make it more elaborate, adding any, or all of the following: Root vegetables including burdock root (*gobo* in Japanese), which gives a hearty, earthy flavor to soup, as well as its tonifying and cleansing powers . . . mushrooms . . . cabbage . . . green vegetables . . . tofu or tempeh . . . leftover cooked whole grains . . . tahini (for a heartier soup) . . . add miso for flavor and body to vegetable or meat stocks.

miso-tahini spread

Another great way to enjoy miso is as a spread, sauce, or dressing.

Timeframe: 2 minutes

Ingredients (for a small portion, about ¼ cup/ 60 milliliters):

1 tablespoon miso
2–4 tablespoons tahini
Juice of ½ lemon (or more)
1 clove garlic (or more), pressed or finely chopped

Process:

Combine the ingredients and mix until well blended. Add more lemon juice, or kraut juice, water, whey, or "pot liquor"—the water left over from cooking vegetables—to reach your desired consistency. Enjoy as a thick spread on bread or crackers, as a sauce for grains or vegetables, or a salad dressing. Miso and tahini are a versatile pair. Or try almond butter, or peanut butter. Experiment and vary!

miso pickles and tamari

Miso is an excellent medium for pickling vegetables. My favorites to pickle in this way are radishes, turnips, and other root vegetables. If they are small (up to about 2 inches/5 centimeters) you can leave them whole; otherwise coarsely chop. Experiment with other vegetables as well.

Timeframe: 1 to 3 weeks (or longer)

Vessel: Wide-mouth jar, bowl, or small crock

Ingredients (for 1-pint/ 500-milliliter jar):

About ¼ pound/125 grams radishes, turnips, carrots, or other vegetables, sliced
½ head of garlic, split into cloves and peeled
Just over 1 cup/250 milliliters salty long-fermented miso

José and Damian Caraballo at The Tempeh Shop in Gainesville, Florida.

Process:

Spread a thin layer of miso on the bottom of the vessel.

Then place vegetables and whole garlic cloves in the miso. Try to keep the vegetables from touching one another, so each piece will be surrounded by miso.

Repeat with another layer of miso and another layer of vegetables.

Cover the top layer of vegetables with miso and press. Weigh it down, or periodically press it down, and leave it to ferment in a moderately cool place.

Taste. Dig out a pickle, slice into it, and taste after about a week. Taste periodically to monitor the evolving flavor. The vegetables will absorb flavor and salt from the miso, and be fermented, as the miso absorbs flavor and water from the vegetables. Both miso and vegetables are transformed by the process. Serve miso pickles in thin slices or chunky, as you like. Use the miso in soups, spreads, sauces, or dressings. Be aware that this miso now has a higher proportion of water and a lower proportion of salt, so though it has gained much flavor its longevity will be diminished.

Liquid may rise to the top; this is sweet, rich miso tamari. Skim or pour it off and savor its complex flavor as a table condiment, or in dressings, marinades, and cooking.

Tempeh mold grown on waru leaves (*Hibiscus tiliaceus*), used to perpetuate the culture in Indonesia.

tempeh

Tempeh is a soybean ferment from Indonesia that has become known as a meat substitute in Western vegetarian cuisines. It is really worth the trouble of making tempeh yourself. The frozen version sold in stores is what I call a "vehicle food," only as good as the flavors you smother it with. Freshly fermented tempeh, on the other hand, has a rich, unique, delicious flavor and texture.

Tempeh was popularized in the North American vegetarian subcultures via The Farm, the most famous of the 1970s hippie communes, which at one time had more than 1,000 residents relying on a soybased diet, which they quickly recognized required fermentation. Folks at The Farm learned to propagate spores of the mold *Rhyzopus oligosporus*, and distributed them widely, along with detailed directions for simple home production, the ones I learned from, available in *The New Farm Vegetarian Cookbook*, a classic vegetarian text still in print. See the appendix for sources of tempeh starter.

Beyond obtaining the spores, the trickiest part of making tempeh can be maintaining a warm environment. I initially learned The Farm method, which mimicked typical Indonesian temperatures, around 85–90°F/29–32°C for 24 hours. The easiest method was waiting for hot summer weather. For years, I used the oven of a propane stove with just the pilot light on, with a Mason jar ring propping the door open just enough so that it doesn't get too hot. You can also use the heat generated by the illuminating lights on many ovens; or an oven with a "proofing" setting. I built a simple incubator that has worked great, using a non-functioning refrigerator, heated by an incandescent lightbulb, regulated by a thermostatic device made for regulating temperatures in a greenhouse. Then a few years ago, I met an Indonesian couple with a tempeh business in California who incubate at 72°F/22°C for 48 hours, using a thermostatic heating unit in a small room. Lately in winter I've been incubating tempeh on a high shelf near the woodstove.

Innovate, make it work. Be sure to maintain good air circulation around the incubating tempeh. It needs oxygen but cannot dry out, so it must be wrapped in a way that holds moisture and yet allows for air circulation. Traditionally tempeh has been wrapped in banana leaves. The typical temperate adaptation is to use plastic bags with tiny holes poked at regular intervals.

soy tempeh

Timeframe: 1 to 3 days

Equipment:

Grain grinder (for the easiest removal of hulls from soybeans)

Clean and unscented towels, or a fan, for drying cooked beans

Ziplock or other plastic bags (3- or 4-quart/ -liter size)

Ingredients (for about 2 pounds/1 kilogram of tempeh):

2 cups/500 grams soybeans

1 tablespoon vinegar (not necessary with a long soak)

1 teaspoon tempeh starter (follow recommended proportions of your source)

Tempeh grown in a banana leaf.

Process:

Dehull the soybeans. The easiest method is to use a grain mill, cracking the beans very coarsely so that every bean is broken but in just a few large pieces, and the hulls start to fall off. When you soak the beans, many of the hulls will rise to the surface. Skim off the hulls now and during cooking. Don't worry if you don't get them all. Dehulling is critical with soybeans, chickpeas, and some other beans, due to their heavy hulls, which the mold cannot penetrate. In the absence of a grain grinder, split the beans after soaking, as described below.

Soak the beans in a large enough pot with lots of water—the beans will double in volume while soaking. The soak is actually a preliminary fermentation in which the beans acidify slightly, making the environment more hospitable for the mold and less hospitable for potential bacterial growth. Soak for about 24 hours unless you are in a particularly hot spot. If you do not soak or soak for a shorter time, add vinegar to the beans after cooking.

Split the soaked beans, if you didn't split them before soaking. Drain the water off the beans and transfer to a plastic bag. Place on a counter and roll repeatedly with a rolling pin, using force, to split beans. Once they are mostly split, transfer to

a bowl and cover with water. Massage the beans underwater to remove the hulls and split any remaining whole beans, then rinse away as many of the hulls as you can.

Cook the beans. Use plenty of water so the remaining hulls will float above the beans. Bring to a boil, without salt, and simmer until the beans are just barely soft enough to eat. For soybeans, 45 minutes should do it. Do not cook them as soft as you would want them to be for eating. The fermentation will continue to soften the beans. As you cook and stir the soybeans, their hulls will rise to the surface of the pot in a foamy froth. Skim off the froth with the hulls and discard.

Drain the cooked beans and dry and cool them. Drain them into a large colander or bowl. Stir frequently to expose different surfaces and encourage rapid cooling and evaporation of surface moisture. Excessive surface moisture encourages bacterial growth and can hinder the desired myceliation by the tempeh mold. Drying and cooling can be speeded by the use of a fan blowing on the steaming beans. Another strategy is hand-drying with towels. Swaddle and pat the cooked soybeans until most of the surface moisture has been absorbed into a towel, or more than one if necessary.

Add starter to the beans. Transfer the beans, cooled to around body temperature but not quite cooled to ambient temperatures, to a mixing bowl. If you didn't soak the beans, add vinegar to acidify the environment and favor fungal growth, and mix thoroughly. Add the spore and mix well, for several minutes, rotating the bowl so the spore is evenly distributed among the soybeans.

Fill bags. Scoop the mixture into sealable plastic bags. Fill the bags about halfway, spreading the beans evenly, and seal the bags. Use an ice pick or fork to poke small holes in the bags every couple of inches, on both sides. The bags hold the moisture in the beans while the holes ensure good air circulation, the conditions necessary for the fungus to thrive. You can reuse the bags by cleaning them after use, drying them thoroughly, and storing them in a special place. Carefully place the bags on a rack in your warm incubation space.

Incubate the tempeh to ferment at 85–90°F/29–32°C for about 24 hours or at around 72–75°F/22–24°C for about 48 hours. No dramatic changes occur during the first half of the fermentation period. Then hairy white mold begins to form in all the space between the soybeans, slowly building in density. It begins to generate heat, as well, so keep an eye on the temperature and adjust the incubation space as necessary. The mold gradually thickens until it forms a cohesive mat holding the beans together. The tempeh should have a pleasant, earthy odor, like button mushrooms or babies. Eventually, the mold will start to show patches of gray or black coloration, originating near the airholes, indicating that it has completed mycelial growth and is ready to eat.

Remove the tempeh from your incubator and allow it to cool to room temperature before refrigerating. Refrigerate or freeze without stacking. If you stack tempeh before it is cool, the mold will continue to grow and generate heat, even in the freezer. Enjoy fresh tempeh for up to about 5 days in the refrigerator. For longer storage, I recommend freezing.

Tempeh is generally not eaten raw. Whereas bacteria are highly beneficial to eat raw, the tempeh mold is not thought to be, and it is typically cooked. To discover fresh tempeh's unique flavor, fry slices of it plain in coconut oil or butter. Or marinate tempeh in a coriander seed brine. Add it to a curry or bake it in a rich barbecue sauce. Try Sweet and Spicy Glazed Tempeh (page 209) or Tempeh Reuben Sandwiches (page 210). Or prepare it however you like it.

black-eyed pea and oat tempeh

The tempeh recipe above is the most basic variety. You can incorporate any kind of legumes, as well as grains, into your tempeh. Here's an example, black-eyed pea and oat tempeh.

Timeframe: 2 to 3 days

Equipment: 3 or 4 small ziplock or other plastic bags (ones), or a baking tray and aluminum foil

Ingredients (for about 2 pounds/ 1 kilogram of tempeh):

2 cups/400 grams black-eyed peas (or other beans)
1 cup/200 grams whole oat groats (or other grains)
1 teaspoon tempeh starter (follow recommended proportions of your source)

Process:

Soak the black-eyed peas in plenty of water, for about 24 hours. Then knead them with your hands to loosen and remove the hulls.

Soak the oats, separately, in just ½ cup/125 milliliters of water, for the same amount of time.

Drain the water off the black-eyed peas and transfer them to a plastic bag. Place this on a counter and roll repeatedly with a rolling pin, using force, to split peas. Once they are mostly split, transfer to a bowl and cover with water. Massage underwater to remove the hulls and split any remaining whole peas, then rinse away as many of the hulls as you can.

Cook the black-eyed peas in a good deal of water so hulls will float to the top and be easy to skim off. Do not cook the beans long. For soaked black-eyed peas, about 15 minutes of simmering should suffice. They should not be soft enough for a pleasant eating experience; the fungus will further soften them. If they lose their form, there will not be air spaces between beans and the tempeh will be impeded. The general rule of thumb is to cook beans to the point where they are just barely edible, meaning you can sink your teeth through them. Figure no more than 25 percent of normal cooking time.

Cook the oats separately. Cook the grain very dry, using just the soaking water. Bring to a boil, then lower the heat and cover until the water has been absorbed, about 20 minutes. Monitor closely to make sure it doesn't burn. You can add any kind of grain to tempeh; just cook it dry so it maintains its form, doesn't add excess moisture to the tempeh, and helps absorb the surface moisture of the beans.

Strain the beans and let them drain well.

Add the cooked oats, still hot.

Mix well, leave in an open bowl, and stir periodically to release steam. If they look wet, with glistening surfaces, use a fan or a towel to further dry them.

Once the beans are dry and cool, add the starter, prepare and fill bags, incubate, and enjoy as detailed in Soy Tempeh, above.

sweet and spicy glazed tempeh with broccoli and daikon

My friend Orchid, a fellow communard from the early days, has been a major source of culinary inspiration for me. This is a delicious and gorgeous dish that he created with tempeh I made.

Timeframe: Less than 1 hour

Ingredients (to serve 3–4 as main dish, 4–6 as side dish):

½ pound/250 grams tempeh
1 cup/85 grams broccoli florets
1 cup/125 grams daikon radish (cut into half-moon slices)
¼ cup/60 milliliters orange juice
2 tablespoons honey
1 tablespoon arrowroot powder
1 teaspoon sesame oil
1 tablespoon rice vinegar
1 tablespoon wine
2 teaspoons chili paste
3 tablespoons tamari, divided
1 tablespoon miso
2 tablespoons vegetable oil
2 tablespoons minced fresh gingerroot
3 tablespoons minced garlic
½ teaspoon ground white pepper

Process:

Cut the tempeh into bite-size pieces and steam for about 15 minutes, in a steamer basket in a saucepan filled with ½ inch/1 centimeter of water and covered.

Add the broccoli and daikon for the last 2 minutes of steaming.

Mix together in a bowl the orange juice, honey, arrowroot, sesame oil, rice vinegar, wine, chili paste, and 2 tablespoons of the tamari. Stir well, making sure that the honey and arrowroot are thoroughly dissolved. In another small bowl, blend the miso with the remaining tablespoon of tamari.

Heat a wok, then add the oil and let it heat. Fry the ginger for about a minute. Add the garlic, and fry 2 minutes or until light brown, then add the white pepper and fry for another 30 seconds. Stir the juice mixture again, add it to the wok, and cook for a few minutes, stirring constantly, until the sauce thickens.

Remove the wok from the flame, add the steamed tempeh and veggies, and stir. Add the miso-tamari mixture and stir again. Serve with rice.

My friend Lagusta Umami's tempeh incubator.

tempeh reuben sandwiches

A great way to enjoy tempeh is in a tempeh Reuben sandwich. This sandwich incorporates four different ferments: bread, tempeh, sauerkraut, and cheese.

Sauté slices of tempeh in a well-oiled pan.

Make sandwiches. Spread Thousand Island dressing (made of ketchup, mayonnaise, and relish) on slices of bread (rye is best), then place sautéed tempeh slices on the dressing.

Cover the tempeh with a generous portion of sauerkraut.

Cover the sauerkraut with a slice of Swiss cheese (or your favorite).

Broil or bake for a minute or longer, until the cheese is melted.

Serve open-faced, with sour pickles (page 60).

Further Reading

Shurtleff, William, and Akiko Aoyagi. *The Book of Miso*. Berkeley, CA: Ten Speed Press, 2001.

——— . *The Book of Tempeh*. Berkeley, CA: Ten Speed Press, 2001.

A tempeh-making enterprise in Indonesia.

10: wines

(Including Mead, Cider, and Other Alcoholic Beverages Made from Simple Sugars)

Certainly alcohol is the oldest, most widespread, and best-known product of fermentation. Fermented alcoholic beverages are perhaps very nearly universal, though there is some confusion about this. Well into the 20th century, many ethnographers propagated the preposterous idea that alcoholic beverages were not found among indigenous (so often dismissed as "uncivilized" or "primitive") peoples.[1] Though traditional practices vary widely, and some groups do not, many indigenous peoples, in almost every part of the world, have long traditions of fermenting alcoholic beverages out of whatever carbohydrate sources they have had. Cultural survival and the historical record have been severely limited by colonial genocides, mass displacements, and rules imposed in many places forbidding natives from fermenting their traditional drinks. Many traditional practices, fermentation among them, have been lost. Yet enough of these ancient fermented alcohol traditions survive to suggest that they have long been extremely widespread, if not quite universal.

The context for making and consuming fermented alcoholic drinks in traditional cultures was, as a general rule, communal and ritualistic. Some cultures created noisy rituals, with the idea that "excited, sometimes even angry, strong energy helped the yeast to work more effectively."[2] Other cultures, with the notion that the ferment needed peace and quiet and could be startled or scared by sounds and movement, approached fermentation processes with quiet

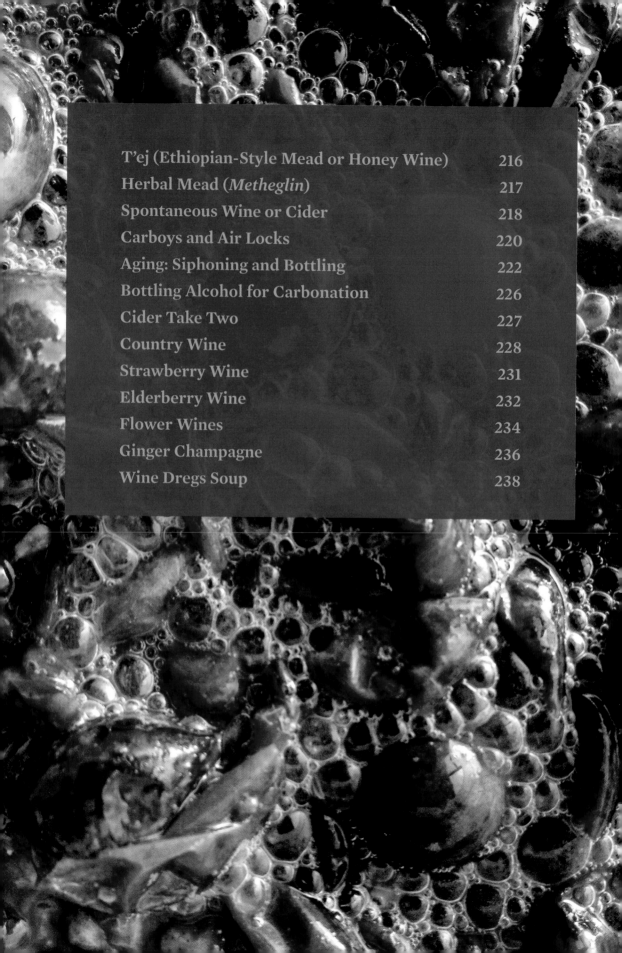

reverence. Either way, the context was ritualistic and sacred. Fermenting your own is a powerful way of reclaiming the ritual sacredness of alcohol fermentation.

When I first tried fermenting wine and beer, I learned from books. But I was put off by the complicated, high-tech methods that most of the books detailed. I especially disliked the emphasis on chemical sterilization, and the predominant practice of killing the wild yeast present on the skins of fruit to assure the success of a particular proven commercial strain of yeast. This practice offends my wild fermentation sensibilities.

I knew that simple, quick, and delicious alcohol ferments were possible, having sampled many different indigenous local brews when I traveled in Africa (long before my specific interest in fermentation developed). Almost every rural village we visited had some ferment to share, among them palm wines and cassava and millet beers. These local ferments were never poured from bottles or stored for long. They were drunk young (not aged) and generally served from open fermentation vessels.

Why was there such a chasm between these low-tech indigenous fermentation traditions I had sampled, and all the information I could find about making beer and wine at home? The home fermentation books and supply shops emphasized specialized equipment, pure strains of yeast, lots of additives, and highly clarified products free of cloudy yeast residue. I do not dispute that these practices can yield wonderful results. But I knew from my African travels that far more accessible methods existed.

The recipes that follow are primarily low-tech wild fermentations. They aim to demonstrate a broad spectrum of possibility. My own alcohol fermentation methods are extremely simple. Experts may scoff at them. To supplement my primitive approach, I also describe the techniques used by a few of my friends. Though the methods vary, along with some of the assumptions behind them, they all produce delicious ferments. Jump in, experiment, and find the process that works best for you.

This chapter starts simple, with wines and meads based on simple sugars that spontaneously ferment into alcohol. It will then move into somewhat more involved methods for longer fermentation to produce stronger beverages, and bottling. In the following chapter, we'll delve into grain-based alcoholic beverages (beers), which are inherently more difficult, requiring an additional enzymatic process to break down complex carbohydrates into simple sugars that can be fermented into alcohol.

Hooch

To illustrate how little is required in the way of specialized equipment or ingredients to ferment alcohol, I'll start with hooch, slang for surreptitiously brewed alcohol. This recipe comes from Ron Campbell, veteran of 18 years in the Illinois prison system. While doing his time, Ron earned the affectionate nickname "Bartles & Jaymes" (a brand name of wine coolers) for his prolific wine-making behind bars. Here's how he did it, in his own words:

First, we sent two to three people to the chow hall to score some fruit cocktail or peaches. This would be used for the "kicker." The kicker sits out one to two days in the open air to collect all the yeast that is abundant in it. [Wild fermentation is everywhere.] We mixed this with six 6-packs of Donald Duck orange juice, along with 1 pound of sugar for each 6-pack, dissolved thoroughly in 1 quart of hot water. Some said I used too much sugar, but nobody ever complained when we drank the finished product.

We poured all of this into a 55-gallon garbage bag, double-bagged it to keep the smell down, and let it sit in a warm place for three days, letting the pressure off whenever needed. We couldn't have an explosion, could we? The rest was waiting, and staying up nights to let the air out. We took shifts to do that. Our homebrew was much too important to have wasted. When three days passed, or the brew was no longer cooking off, we took it and strained the fruit out. We could usually tell when it was done, because we would have to burp the bag only once every two to three hours, instead of every thirty minutes or so. We also tasted it for potency, by sipping a small amount and letting it sit in the front of the mouth while inhaling through the lips. We could taste the alcohol this way.

The whole process was risky, because it was obviously against the rules, and punishable by isolation time if caught. Years ago, if you stayed under five gallons you didn't have to worry about a major case if caught, but they're now taking people to court for any amount. I only got caught once, and that was only a few weeks before my release. I sat in solitary for a month, and went home. My last batch was shared with a group of guys in solitary. We saved our breakfast juices, sugar, jelly, and fruit for days, and made about 3 gallons. Other people in prison use ketchup, or tomato purée, but I always preferred the fruit. It's an acquired taste, but it sure does the job!

t'ej (ethiopian-style mead or honey wine)

I first learned how to make t'ej in a cookbook called *Exotic Ethiopian Cooking: Society, Culture, Hospitality & Traditions* by Daniel Jote Mesfin. Following these basic proportions and steps, I have made many excellent meads. Though t'ej is traditionally consumed young (like most traditional beverages), ready to drink in a matter of weeks, mead improves with age, and can be fermented longer, bottled, and aged. See Aging: Siphoning and Bottling, page 222.

Timeframe: 2 to 4 weeks

Equipment:

1-gallon/4-liter (or larger) ceramic crock, wide-mouth jar, or plastic bucket
1-gallon/4-liter glass jug (the kind you can buy apple juice in)
Air lock and bung (from a beer and wine supply shop for a few dollars; these are helpful but not necessary)

Ingredients (for 1 gallon/4 liters):

3 cups/1 kilogram honey (raw if available)
Handful (or more) organic fresh or dried berries or other fruit with edible skin (optional)

Process:

Combine the honey with ½ gallon/2 liters dechlorinated water in the crock or jar. You will add more water later to bring the total volume to a gallon, but for now you want to leave room in the vessel for vigorous stirring.

Stir well, until the honey is thoroughly dissolved.

Add the fruit, if desired, and stir some more.

Cover with a towel or cloth.

Ferment in a warm spot.

Stir as often as you think of it, at least twice a day. Stir vigorously! You're oxygenating the yeast, and distributing it. Trust that the yeast indigenous to the honey and the fruit will flourish, and that other yeasts will be drawn to the sweet honey-water from the air. After 3 or 4 days (more if it's cold, less if it's hot), the brew should be bubbly and fragrant. Keep stirring! Leave the fruit in about a week once bubbling is vigorous, then strain.

Strain out the fruit and transfer the bubbly honey-water into a clean glass jug. Add water to fill the gallon jug to the point where the neck narrows. Cork with an air lock if you can easily find one (see the illustration on page 221). If not, cover the bottle with a balloon, condom, or any jar lid that can rest on it loosely and slow airflow without holding pressure in.

Ferment for 2 to 4 weeks, until bubbling slows. This is "instant" gratification wine. Drink it now, or age it (see Aging: Siphoning and Bottling, page 222). Delicious, intoxicating alcoholic beverages can be as simple as this.

Variations: Plums, peaches, grapes, pineapple, or any fruit you like . . . coffee-banana, using coarsely ground roasted coffee beans and bananas . . . and any kind of medicinal or culinary herbs, as described below.

herbal mead (*metheglin*)

Most meads around the world incorporate various botanical ingredients, and in the mead-making revival foragers, wildcrafters, herbalists, and alchemists are all working with herbal meads. In Ethiopia, t'ej is traditionally made using a bitter plant called gesho, or woody hops. I have never used this herb, and have had fine results without it. There are other herbal bittering agents, including hops and yarrow, among many. Beyond bittering agents, any medicinal or culinary herb may be used. Make a decoction or infusion of one or more herbs in hot water, then mix that with honey; or infuse the herbs into the honey first, then add water; or keep it all raw and mix fresh herbs with honey and cold water. I love to make hibiscus mead, infusing a few handfuls of dried hibiscus in hot water, then adding the infusion to honey and adding some raw dried hibiscus as a starter. Another memorable batch was lemon herbs, in which I added a handful each of fresh lemon balm, lemon verbena, lemon thyme, lemongrass, and lemon basil at the beginning of the process. Leave the herbs in the crock for about a week, stirring frequently, then strain them out, transfer the wine to a clean gallon/4-liter jug, and air lock. Use any other herbs you like; experiment.

spontaneous wine or cider

Freshly pressed raw fruit juice spontaneously ferments easily and quickly. This is how wine has always been made, from the juice of pressed grapes; cider from pressed apples; perry from pressed pears; and so forth.

Not every fruit neatly juices; some express thick pulps. Grapes easily release their juice when you simply squeeze them by hand or apply moderate pressure. I like to leave skins in as juice begins to ferment for red color and tannins, then strain and press them after a week or so of fermentation. It takes about 15 pounds/7 kilograms of grapes for a gallon/4 liters of juice. Apples and pears cannot be hand-pressed, but require a cider press, with similar proportions of fruit. You may certainly juice using an electric juicer.

If you want to ferment packaged commercial juice you can, but understand that generally the juice has been pasteurized, so its indigenous wild yeasts are gone. For best results, add to the pasteurized juice a little fresh raw organic fruit with skins as a source of yeast and bacteria.

This process, which takes only about a week, results in a mildly alcoholic beverage that is still somewhat sweet. This is the way most alcoholic beverages have been fermented through time, in open vessels, and enjoyed young. If the beverage continues to ferment in the open vessel, as the alcohol fermentation slows, vinegar organisms start to ferment the alcohol into vinegar. To continue the process and produce a dry alcoholic beverage requires protecting the fermenting juice from air, since the vinegar organisms need oxygen (see Carboys and Air Locks, page 220).

Timeframe: About 1 week

Vessel: Crock, bowl, or bucket with a broad surface area, more than 1 gallon/4 liters in capacity to allow for vigorous stirring

Ingredients (for 1 gallon/4 liters):

1 gallon/4 liters fresh grape, apple, pear, or other fruit juice (fresh is best but if you use commercial juice read labels to be sure it is pure juice and does not contain preservatives)

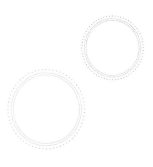

Process:

Ferment the juice at room temperature, in a crock, bowl, or bucket with a broad surface area, with enough room to allow for vigorous stirring. Cover with a cloth to keep flies out but allow for air (and yeast) access.

Stir frequently, at a minimum twice a day but more if possible. Stir vigorously. One of the ways that the stirring stimulates the process is by introducing air and oxygen, and the more vigorously you stir, the more air you mix in. Stirring also distributes airborne yeasts that land on the surface and any yeast activity, and prevents unwanted surface growth. Stir, stir, stir.

Observe bubbling. At first you will notice a few bubbles. Keep stirring frequently and the bubbling will grow in intensity. After a week or so the bubbling will peak and begin to slow.

Taste as the fermentation proceeds. Over the course of 10 days the stages might be described as "sweet, mildly alcoholic," then "stronger, losing its sweetness, not at all sour," then eventually "starts to have a sour edge." Homebrewing can be as simple as this.

Cutting a mature maguey plant in Mexico to access the center in order to collect sap, or *aguamiel*, to ferment into *pulque*.

carboys and air locks

The alcoholic beverages presented thus far can all be fermented exclusively in open vessels, and enjoyed relatively quickly. In an open vessel, it is only a matter of time before the beverage becomes vinegary. Alcoholic beverages intended for aging are generally completed in air-locked vessels. In the early stages of fermentation, when yeast activity and bubbling are most vigorous, the surface of the ferments is protected by the carbon dioxide continually being released at the surface, so even if vinegar bacteria are present, they lack access to the oxygen they need to metabolize alcohol into acetic acid. It is only as the bubbling subsides that the vinegar-producing aerobes can become established.

Most traditional alcoholic beverages have been drunk only partially fermented, lightly alcoholic, still sweet, and sometimes sour. To ferment to dryness (converting all the sugars to alcohol) and avoid souring requires technology to minimize surface area and block access of fresh air to it. This simple technology is a vessel called a carboy, and a plastic device called an air lock. A carboy is a large bottle with a narrow neck, which minimizes surface area in contact with the air. For 1-gallon/4-liter batches, glass juice jugs confer the same advantage.

The carboy is then plugged with an air lock, a device that allows the carbon dioxide produced by fermentation to escape while preventing lower-pressure air from outside from entering the vessel. There are various designs, but they all use water to block the free flow of air, while still allowing pressure to release. In long-term ferments using air locks, be sure to check them periodically, as the water can evaporate out of them and break the air lock; just add a little water as necessary. Air locks are inexpensive and available from wine- and beer-making supply shops and Internet sources.

If you don't have an air lock, a balloon or condom stretched over the mouth of the fermenting vessel is a good alternative. It prevents air from entering the vessel and absorbs the pressure of the carbon dioxide released in fermentation by inflating. Just be sure to manually release the pressure as needed (it may diffuse through) or the balloon/condom may fly off or burst.

Wine fermenting in a barrel at Pratale, a farm in Umbria, Italy.

aging: siphoning and bottling

T'ej is alcoholic and delicious after a few weeks; however, most mead or wine is far better after a few years. Meads or wines to be aged or stored for any length of time need to be bottled. Even before bottling, once vigorous fermentation slows, it's best to siphon wine or mead from the initial fermentation vessel into a clean one, leaving the sediment, or lees, behind. This process is called racking. The siphoning agitates and aerates the fermenting liquid, enabling the yeast to complete fermentation, and the removal of the sediment prevents it from imparting any undesirable flavor.

Commercial wines are full of strange clarifying agents, including egg whites, milk caseins, gelatin, and isinglass, an extract from the bladder of sturgeon (you don't read about these because alcoholic beverages are not required to be labeled with ingredients like other foods and drinks).[3]

Wine-making shops and websites sell siphoning tools, which consist of flexible plastic tubing attached to a few feet of hard plastic tubing. This hard tube goes into the carboy, to a point above the sediment, and is much easier to control than flexible tubing. In the absence of this specific tool, any flexible plastic tubing will do.

Before siphoning, set your carboy on a table or counter, and let it sit undisturbed for a few hours so any sediment that dispersed when you moved it has a chance to settle. Place another clean fermentation vessel on the floor or a lower surface. For this to work, gravitationally, the vessel you are filling needs to stay lower than the point you are siphoning from. Be sure to have a glass nearby, so you can enjoy a taste of your wine. When you are ready, remove the air lock from the carboy, and place the hard tube end of the siphon into the carboy, with the end in the wine but higher than the level of the sediment. Hold it (or better yet, have a second person hold it) at that level as you siphon. Place your mouth on the exposed end of the hose, and suck until you taste your wine. Then place a clean finger over the end of the hose to hold the liquid in the siphon, bring it to the mouth of the clean carboy or jug, release your finger, and fill. When you leave sediment behind, the

new carboy or jug will not be full to the point where the neck narrows, so mix some fresh honey- or sugar-water at the same proportions as the original batch and top off as necessary.

Place an air lock in the new carboy and leave it to continue to ferment. In general, ferment wines for at least three to six months before bottling. If you bottle them before fermentation is complete, you run the risk of having corks pop out. Even if there is no visible bubbling or release of air after a few weeks, slow fermentation continues for months.

Meanwhile, save bottles from (corked, not screw-top) commercial wines and pop-top (not screw-top) beers for your bottling, or collect them at a local recycling center. When you are ready to bottle, clean them thoroughly with soap and hot water, using a flexible bottle brush, if necessary, to remove crud. Rinse the bottles thoroughly; you don't want soap residue in your wine. Thorough cleaning is sufficient for me, but some meticulous wine makers steam bottles standing upside down in a big pot, covered, for about 10 minutes.

Set your carboy on a table or counter, arrange clean bottles nearby, on a tray on a lower surface or on the floor, and siphon into the first bottle. As each bottle fills (not to the rim, but to about 2 inches/5 centimeters below it), clamp the hose, crimp it by folding it on itself, or block it with your finger, to stop the flow as you move the siphon to the next bottle. Somewhere in there, fill up a glass to enjoy. Fill bottles until you are about to reach the yeasty sediment.

Once your wine is in bottles, you need to cork them. Traditional corks come from the bark of trees native to the Mediterranean (which regenerates); some wine makers prefer synthetic corks. Both are available at wine-making suppliers. Corks are fatter than the necks of the bottles, so you will need a corking tool to force them into the bottles. There are a number of cleverly designed contraptions for this. Soak corks in boiled water for a few minutes to sanitize and soften them.

Aging mellows wines. Store wine in a cool dark place (such as a cellar). With traditional corks, leave bottles upright for a week or so until the corks fully expand and seal, then store bottles on their sides, so the wine keeps the corks moist and expanded. (This is not necessary with synthetic corks.) Mark your wines clearly so you can distinguish different vintages.

bottling alcohol for carbonation

Corking wine in bottles as described above is only appropriate for flat ciders, wines, or meads. Fermentation must be complete before bottling; if it continues in the bottle, pressure will build and the cork will be forced out. It has happened to me more than once! Sparkling beverages, including carbonated beers, call for bottles with secure lids that can take some pressure.

The easiest bottles, if you can find them, are rubber-gasket "bail-top" bottles that Grolsch and some other premium beers use. Save these when you come across them, and collect them from recycling centers. Also collect beer bottles with lips that hold "crown caps," the kind of beer caps you need to open with a bottle opener. Brewing suppliers sell caps and capping devices, so you can reuse these bottles indefinitely. You can also use heavy champagne bottles, designed to withstand pressure. These bottles use special corks called champagne stoppers, secured by champagne wires (or you can improvise with any available wire).

Another option is to bottle in 1-, 2-, and 3-liter plastic soda bottles with screw tops—an unorthodox and perhaps inelegant method, but resourceful and effective, not so much for aging but for more short-term enjoyment. Plastic bottles also make it easy to monitor—by squeezing—how carbonated a beverage is getting.

Beware of over-pressurizing bottles! If there is too much sugar left to ferment in the bottle, the bottles can explode, as discussed in Bottling and Carbonation in the context of more lightly fermented beverages in chapter 6. Generally sparkling alcoholic beverages are fermented to dryness, then "primed" by the addition of a tiny controlled amount of sugar at the time of bottling. I determine whether the sugars are all fermented simply by tasting. If the wine is still sweet, it is not ready to bottle. Only bottle it if it tastes like all the sweetness has fermented away. If you want to get technical about it, use a tool called a hydrometer.

When your beverage is ready for priming, siphon it into a clean vessel, leaving the yeasty sediment behind. The amount of sweetener to add is 1 cup/250 milliliters for a 5-gallon/20-liter size or 3 tablespoons for a 1-gallon/4-liter size. Add sweetener by first removing about 1 cup/250 milliliters of the beverage, then mixing the sweetener into that. Once it's well dissolved, stir this mixture into the rest of the beverage to distribute the priming sugar evenly. Then bottle, cap, and leave bottles to ferment at least 2 weeks before drinking, or age longer.

cider take two

As it turns out, one of my editors, Ben Watson, is a longtime cider maker and the author of the book *Cider, Hard and Sweet*. Ben felt that my earlier recipe for short-fermented Spontaneous Cider doesn't do cider justice. "Hard cider that is truly fermented to dryness can require up to six months to make and mature before bottling," he wrote on a Post-it note attached to my original manuscript. I sure do enjoy good hard, dry cider, so I am including what Ben calls in his book "Cider 101."[4]

Hard cider was the favorite drink of colonial New England. Apple orchards provided the primary source of fruit to ferment into alcohol for the settlers. In Massachusetts in 1767, cider consumption was greater than 35 gallons/140 liters per person.[5] Cider faded in popularity as America's agrarian society urbanized, and only now is it seeing a resurgence.

This process produces a dry, still (uncarbonated), traditional farmhouse cider.

Timeframe: 6 months or more

Vessel: 1-gallon jug with air lock

Ingredients (for 1 gallon/4 liters):
1 gallon/4 liters fresh unpasteurized apple cider (without chemical preservatives)

Process:

Fill the jug nearly full of sweet cider. Reserve about 2 cups/500 milliliters of the cider to add later and leave it out of the gallon jug to leave a little room for the ferment to froth.

Cover the container with plastic wrap and place it in a cool spot out of direct sunlight. After a few days, the cider should begin to froth up vigorously and "boil over."

Remove the plastic wrap and cover with a cloth. Let the cider continue to ferment. Wipe off the sides of the container every day to remove any scummy residue until this vigorous fermentation subsides (which may take several weeks, depending on temperature).

Add the reserved cider to fill the vessel, leaving about 2 inches/5 centimeters of head space at the top. Fit the jug or carboy with an air lock filled with water.

Ferment for one or two months, until the steady glub-glub of escaping carbon dioxide slows down considerably and the cider begins to clear. There will be a lot of sediment on the bottom of the container.

Rack the cider off into another clean jug, leaving the lees, or sediment, behind. Place an air lock filled with fresh water on the top. Let the cider continue to age and mellow for one or two months.

Bottle. Approximately four to five months after you've started, the cider should be completely fermented to dryness, or nearly so, and ready for bottling. The cider's flavor will improve if it is aged in the bottle for another month or two before drinking.

country wine

Though the word *wine* comes from the word *vine*, and wine classically is made from grapes, wine can be made by fermenting any sweet substance, and wines from sweetened infusions of all kinds of fruits, vegetables, and flowers are known as country wines.

Living in a rural community where many different people have experimented with the simple techniques of making wine, I have had the great privilege of sampling an awesome array of far-out country wines. My friends Stephen and Shana made tomato wine, which was terrific, though not particularly tomatoey, and jalapeño wine, which was hot and delicious. The only limit on what can be made into wine is your imagination. To give you a sense of the variety that is possible, I took an inventory of the wines in our communal root cellars. The fruit wines I found were blueberry, "black and blueberry," mulberry, sweet cherry, sour cherry, strawberry, apple, plum, muscadine (a variety of grape), persimmon, elderberry, nectarine, cantaloupe, sumac, "mystery fruit wine," hibiscus-strawberry, peach, wild grape, prickly pear, banana, and pear and apple-pear champagne. Then there were the flower and herb wines: daylily, dandelion, elderflower, phacelia, trillium, morning glory petal mead, lilac petal mead, echinacea, stinging nettle, mugwort, wild cherry bark, "hops-chamomile-valerian-catnip-sorghum honey wine," and garlic-anise-ginger. And there were vegetable wines including carrot, corn, potato, beet, sweet onion (an exceptional cooking wine), and category-defying redbud with orange and plum, almond, and watermelon-chamomile. Anything tasty or aromatic that you have an abundance of can be made into wine.

The basic process for country winemaking is to ferment a sweet infusion of the fruit or flower or vegetable or whatever you are using

to flavor it. Methods vary: I typically do it all raw and at room temperature with fruit; or using hot water with herbs as infusions or decoctions. Some people use hot water with fruit, or use steam-juicing devices.

One major variable in wine-making is the amount of sweetener added to the unfermented mixture (the must). To my palate, dry wines taste better than sweet wines. Less can be more. Up to a point, additional sweetener can yield higher alcohol content. After that point, adding more sugar just makes the wine sweeter. One of the ironic twists of alcohol fermentation is that as yeasts produce alcohol and the alcohol level rises, the environment becomes less hospitable to yeasts, and they die off. The alcohol level that yeast can survive varies somewhat with different strains; champagne yeast, for example, is selected for its relatively high alcohol tolerance. This is one of the unpredictable aspects of wild fermentation.

Another major variable is the type of sweetener used. You can ferment any sweetener. I generally prefer to use honey rather than cane sugar, mostly because it does not require importation or refinement. For a beautiful and informative ode to honey, check out Stephen Harrod Buhner's *Sacred and Herbal Healing Beers*. He points out that ancient honey ferments included not only honey but also the other related substances and beings found in the hive (bee pollen, propolis, royal jelly, and even angry bees, full of venom), and he catalogs the great health benefits of every one of these whole-hive components. The one great advantage of cane or beet sugar in wine-making, however, (other than its price, which no other sweetener can approach) is that its flavor and color are neutral, allowing the flavors and colors of flowers and berries to shine without rivalry. Honey exerts more of its own flavor and color influence over wines. Maple syrup, sorghum, rice syrup, agave, molasses, and other sugars can be used, as well; each sweetener imparts its own unique flavor and qualities to ferments.

Ye Olde Cider Bar List

Draught Cider

	ABV	Half	Pint
Sam's Medium	6%	£1.20	£2.40
Sam's Dry	6%	£1.20	£2.40
Sam's Autumn Scrump	7.5%	£1.55	£3.10
Thatchers Black Rat	6%	£1.25	£2.60
Thatchers Diesel	6%	£1.25	£2.60
Westons Old Rosie	7.3%	£1.55	£3.20
Westons Country Perry	4.5%	£1.55	£3.20
Wiscombe Suicider	8%	£1.60	£3.20

Keg Cider

	ABV	Half	Pint
Westons Stowpond Press	4.5%	£1.50	£3.10
Thatchers Gold	4.8%	£1.50	£3.10
Sam's Pound House	6%	£1.55	£3.10
Westons LBW	7.3%	£1.60	£3.30

Bottled Cider

	ABV	Bottle
Westons Vintage	8.2%	£3.40
Westons Extra Dry Oak	6%	£3.30
Westons Med / Dry Oak	6.5%	£3.30
Thatchers Katy	7.4%	£3.30
Thatchers Old Rascal	4.5%	£3.30
Kingstone Press	5.3%	£3.30
Gaymer's Olde English	4.5%	£2.50
Sheppy's Tremlett's Bitter	7.2%	£2.90
Sheppy's Kingston Black	7.2%	£2.90
Sheppy's Dabinett	7.2%	£2.90
Westons L.A	0.5%	£1.80
Norcotts Elderflower Cider	4%	£3.40
Westons Perry	7.4%	£3.40

House Wine, Sherry & Port
Same Price As Country Wines Per Glass

Country Wines

	ABV	125ml	175ml
		£2.60	£3.00

Sweet
- Cherry
- Ginger
- Mead

Medium / Sweet
- Apricot
- Blackcurrant
- Peach

Medium
- Blackberry
- Raspberry
- Sloe
- Strawberry

Medium / Dry
- Quince

Dry
- Elderflower
- Nettle

Off / Dry
- Cowslip
- Damson
- Elderberry
- Gooseberry

Also Available as Cooler's £3.30

Soft Drinks

	Half	Pint
Coca-Cola	£1.30	£2.00
Diet Coke		
Schweppes Lemonade		
Bitter Lemon		
Ginger Beer		
Apple Tango	£1.30 can	
Cherry Tango	£1.30 can	
J20's	£2.20 Bottle	
Cordial & Soda	50p	£1.00

strawberry wine

Strawberry wine is a classic country wine, and so delicious. Use this recipe as a general guideline for other fruit-based country wines.

Timeframe: For a sweet young wine, 1 to 2 weeks; for a dry wine, 3 to 6 months; for an aged wine, 1 year or more

Equipment:

Crock, bowl, or bucket of more than 1-gallon/4-liter capacity to allow for vigorous stirring

1 gallon jug or carboy with air lock, if fermenting to dryness

Ingredients (for 1 gallon/ 4 liters):

2–3 quarts/2–3 kilos of strawberries. The fruit is the source of the yeasts, so use organic or no-spray berries, always raw. Fresh are best but frozen is fine too. The more berries you use, the stronger the berry flavor.

2 cups/500 grams sugar

Process:

Prepare the berries. Wash well and remove the stems. I prefer not to crush or chop berries. It is their essence and sweetness I am after, which will infuse into the solution without crushing, not their pulp and pectins, which I want to leave behind as much as possible.

Mix the sugar solution. Add sugar to 1 gallon/4 liters dechlorinated water and stir until the sugar is fully dissolved.

Fill a vessel. Use a broad open vessel, with plenty of room for vigorous stirring. Add the berries and sugar solution. Loosely cover with a cloth; secure if necessary to keep flies out.

Stir frequently, at least 2 times a day, or 10 times. After a few days, bubbling will become evident.

Keep stirring! After about a week of vigorous bubbling, the berries will be spent.

Strain and discard the berries.

Enjoy the wine now, lightly fermented, still-sweet. This is very easy, and pretty much how many people throughout history have enjoyed alcohol.

Or you can ferment to dryness in an air-locked jug or carboy, with a narrow neck. If the wine does not fill the vessel to its narrow neck, add sugar-water as necessary to fill. Ferment for at least a couple of months, until bubbling ceases. Siphon into a secondary vessel. If bubbling restarts, ferment until it ceases. Bottle. Age six months or longer.

Variations: Elderberry . . . blueberry . . . blackberry . . . cherry . . . plum . . . peach . . . With larger fruits, cut each fruit into a few pieces.

This is how I make almost all of my country wines. My methods are extremely simple. Just to illustrate the diversity of techniques people can use, the following recipes document quirky methods used by a few of my friends.

elderberry wine

This is the method my friend and neighbor Sylvan uses to make consistently excellent wine from delicious, nutritionally rich, and immune-boosting elderberries, the most abundant and easily available fruit in our area.

Timeframe: 1 year or more

Equipment:

Crock, bowl, or bucket of at least 1-gallon/
    4-liter capacity to allow for vigorous stirring
1 gallon jug or carboy with air lock

**Ingredients (for 1 gallon/
5 liters):**

3 pounds/1.5 kilograms elderberries, 2
    quarts/2 liters after destemming, or more!
1 packet wine or champagne yeast
4 cups/1 kilogram sugar

Process:

Prepare the berries. Destem and clean the berries. This is a good job to do with helpers. Collect a bowlful of destemmed berries at a time, cover with water, and stir. Ripe berries sink while leaves, insects, and overripe berries float to the top. Skim off what floats with a strainer, pour off the water, and place the clean berries in a bucket or crock. Repeat until all the berries are clean. "The more berries, the richer the flavor," says Sylvan.

Boil water. Be ready with ½ gallon/2 liters, but only add as much water as you need to cover the berries. Cover with a towel and leave it overnight to steep and cool.

Add the yeast. Remove 1 cup of the liquid, dissolve a packet of yeast in it, and leave for a few minutes, until it appears bubbly and active. Then add it to the berries and water, stir, and cover.

Ferment 2 to 3 days, stirring often. No sugar has been added yet. "The yeast should feed on the sugar in the fruit before you give it something else to feed on," explains Sylvan. During this time, the wine gets somewhat frothy, but not nearly as active as it will get when sugar is added.

After 2 or 3 days, add the sugar. Pour the sugar into a cooking pot, then add just enough water to liquefy; heat slowly, stirring constantly, until the sugar dissolves into a clear syrup. Cover the syrup until it cools, then add it to the elderberry mash.

Ferment 5 to 7 days, covered, stirring often, until vigorous bubbling begins to slow.

Strain and transfer. Strain this initial fermenting concentrate through a cloth or mesh in a colander. Transfer to a narrow-necked jug or carboy, which it will only fill partway since we have not

added all the water yet. Return the berry solids to the initial open vessel and cover with fresh water. After a few moments, strain this and gently press the berries. If necessary add a little more water to fill the jug to the point where the neck narrows, but not up the neck. Leave a little head-room for foam. Insert the air lock.

Ferment at room temperature for the first month or two. At first, place the jug on a pan to contain the mess in case it gets so frothy that it overflows. If this should occur, temporarily remove the air lock and clean it and the mouth of the carboy. Fermentation will slow gradually.

Rack. After two months in a warm spot, siphon the wine into a clean jug, leaving the sediment behind. Insert an air lock and relocate the carboy to a cool, dark location. Ferment there for at least nine months. Periodically check to make sure the water hasn't evaporated out of the air lock, and refill and clean the air lock, as necessary.

Bottle, age if you like, and enjoy.

Harvesting grapes to process into wine at Pratale, a farm in Umbria, Italy.

flower wines

"Wine made from flowers preserves the exquisite flavors and benevolent properties of the blossoms from which it is made. It also preserves the memories of fine, clear, sunshiny days—alone or with Someone Else—in woods, meadows, and hills, picking millions of tiny flowers for hours until they become etched on the insides of the eyelids." These wise words were written by my friend and neighbor Merril Harris, in an article, "Nipping in the Bud: How to Make Wine from Flowers," published in *Ms. Magazine* nearly 50 years ago.

Dandelion wine is the classic flower wine, made with the bright-yellow flowers of the plentiful and easy-to-find weed. Don't believe the hype of the manicured lawn lobby; dandelion is not only beautiful and tasty, but also a potent liver-cleansing medicine. Many other flowers can transfer their delicate bouquets and distinctive essences into wines, as well, including (but certainly not limited to) rose petals, elderflowers, violets, marigolds, yarrow, red clover blossoms, and daylilies.

"Begin by gathering your flowers," writes Merril, "perhaps the most pleasurable part of the winemaking process." As a general guideline, pick about a gallon of flowers per gallon of wine you intend to make. If you cannot gather this many in a single outing, freeze what you gather until you accumulate enough. Be sure to pick flowers from places that have not been sprayed, which usually means not roadsides.

Timeframe: 1 year or more

Equipment:

Crock, bowl, or bucket of at least
1-gallon/4-liter capacity to allow for
vigorous stirring

1-gallon/4-liter jug or carboy with air lock

Ingredients (for 1 gallon/ 4 liters):

1 gallon/4 liters flowers in full bloom, yielding
about ½ pound/250 grams petals

4 cups/1 kilogram sugar

2 lemons (organic, because you will use
the peel)

2 oranges (organic, because you will use
the peel)

1 pound/500 grams raisins (golden raisins will
preserve the dandelion's light hue better
than dark raisins)

½ cup/125 milliliters berries (for wild yeast) or
1 packet wine yeast

Process:

Prepare the flowers. As much as possible, separate
the flower petals from the base of the blossoms,
which can impart bitter flavors.

Make the infusion. Place flower petals in a crock,
reserving about 1 cup/250 milliliters to add later
in the process. Add the sugar, the juice, and thinly
peeled rinds of the lemons and oranges (to add
acidity), and the raisins (to introduce astringent
tannins). Then pour 1 gallon/4 liters of boiling
water over these ingredients, and stir until the
sugar is dissolved. Cover the crock to keep flies
away, and leave to cool to body temperature.

Add the yeast. Add the reserved flower petals and
berries to introduce wild yeasts. (Or to use
commercial yeast, remove 1 cup of the cooled
mixture, dissolve a packet of yeast into it, and
once it starts to bubble vigorously return it to the
crock.) Cover the crock.

Ferment, stirring as often as you think of it, for 3 to
4 days.

Strain through a cloth or mesh and squeeze moisture
out of the flowers.

Transfer to a jug with an air lock, and ferment about
three months, until fermentation slows.

Rack by siphoning into a clean vessel, leaving the
sediment behind.

Ferment at least three more months.

Bottle.

Age at least three months to mellow wine; longer
is better.

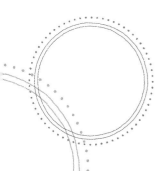

ginger champagne

Any country wine or mead can be carbonated by priming (see page 226). My friend Dashboard (then known as Nettles), with whom I built and shared a home, made this ginger champagne in 1998, anticipating the imminent arrival of the new millennium in 2000. Lucky for us, Dashboard recorded his ingredients and steps in our beloved kitchen journal, and he helped me re-create the recipe to pass on to you.

Sparkling wines use a specific variety of yeast—champagne yeast—that can tolerate higher levels of alcohol. After all the sugar is converted to alcohol and it is ready to be bottled, a little extra sugar is added so that fermentation continues in the bottle, trapping carbon dioxide and creating the sparkle. Since significant pressure builds in the bottle, champagne is bottled in heavy bottles. Special corks that you can grasp are available from wine-making suppliers, called champagne stoppers, and you have to secure the stoppers with champagne wires (or you can improvise with any available wire).

Timeframe: 1 year

Equipment:

1 jug with air lock
5 champagne bottles with stoppers and
  wires, or beer bottles

Ingredients (for 1 gallon/ 4 liters):

12–24 inches/30–60 centimeters/125–250
  grams fresh gingerroot
4 cups/1 kilogram sugar
Juice of 1 lemon
1 teaspoon vanilla extract
1 package champagne yeast

Process:

Make a ginger infusion. Slice, chop, or grate the
  ginger. The amount used will determine the
  intensity of ginger flavor. Place it in a large pot
  with the sugar and 1 gallon/4 liters of water. Cover,
  bring to a boil, and simmer for 1 hour, stirring
  occasionally. After 1 hour, turn off the heat.

Add the lemon juice and vanilla.

Cover and cool to body temperature.

Add the yeast. Strain 1 cup/250 milliliters of the
  cooled infusion into a measuring cup and dissolve
  a packet of yeast into it. Strain the rest of the
  mixture into the jug. Once the cup with the yeast
  starts to bubble vigorously, add it to the jug and
  insert the air lock.

Ferment two to three months at room temperature,
  until fermentation slows.

Rack by siphoning the wine into a clean jug, leaving
  the yeasty sediment behind. Since you are losing
  some volume, top off with sugar-water mixed at
  a ratio of ¼ cup/60 milliliters sugar per cup/
  250 milliliters water. Replace the air lock and
  ferment about six more months, until bubbling
  has ceased altogether.

Prime with a small amount of sugar to reactivate the
  yeast, now dormant since it has consumed all the
  available sugar and converted it into alcohol and
  (escaped) carbon dioxide. The priming sugar
  ferments in the bottle, carbonating the champagne. Don't use too much sugar or the
  champagne will be spewing and bottles can
  explode! First, siphon the wine into a clean open
  vessel, leaving behind the sediment. Add 4
  teaspoons sugar and stir well to dissolve.

Fill the bottles.

Cork with champagne stoppers, and secure the
  stoppers with champagne wires.

Wait at least a month for the final fermentation to
  complete. Champagne can store for years, ready
  to make any occasion a celebration.

Chill bottles before opening to minimize spewed
  champagne.

wine dregs soup

When you rack and bottle wines, you are left with yeasty sediment at the bottom of the fermenting vessel. This sediment is not pretty, so generally it is not bottled or served. But all that yeast, deceased as well as living, is full of B vitamins. Wine dregs make a rich and flavorful addition to soups and stews. Cook it for a while to cook off the alcohol.

Further Reading

Buhner, Stephen Harrod. *Sacred and Healing Beers: The Secrets of Ancient Fermentation*. Boulder: Siris Books, 1998.

Garey, Terry A. *The Joy of Home Winemaking*. New York: Avon, 1996.

Spence, Pamela. *Mad About Mead! Nectar of the Gods*. St. Paul: Llewellyn Publications, 1997.

Vargas, Pattie, and Rich Gulling. *Making Wild Wines and Meads: 125 Unusual Recipes Using Herbs, Fruits, Flowers, and More*. Pownal, Vt: Storey Books, 1999.

Watson, Ben. *Cider, Hard and Sweet*. Woodstock, VT: Countryman Press, 1999.

Zimmerman, Jereme. *Make Mead Like a Viking: Traditional Techniques for Brewing Natural, Wild-Fermented, Honey-Based Wines and Beers*. White River Junction, VT: Chelsea Green Publishing, 2015.

Pulque in Mexico.

11: beers

Beers are alcoholic beverages made primarily from grains. In contrast with the honey-, sugar-, and fruit-based beverages we've covered so far, all simple carbohydrates that spontaneously ferment into alcohol, grains are complex carbohydrates that must be digested first into simple carbohydrates before yeast can ferment them into alcohol. This requires an additional step; therefore beer-making is always a more complex process.

In the Western tradition, this is accomplished by malting, which means germinating, or sprouting, the grain. The germination releases enzymes that break down complex carbohydrates into simple sugars, a process intended to nourish the emergent plant but one that, as fate would have it, ends up nourishing yeast instead to produce alcohol. Directions for sprouting grains are found on page 246. I'll walk you through a couple of beers that are started from whole grains, transformative processes beginning simply with dried grains. Most homebrewers do not actually malt their own grain, however. Commercially available malted grains are probably more efficient to use, widely available, much easier, and produce flavorful, distinctive brews.

There are two other ways that people use to convert the complex carbohydrates of grains into simple sugars to ferment into beers. One is through the action of molds. Across Asia, rice and other grains are fermented into alcoholic beverages like saké using *Aspergillus* and other molds, which contain enzymes that break complex carbohydrates into simple sugars. Koji, used for amazaké in chapter 8 and for miso in chapter 9, as well as saké, is a Japanese example. The other method people use for this important carbohydrate conversion is to chew grains and saturate them with saliva, which also contains enzymes that digest complex carbohydrates. Perhaps you have noticed that if you chew long enough on a morsel of starchy food it starts to taste sweet. Digestion begins in the mouth, and your body wastes no

time breaking down food into simpler nutrients. Chewing on grains and spitting them out is a low-tech and ancient means of carbohydrate conversion for beer-making. This is exactly how we'll make our next ferment, chicha, which is followed by examples of beers produced using molds and malting.

Barrels of aging beer at Allagash Brewing Company in Maine.

chicha
(andean chewed-corn beer)

I start with this because chewing is the simplest means of achieving carbohydrate conversion, and thought to be the most ancient. The word *chicha* actually describes a broad range of South American beverages, mostly alcoholic but some not, mostly corn-based but some not, and with many other varied ingredients. Chicha was considered by the Incas "the vehicle that linked man to his gods through the fecundity of the earth."[1] The chewed variation is not extremely widespread at this point, but the tradition is said to persist in some Andean communities. This chicha has a light, delicious, corny flavor.

An integral part of this chicha-making process is chewing the corn to saturate it with enzyme-rich saliva. (Later in the process the brew is boiled for an hour, killing any "germs" in the saliva.) The salivated corn gobs are called *muko*. Traditionally, muko has been produced communally by old people and children sitting in a circle and telling stories.

Recruiting people to chew corn with me has been very interesting. To me it seems adventurous and weirdly intimate to chew food, spit it out, and intermingle it. Some of my friends have been excited to try this simple process and join a circle of chewers. But the squeamish ones were utterly repulsed by the thought of it. We intrepid chewers derived much pleasure from the emphatic refusals of the saliva-phobes. If you embark upon a chicha-making adventure, the sensational accounts of it are likely to persist long after you've exhausted your supply of delicious corn beer.

This recipe uses berries to start the fermentation, yielding a variation of chicha called frutillada with bright color as well as flavor. Black raspberries gave a batch of mine a salmon hue.

Timeframe: About 2 weeks

Ingredients (for 2 quarts/2 liters):

4 cups/700 grams whole-kernel corn (use nixtamalized as described on page 151; or whole kernels that have not been nixtamalized)

1 cup/180 grams polenta or grits

½ cup/70 grams organic berries

Process:

Cook the corn. Whether you use nixtamalized or not, cook the corn for 1 to 2 hours, until it is soft enough to chew. It will be cooked further. Cool to a comfortable temperature.

Chew the corn. Get several friends to help you with this process, which can only proceed one mouthful at a time. Take a spoonful of the corn at a time into your mouth. Gently chew the corn, mixing it with saliva, as you hold it together in a mass and form it with your tongue against the roof of your mouth. Then spit out the formed ball. The biggest problem people seem to encounter is the corn becoming too liquid and dispersing in their mouths. This recipe calls for a bit more corn than you actually need, as some will inevitably be swallowed as you chew.

Dry the corn balls in the sun, a dehydrator, or a warm oven. Do not allow it to exceed a temperature of 155°F/68°C. Once dried, muko is stable and storable, so it is possible to chew just a little at a time and accumulate the quantity you need over time.

Mix the mash. In a cooking pot, mix the dry corn balls with the polenta or grits and 2 quarts/2 liters of water. The enzymes in the chewed corn balls can convert the carbohydrates in the added polenta or grits.

Heat this mixture to 155°F/68°C, at which temperature the enzymes become highly active. Break up the chunks of chewed corn, and hold the mixture at this temperature for 20 minutes. Cover the pot, remove from the heat, and leave it for a few hours until the corn mash cools.

Strain and press, discarding the solids.

Boil the remaining liquid for 1 hour, then cool.

Ferment in a crock, with berries added to introduce yeast. Stir well and cover to keep flies out.

Stir frequently. Keep stirring for about a week, as fermentation develops, builds in vigor, peaks, and begins to slow down.

Strain out the fruit.

Enjoy the chicha fresh like this, or . . .

Bottle. Leave the bottles at ambient temperature for another day to carbonate, if desired.

In Costa Rica, Mauricia Vargas shows me how she makes a starter, in her indigenous Bribri tradition, for brewing chicha.

rice beer

Saké is the most widely known example of a beverage fermented from rice, and also the most elaborate and refined in process. Sometimes saké is described as rice wine, but because the defining characteristic of beer is that it is made from grain, I think of it as rice beer. This rice beer, like chicha and most indigenous brews around the world, is opaque rather than clear, a starchy suspension like a thin gruel. Similar beverages, varying in starters, specific processes, and ingredients, are fermented all across Asia from rice and other grains.

   This simple and accessible method for making your own rice brew uses as a starter what are commonly called Chinese yeast balls, widely available in Asian markets and online.

Rice beer with sweet potatoes.

Timeframe: 5 to 10 days, depending upon temperature

Vessel: Crock, jar, or glass or ceramic bowl with a capacity of at least 1 gallon/4 liters

Ingredients (for 2 quarts/ 2 liters):

4 cups/1 kilogram rice
1 Chinese yeast ball

Process:

Cook the rice at normal proportions without any salt. Presoak it if you wish.

Cool until still warm but comfortable to the touch.

Transfer to a crock or other open vessel.

Add water. Use about 1 quart/1 liter, and make sure it's dechlorinated.

Break up the rice. Use your hands to gently squeeze the rice, breaking up clumps and separating individual grains.

Add the yeast ball. Crush it into powder with a mortar and pestle, or by pressing it with the back of a spoon against a sturdy bowl. Mix the powder into the rice and water. Cover the vessel with a cloth or loose-fitting lid.

Ferment in a warm spot.

Stir several times a day, to help redistribute and spread enzyme and yeast activity. At first, all the water you added is absorbed by the rice, but as enzymatic digestion progresses, liquefaction occurs gradually and the rice is soon floating in liquid.

Taste. Rice beer is quite delicious throughout its development, at first very sweet and gradually more alcoholic. Ferment until most of the rice grains have sunk to the bottom. This may take just a few days in a warm environment, or as long as 2 weeks in a cool one.

Strain through a fine-mesh colander or cheesecloth. Press it well to get out all the juice that you can. Pour a cup of water gently over the residue and press again. Try the still-flavorful pressed residue in pancakes, breads, and other cooking. Enjoy rice beer fresh like this, or . . .

Bottle. Leave the bottles at ambient temperature for another day to carbonate, if desired.

Drink. Refrigerate for short-term preservation or pasteurize for longer-term storage; otherwise lactic acid bacteria from the mixed culture will continue to acidify.

Stronger. To make stronger rice beer, cook another 4 cups/1 kilogram rice, cool it, pour the rice beer over the fresh rice, and let the process repeat itself.

Variations: Cook the rice with spices . . . Add cooked sweet potato to the warm rice mash . . . Try mixing in other grains.

sprouting grains

Sprouting grains, also known as malting, makes them much sweeter. The power of germination creates enzymes that break down the complex carbohydrates of the grain into simple sugars. Germination starts with soaking grains (or other seeds) in water. But if you leave them submerged too long they will ferment (and eventually rot) rather than germinate. Germination requires oxygen as well as water, so seeds must be drained to have access to oxygen; then repeatedly rinsed and drained to keep moist. When used with unmalted grains, enzymes from the malt can break down more carbohydrates, especially at elevated temperatures.

Recipes that involve sprouting refer to these directions, and each specifies the type and amount of grain to use.

Timeframe: 2 to 5 days

Vessel: If you have something specifically designed for sprouting, use it. I sprout in a wide-mouth 1-gallon/4-liter jar with a piece of mesh stretched over the mouth, secured by a rubber band.

Process:

Soak whole grains in water, in a jar as described above, for about 24 hours at room temperature.

Drain. Discard the water. Set the jar upside down in a place where it can drain well. I like to rest it in a measuring cup. The important thing is that the jar rests safely above wherever the water drains, so the grains won't sit in water.

Rinse the sprouts with fresh water at least twice a day, morning and evening, more often if you think of it. In hot weather especially, rinse often. The aim is to keep the sprouts from drying out or molding. You'll know the grains have germinated when you see little tails emerging from them. Be sure to keep rinsing the sprouts at least twice a day. Once the sprout reaches about three-quarters the length of the seed, the fermentable sugars and desired enzymes are at their peak. Use them soon, store in the refrigerator for a few days, or dry for longer storage. If the grains continue to sprout, they will rapidly lose sweetness.

Learning to make an indigenous Bribri starter for brewing chicha with the Vargas family of Finca Loroco in Costa Rica.

bouza (egyptian beer)

Bouza is an ancestor of the beer we know and love, which lives on in various forms in contemporary Egypt, East Africa, Turkey, the Balkans, and beyond. Like most indigenous beers, bouza is a cloudy, starchy suspension. Fizzy, tart, and mildly alcoholic, bouza made by roughly the process described here is more than 5,000 years old, but the particulars of this recipe are my own interpretations, based upon information from several sources, most notably an article in the anthropology journal *Food and Foodways*.[2]

Bouza requires only two ingredients, grains (wheat, barley, or potentially others) and water, manipulated in several different ways. The process for bouza vividly illustrates the bread–beer connection. Wheat formed into loaves of bread is part of the process, and traditionally a way yeast was stored for bouza-making was in partially cooked loaves, where the center remained raw and alive. "In essence, making bread was a convenient way to store the raw materials for brewing beer," reports *Archaeology* magazine.[3]

Timeframe: 4 to 7 days

Vessel: 1-gallon/4-liter crock or other open vessel

Ingredients (for 1 gallon/ 4 liters):

4 cups/1 kilo wheat berries
1 cup/250 milliliters vigorous sourdough starter (see page 158)

Process:

This process is actually three distinct processes—Malting, Making Loaves, and Brewing—that all start with a single first step that gets it all going, soaking.

Soak the wheat berries. Cover with plenty of water so they will remain covered as they expand. Soak for about 24 hours.

Drain and divide the soaked wheat berries into two roughly equal parts. Half will be malted or sprouted; the other half will be ground into dough, fermented, and baked into loaves.

Malting:

Sprout half the soaked wheat, following process as described in Sprouting Grains, page 246. Sprout 2 to 3 days, protected from direct sunlight, rinsing frequently, until the tails are about three-quarters the length of the grains. For bouza, generally the malted grains are used fresh, but they can be dried for storage.

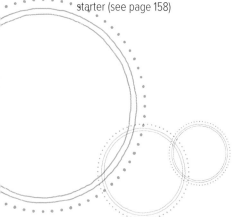

Making Loaves:

Coarsely grind the other half of the soaked wheat. Use a food processor, hand grinder, or mortar and pestle. Add ½ cup/125 milliliters bubbly sourdough starter and a little water as necessary to form a cohesive dough. Place the dough in a bowl, and place the bowl inside a plastic shopping bag, loosely secured, to keep the dough from drying.

Ferment for 12 hours or longer in a warm spot, stirring a few times.

Form the dough into a few small round loaves. Place the loaves on an ungreased baking sheet.

Ferment the loaves for about an hour before baking.

Preheat the oven to 300°F/150°C.

Bake the loaves for about 15 minutes, so the outside is cooked but the center is still raw, with live yeast. Cool and store, protected from rodents, until the grain is malted and you are ready to brew bouza.

Brewing:

Heat water (1 gallon/4 liters) to about 170°F/77°C.

Coarsely grind the sprouted grains using a food processor, hand mill, or mortar and pestle.

Combine. Pour the hot water into a crock. This will warm up the crock and cool the water to around 155°F/69°C. Break up the baked loaves into a few pieces and add them. Add the ground sprouted grains. Cover and leave to slowly cool to ambient temperature.

Add ½ cup/125 milliliters of vigorous sourdough starter. Cover the crock with a cloth and stir frequently.

Ferment for 2 to 3 days.

Strain out the solids. Enjoy bouza fresh, or bottle it and allow it to ferment another day to carbonate. Bouza will keep for a week or so in the refrigerator.

The "coolship" at Cantillon Brewery in Brussels, Belgium, used to collect wild airborne yeast.

african sorghum beer

Sorghum beer is a traditional beer of much of sub-Saharan Africa. An opaque suspension like other indigenous beers, it is fresh and inviting with its sweet-alcoholic-sour flavor. "Opaque beer is more a food than a beverage," states a report of the United Nations Food and Agriculture Organization. "It contains high proportions of starch and sugars, besides proteins, fats, vitamins and minerals."[4]

Timeframe: 4 to 5 days

Vessel: 1-gallon/4-liter crock or other open vessel

Ingredients (for 1 gallon/ 4 liters):

5 cups/1 kilo sorghum, divided in half

Process:

Sprout half the sorghum, as described in Sprouting Grains, page 246. Rinse for 2 to 4 days, until tails emerge from the sprouts about ¾ inch/2 centimeters long.

Dry malted sorghum in the sun, or using a dehydrator, fan, and other method of low-heat drying. After drying, the malted grain is stable for dry storage and is often aged for several months before use.

Coarsely grind dry malted sorghum using a mill, mortar and pestle, or other means. Also coarsely grind unmalted sorghum, keeping it separate.

Make sorghum porridge. Boil ½ gallon/2 liters water. Stir in the ground unmalted sorghum and continue stirring to achieve a porridge-like consistency. Remove from the heat and allow to cool to 140°F/60°C, cool enough to comfortably touch, but still quite warm.

Add half the malted sorghum grits/flour, reserving half to add later. Stir the malt into the porridge thoroughly. The enzymes in the raw malt are highly active at this temperature, digesting complex carbohydrates into simple sugars. Leave in a warm or insulated spot, protected from flies. After a few hours, when the mash cools to below 110°F/43°C, add half of the remaining malt (leave the other half for one more later addition) and stir well to distribute.

Ferment in a warm spot for 12 to 24 hours (depending upon temperature), during which time lactic acid bacteria proliferate, lowering pH.

Cook the soured mash. Combine the soured mash with ½ gallon/2 liters more water, bring to a boil, and gently simmer for 2 to 3 hours to caramelize the sugars, adding water as necessary to maintain a gruel-like starchy suspension. Cool to body temperature, then add the final portion of raw ground malted sorghum to introduce yeasts for the final alcohol fermentation (or substitute a packet of yeast).

Ferment in a warm spot protected from flies. In the tropics, fermentation time is measured in hours. In my temperate zone, I have typically fermented 2 or 3 days, then strained it through cheesecloth and bottled it in plastic soda bottles to ferment a few more hours to trap carbonation. Fresh sorghum beer is alive and pressurizes quickly, so always use caution not to overcarbonate.

Chinese yeast balls.

Brewer Ben Millstein at his Kodiak Island Brewing Company.

tesgüino

Tesgüino is an indigenous beer of Mexico, made from malted corn. It's delicious and easy to make.

Timeframe: 1 week to 10 days

Vessel: 1-gallon/4-liter crock or other open vessel

Ingredients (for ½ gallon/ 2 liters):

3 cups/500 grams dry whole organic field corn (not fresh sweet corn)

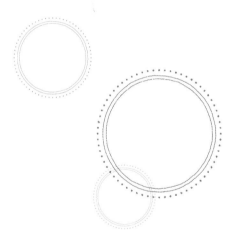

Process:

Sprout the corn, as described in Sprouting Grains, page 246. Soak for at least 24 hours, then rinse for 3 or more days, until the sprouts reach a length of about 1 inch/2.5 centimeters.

Coarsely grind the malted corn into a paste using a mill, food processor, mortar and pestle, or other means. Reserve about ½ cup/125 milliliters of the malt paste raw to add after brewing.

Mix the rest of the sprouted corn paste with ½ gallon/2 liters hot water. Heat the water to about 145°F/63°C to help the enzymes break down complex carbohydrates. Leave to slowly cool to body temperature.

Bring the corn mixture to a low boil and simmer for at least 6 hours, the longer the better. Maintain a low flame, stir frequently, and add water as necessary. As the hours pass, the tesgüino smells better and better.

Strain out the solid chunks once you decide it has cooked long enough.

Transfer the tesgüino to a crock or other open vessel and cool to body temperature.

Add the reserved raw malt paste as a source of yeast, and stir it in well. I have found this method reliable. A more traditional way of introducing yeast is to use a vessel dedicated to this purpose and never washed. You could simply add a packet of yeast at this point, or some bubbly sourdough starter, or, if you get into a rhythm of this, a previous batch.

Ferment in a warm spot protected from flies. Stir frequently. Observe the slow development of bubbling, then its increasing vigor. Keep stirring! When the bubbling has peaked and begins to slow, about a week after the beginning of fermentation (maybe less or more), the tesgüino is ready to drink.

Enjoy fresh, or bottle it in plastic soda bottles, ferment them a few more hours to trap carbonation, and refrigerate.

Some Thoughts on Homebrewing

The basics of brewing beer are not so different from any of these last few recipes. Take coarsely ground malted barley, add it to hot water, and it becomes the mash. Hold the mash at successively higher temperatures, at which different enzymes optimize, yielding flavor complexity. Once the mash reaches about 170°F/77°C strain out the spent grains and "sparge," gently rinsing them with hot water to capture residual sugars. Boil the sweet, fragrant strained liquid, now called wort, for an hour or more. Add hops and other flavorings at various stages of the boil. Cool. Add yeast or use some other method of introducing yeast into the cooled wort. Ferment.

This brewing process can certainly be done with improvisational tools, but it has given rise to great technical inventiveness. Brewing systems at every scale are wonders of engineering, plumbing, and ingenuity. Like many people I have felt intimidated by the equipment, the jargon, and the accompanying compulsiveness about sterilization. "There is a lot of talk about the necessity for the use of chemicals to keep everything sterile, the need for other chemicals to make the beer work well, the crucial necessity for Teutonic authoritarian temperature controls, and the importance of complex understandings of minuscule differences in grains, malts, hops, and yeasts," writes Stephen Harrod Buhner in *Sacred and Herbal Healing Beers*. "Generally, this frightens off a lot of people and takes all the fun out of brewing."[5]

Long ago I borrowed a motto from an old friend who homebrews, Tom Foolery: "Cleanliness, not sterility." Really, if you think about it, in your home, sterilization is a fantasy. Sure, there are all kinds of chemicals that can fleetingly sterilize. But then after you rinse whatever it is with non-sterile water and dry it in non-sterile air or with a non-sterile towel, it is no longer sterile. It's important to be clean, and to use clean vessels and utensils and have a clean working area. But good beer does

not require sterility, and in some cases actively cultivating environmental exposure to wild bacteria and yeasts can result in exciting flavors. Don't worry. As Charlie Papazian counsels in *The New Complete Joy of Home Brewing*: "Relax. Don't worry. Have a homebrew. Because worrying is like paying interest on a debt you may never have owed." Profound advice.

My earliest experiences of brewing beer skipped the complicated process of extracting sugars from grains, relying instead on malt syrup from a can, added to hot water, then cooked with hops and/or other herbs, cooled, pitched with yeast, and fermented. This is certainly an accessible way of making beer, but didn't really satisfy my curiosity about the basic transformative processes. My first introduction to brewing beer from grain was not until I was writing the first edition of *Wild Fermentation*. In March 2002, my dear friend and fellow fermentation experimentalist Patrick Ironwood first walked me through the process.

Patrick has been brewing since age 15, when his parents gave their budding do-it-yourselfer a homebrew kit and he made his first batch of beer for them. Twenty years later, Patrick was brewing in 30-gallon/120-liter batches and storing his beer in kegs. Beer-making has much specialized equipment and paraphernalia. The people who get into brewing beer tend to be techies. Patrick and several other homebrewers I have met have gone so far as to weld modifications to their equipment. I have also had the opportunity to visit many small breweries, and I can only marvel at the complexity of it all!

Absolutely, become part of the homebrew movement. Make excellent beer. Enjoy it and share it. I would especially encourage folks in the direction of experimenting with wild fermentation or mixed cultures rather than pure strain yeasts, and these are the kinds of funky sour beers I get most excited about. But if you wish to explore the complexity of brewing beer from malted barley, then you need to consult a more specialized book than this one. Thankfully, many excellent guides are available.

Further Reading

Buhner, Stephen Harrod. *Sacred and Healing Beers: The Secrets of Ancient Fermentation*. Boulder, CO: Siris Books, 1998.

Mosher, Randy. *Radical Brewing*. Boulder, CO: Brewers Publications, 2004.

Palmer, John. *How to Brew: Everything You Need to Know to Brew Beer Right the First Time*. Boulder, CO: Brewers Publications, 2006; available free online at www.howtobrew.com.

Papazian, Charlie. *The Complete Joy of Homebrewing, Fourth Edition: Fully Revised and Updated*. New York: William Morrow, 2014.

Sparrow, Jeff. *Wild Brews: Beer Beyond the Influence of Brewer's Yeast*. Boulder, CO: Brewers Publications, 2005.

A brewer in a Himalayan village, Kalap, Uttarahkand, India, with the starter he uses, the local equivalent of Chinese yeast balls.

12: vinegars

Most of my experience with vinegar-making has been from wine-making gone awry. I imagine that is how vinegar first came into being, for alcohol ferments left in contact with the oxygen-rich air inevitably develop bacteria of the genus *Acetobacter*, which digest alcohol into acetic acid, but only in the presence of oxygen. The word *vinegar* comes from the French *vinaigre*: *vin*, wine, and *aigre*, sour. Vinegar is an excellent consolation for your wine-making failure. It is a preservative in its own right, healthful, with many delicious uses in cooking.

There are different types of vinegar, generally distinguished by the source of the alcohol from which the vinegar is made. Wine vinegar is made from wine; apple cider vinegar from apple cider; rice vinegar from rice wine; malt vinegar from malted grain beverages such as beer. Beyond these widely known styles, vinegar can be made from any fruit, like alcohol. Vinegar can be delicious and quite varied. Yet the cheapest and most commonly used vinegar is colorless and flavorless: distilled white vinegar, made from distilled alcohol, diluted by water.

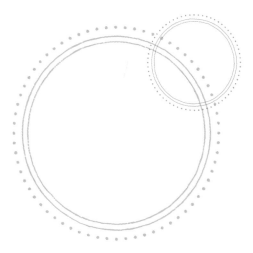

banana vinegar

No vinegar is easier or faster to make than banana vinegar, which pretty much makes itself. Just bananas, no other ingredients.

Timeframe: 5 days to 1 week

Ingredients (for about ⅓ cup/80 milliliters):

3 overripe bananas

Process:

Peel the bananas.

Mash the bananas into a pulp.

Ferment the bananas in a bowl covered with a cloth.

Stir frequently, renewing the surface to prevent surface growth.

Observe. The banana mash will begin to liquefy and ferment.

Taste after a few days. Taste periodically until the vinegar becomes sufficiently acidic.

Strain out the solid remains.

Bottle in a narrow-necked sealable bottle.

wine vinegar

If a little homemade or commercial wine remains at the bottom of a bottle at the end of an evening, toss it into a non-reactive vessel with a broad surface area, such as a bowl, a crock, or a jar. Bear in mind that vinegar fermentation is an aerobic process that requires a steady flow of fresh air with oxygen. Ferment it in a wide, open vessel, with a large surface area exposed to the air. Cover it with cloth to keep out flies and particles, and store it out of direct light and away from alcohol fermentation projects. For best results, ferment the wine completely with an air lock before deliberately exposing it to aerobic vinegar organisms. Also, don't use vessels for vinegar-making and wine-making interchangeably. If one of your homemade wines turns out sour, call it vinegar and use it in cooking and salad dressings.

My friend Hector Black, who planted an impressive blueberry orchard, makes blueberry wine vinegar in a big oak barrel. His blueberry wine vinegar is thick and fruity. The barrel lays on its side to maximize the surface area in contact with the air. The hole in the barrel (the "bunghole") is stuffed with cheesecloth. This year Hector tried something new that he says sped the process: He used a small electric air pump designed for an aquarium to pump air into the developing vinegar. Since the vinegar-making organisms are aerobic, this stimulates them and increases their action.

The acidity of finished vinegar correlates with the alcohol content of the wine from which it was made (and with the sugar concentration of the original prefermented solution). The time it takes for wine to become vinegar will vary quite a bit, depending upon the type of sugar, alcohol content, temperature, and aeration. Figure roughly 1 to 3 weeks in summer, longer in winter. Taste the vinegar periodically to monitor its progress. Once you can taste that most of

the sweetness/alcohol has converted to acetic acid, bottle the vinegar in small narrow-necked bottles that seal tightly. If living vinegar is not protected from oxygen, then it can begin to de-acidify as acetobacter consumes the acetic acid it just produced and metabolizes it into water and carbon dioxide.

You may observe a film or disk collecting on the surface of the vinegar. This is called the mother-of-vinegar, or mother for short. It is a mass of vinegar-making organisms that can be transferred to your next batch of vinegar as a starter. There is no need to be afraid of the mother; it is harmless and even edible. Vinegar may also contain solid blobs below the surface, which are cast off from the mother-of-vinegar. You can either strain these out or consume them with your vinegar.

apple cider vinegar

In chapter 10, I described the simplest alcohol fermentation process I know, leaving fresh apple cider to spontaneously ferment, producing hard cider in less than a week (see page 218). If you leave that same jar on your counter for a couple more weeks, exposed to air, it will become apple cider vinegar just as spontaneously. You can help it along by transferring it to a wide container where its surface area (and resulting flow of oxygen) is increased. Another way to speed the process is to introduce as a starter a small proportion of live unpasteurized vinegar, a previous batch or something commercially available, like Bragg's.

Folk medicine of many traditions uses apple cider vinegar as a fortifying tonic. Even Hippocrates, the Greek physician whose oath every contemporary American doctor must swear, prescribed vinegar as a remedy.

vinagre de piña (mexican pineapple vinegar)

Pineapple vinegar, *vinagre de piña*, is delicious and super-acidic. Many Mexican recipes call for pineapple vinegar, though you could use this in place of any kind of vinegar. Since this uses only the skin of the pineapple, you get to eat the pineapple flesh. This recipe was inspired by a recipe in *The Cuisines of Mexico* by Diana Kennedy.

Timeframe: 3 to 4 weeks

Ingredients (for 2 cups/ 500 milliliters):

2 tablespoons sugar
Peel of 1 pineapple (organic, because you use the skin; overripe fruits are fine)

Process:

Combine the sugar with 2 cups/500 milliliters of water in a jar or bowl. Stir to dissolve. Coarsely chop and add the pineapple peel. Use a small plate to weight down the pineapple and keep it submerged. Cover with a cloth to keep flies out.

Ferment at room temperature. Stir daily while the pineapple peels are in it.

Strain out the pineapple peels and discard after about 1 week, when you notice the liquid darkening.

Ferment the liquid 2 to 3 weeks more, stirring or agitating periodically.

Bottle and enjoy.

shrub

Shrub is a refreshing soft drink that was popular in the United States prior to the availability of carbonated sodas. Traditionally, it was made by soaking fresh berries in vinegar for up to 2 weeks, then straining out the berries and adding sugar or honey. This concentrate was stored, diluted with water as needed, and served over ice. If you have fruity wine or cider vinegar, it's easier to just mix it with fruit juice. Try mixing 1 part vinegar to 3 parts fruit juice and 3 parts water. You can make it more soda-like by using seltzer in place of water. Adjust proportions to taste. Sweet and sour flavors combine well.

fruit scrap vinegar

Just as the peel of pineapple makes delicious vinegar, so can any fruit
scraps: peels and cores from apple-pie-making; fallen, bruised fruit; or
the dregs of a bunch of grapes or berries (what's left after the finer
specimens have been eaten). Vinegar is a recycling opportunity. Just
pour sugar-water (2 tablespoons sugar dissolved in 2 cups/500 milliliters of water) over the fruit, and proceed as for pineapple vinegar. You
could use honey instead of sugar, if you prefer, but the process might
take a little longer.

anaerobic

switchel

Switchel is another vinegar-based soft drink, generally flavored with ginger. It can be sweetened by maple syrup, molasses, sorghum, honey, and/or other sweeteners. Switchel is refreshing and energizing, and has been associated with hay harvests and other physical work requiring great stamina.

Timeframe: 15 minutes

Ingredients (for ½ gallon/ 2 liters):

2 inches/5 centimeters/20 grams of fresh gingerroot, grated

¾ cup/185 milliliters apple cider or other fruity vinegar

¾ cup/185 milliliters maple syrup and/or other sweeteners

Water

Process:

Combine the ginger and 3 cups/750 milliliters of water.

Simmer about 10 minutes. Cool to near body temperature.

Strain out the ginger.

Add the vinegar and sweetener. Stir to fully dissolve.

Store this concentrate in the refrigerator.

Serve chilled, mixing equal parts concentrate and water (or carbonated water).

Taste and add additional sweetener, vinegar, or water as desired.

Variation: Switchel is very similar to a restorative tonic drink my friend Ha! prepared using vinegar, lemon juice, and molasses: Mix 1 tablespoon molasses, 2 tablespoons cider vinegar, and 3 tablespoons lemon juice into 1 cup/250 milliliters of hot water. Drink warm.

horseradish sauce

Horseradish is a potent root; when you eat it, its heat spreads from your mouth into your sinus cavity. I learned to love it on matzo as a kid, since it is used in the Passover seder ritual to symbolize the bitterness of oppression. I still love it on matzo, but also on sandwiches and nori rolls, and in sauces, dressings, and kimchis.

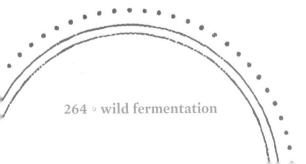

Horseradish sauce is very simple to prepare: First, grate fresh horseradish root finely. Whether you do this by hand or by machine, be aware that the fumes released as horseradish is grated are intense. Breathing it directly can be overwhelming, particularly as you open a sealed food processor. Salt grated horseradish, pack it tightly, cover with just a little vinegar, and let it infuse for a few hours or a few weeks.

Alternatively, you can ferment horseradish with a little honey- or sugar-water. Pour just a little sweetened water over grated horseradish. Stir well, cover with a cheesecloth or mesh, and ferment for 3 to 4 weeks. This involves the horseradish in both the fermentation that creates alcohol from sugars, and the fermentation that creates vinegar from alcohol. I like to think that the fermenting microorganisms are getting as much of a charge from the horseradish as I do.

infused vinegars

Vinegar's acidity makes it an effective solvent and preservative for extracting flavors and phytochemicals from foods and herbs. The flavors and medicinal compounds melt into the vinegar. Depending on what you infuse, you'll have distinctive vinegar for salad dressings or potent plant medicine (or both). Place whatever it is you want to infuse into the vinegar in a jar, cover with vinegar, and put a top on the jar. Vinegar will make metal tops corrode, so use plastic, or place a layer of waxed paper between the bottle and a metal lid. Leave the vinegar to infuse in a dark spot for a few weeks (or longer). Strain the vinegar and discard the spent plant material. If the vinegar is light and you can see through it, place a fresh bit of whatever you infused in the vinegar when you bottle it. Put it in a sleek bottle and give it as a gift. Food boutiques are full of gorgeous bottles of infused vinegars at premium prices.

Here are a few ideas of foods and herbs to extract in vinegar: garlic; rosemary; thyme; tarragon; hot chili peppers; berries; mints; basil; dandelion roots, leaves, and/or flowers . . . anything you like.

vinegar pickling: dilly beans

Pickling food in vinegar is not a fermentation process. In brine pickling, covered in chapter 5, vegetables are preserved by lactic acid, which is produced by the action of microorganisms on the vegetables. Vinegar pickling makes use of a fermented product, vinegar, but the acidity of the vinegar, along with heat processing, prevents microorganism action. Vinegar pickles contain no live cultures. According to Terre Vivante, a French eco-education center focused on organic gardening and preservation of Old World food preservation techniques, "Pickles were always lacto-fermented in times past, and then transferred to vinegar solely to stabilize them for commercial purposes."[1] Indeed, the great advantage that vinegar pickling has over lacto-fermentation pickling is that vinegar pickles will last forever (well, almost), while brined pickles will last for weeks or months, but rarely for years, and definitely not forever. Cookbooks are full of vinegar pickling recipes, so I will offer just one: the dilly beans my father makes from his garden every summer and serves to his family and friends all year long.

Timeframe: 6 weeks

Equipment: Sealable canning jars: 1½-pint/750-milliliter size is best, as its height perfectly accommodates the length of string beans

Ingredients:

String beans
Garlic
Salt (my dad swears by coarse kosher salt, but sea salt is fine, too)
Whole dried chili peppers
Celery seed
Fresh dill (flowering tops are best, or leaves or seeds)
White distilled vinegar

Process:

Prepare the jars. Guesstimate how many jars you'll fill with the string beans you have. Thoroughly clean the jars and line them up.

Pack the jars. Into each jar, place 1 clove garlic, 1 teaspoon salt, 1 whole red chili pepper, ¼ teaspoon of celery seed, and a flowering dill top, small bunch of dill leaves, or 2 teaspoons dill seeds. Then fill the jar with beans standing on end, stuffing them as tightly as you can into the jar.

Prepare the vinegar solution. For each jar you have filled, measure 1 cup/250 milliliters of vinegar and 1 cup/250 milliliters of water. Boil the vinegar-water mixture, then pour it into the jars over the beans and spices, to ½ inch/1 centimeter from the top of the jar.

Heat-process. Seal the jars and place them in a large pot of boiling water for a 10-minute heat processing.

Age. Leave the dilly beans for at least 6 weeks for the flavors to meld, then open the jars as desired and enjoy. My father serves these dilly beans as an hors d'oeuvre. Heat-processed pickles can be stored for years without refrigeration.

vinaigrette

This is my version of the classic salad dressing. It's the first thing my mother taught me to make, and my job as a child was to make it whenever we ate salad. My mother taught me to use at least as much vinegar as oil, lots of mustard, and lots of garlic. Salad dressing is easy; it always surprises me that people buy it prepared.

Timeframe: 10 minutes

Ingredients (for 1 cup/250 milliliters):

¼ cup/60 milliliters vinegar
¼ cup/60 milliliters extra-virgin olive oil
¼ cup/60 milliliters kraut juice or pickle brine
4–8 cloves garlic, crushed into a pulp
2 tablespoons spicy mustard
1 tablespoon miso
1 teaspoon mustard powder
Salt and pepper to taste

Process:

Combine the ingredients in a jar, cover, and shake well. Often I make salad dressing in mustard jars, incorporating the hard-to-remove last bit of mustard. If salad dressing sits and infuses, it only gets better. I like to pre-dress salads, and even let them wilt a bit. If there's a pool of dressing when the salad is done, return it to the jar and reuse.

Variations: Add yogurt, kefir, or tahini for a creamy vinaigrette . . . add honey to sweeten . . . add horseradish sauce . . . toasted sesame oil . . .

Further Reading

Diggs, Lawrence J. *Vinegar: The User-Friendly Standard Text Reference and Guide to Appreciating, Making, and Enjoying Vinegar*. Lincoln, NE: Authors Choice Press, 2000.

Malle, Bettina, and Helge Schmickl. *The Artisanal Vinegar Maker's Handbook*. Austin, TX: Spikehorn Press, 2015.

Thacker, Emily. *The Vinegar Book*. Canton, OH: Tresco Publishers, 1996.

13: cultural reincarnation

Fermentation in the Cycles of Life, Soil Fertility, and Social Change

Fermentation is a lot bigger than its food-transforming aspect. Microorganisms decompose dead animal and plant tissue into elements that can nourish plants. As the early microbiologist Jacob Lippman eloquently stated in his 1908 *Bacteria in Relation to Country Life*, microorganisms

> are the connecting link between the world of the living and the world of the dead. They are the great scavengers intrusted [sic] with restoring to circulation the carbon, nitrogen, hydrogen, sulphur, and other elements held fast in the dead bodies of plants and animals. Without them, dead bodies would accumulate, and the kingdom of the living would be replaced by the kingdom of the dead.[1]

This image helps me to accept death and decay. It is clear evidence on the physical plane that life is a cyclical process, with death as an indispensable part. It makes the harshest reality of life more understandable, more acceptable.

During the same years that I developed my fascination with fermentation, I spent a fair share of time pondering my own decay and death. How could I not imagine it after testing HIV-positive before

any effective treatments were available? Nobody has said this more eloquently than the late poet Audre Lorde:

> Living a self-conscious life, under the pressure of time, I work with the consciousness of death at my shoulder, not constantly, but often enough to leave a mark upon all of my life's decisions and actions. And it does not matter whether this death comes next week or thirty years from now; this consciousness gives my life another breadth. It helps shape the words I speak, the ways I love, my politic of action, the strength of my vision and purpose, the depth of my appreciation of living.[2]

As I wrote the first edition of this book, I turned 40. My age-group peers were talking about mid-life. At the time (and now, a decade and some later), it did not seem implausible that I could be at the mid-point of my life, and that I will celebrate my 80th birthday in the year 2042. I love life and I believe in the infinity of possibility. But I am a student of observation and realism and probability, and at 40, 40 more years seemed extremely unlikely. Over how many decades are the medicines that saved me from the downward spiral of AIDS sustainable? They impact upon many systems of the body and may take a toll over time. Though people with AIDS are living longer, friends keep dying of it. I have had ample opportunity to get used to the idea that this is the latter period of my life. I wonder: Is this resignation? Is this the loss of will to survive?

Revising the book at 53, I feel very open to a long life. My father is a robust 82, and I can picture 90, thanks to the inspiration of a dear nonagenarian friend, Hector Black, and time with a couple of other 90-something powerhouses, who remain very engaged in the world and clearly feel that they still have much to live for. But when it comes to longevity, one absolutely never knows. Death happens. It can come peacefully at 112, or it can come abruptly when you are least expecting it, like an accident or a mass shooting. It can be an individual experience, like a degenerative disease, or a shared tragedy, like an epidemic, war, or genocide. You never know what will happen. Whatever decisions you might make in the pursuit of long, healthy life, you ultimately have limited influence in the matter.

I feel there is wisdom in making peace with death. It will come. All any of us can do is embrace life as best we can, and when we die, I know, I believe, I have faith, that all that we are will continue to be part of the cycle of life, fermenting and nourishing and becoming myriad other life-forms. My fermentation practice is a daily affirmation of this faith.

Getting Acquainted with Death

Our society distances us from death. We have created impersonal institutions to handle the transition. What are we so afraid of? I feel lucky to have been present with my mother, at home, when she died. She had been unconscious for about a week, at the end of a long struggle with cancer; edema (fluid accumulation) bloated her legs and slowly rose higher on her body. Her breathing grew labored as her lungs filled with fluid. Our family gathered around her in a death watch. Her breaths became shallower and spasmodic, until one involuntary muscle contraction was the last. We sat with her for a while and cried, trying to grasp the enormity of the event. The men who came to our apartment for her body in the middle of the night were right out of central casting, pale and grim. They lifted my mother's bloated body into a bag on a stretcher and rolled it to the elevator. To get it into the elevator they had to stand it up, and my mother's body fell like a lead weight. Death was graphic and real.

Since then I have spent time with three other bodies postmortem. One was Lynda Kubek, a friend who died of breast cancer. In the period before she died I was part of her caretaking team. What I remember most vividly about caretaking Lynda is applying clay compresses to a baseball-size tumor protruding from her armpit. Cancer is such an abstract concept, so internal and hidden and shrouded in euphemism, yet that tumor was so very concrete.

When Lynda died, her body was left on her bed for 24 hours before her home burial. By the time we arrived the morning after her passing, friends and family had created a shrine around her, with flowers and incense and photos and fabrics. It was truly beautiful, and felt like an appropriate transition between life and burial. We sat with Lynda's body for a while. It was a very peaceful time. Afterward we went swimming in a nearby pond, and when I came up from diving in, there was a snakeskin floating on the surface of the water. It was a powerful affirmation for me of the idea that death is part of the process of life, nothing to fear.

Tennessee is one of the few states that allow home burial, and Lynda's nephews spent the day digging her grave; a carpenter friend built a simple pine casket. Late that afternoon, her assembled friends and family processed with songs and drums and chants to her grave site and laid her to rest. It felt so good that no commercial establishments—cemetery, funeral home, crematorium—were involved. It was people taking care of their own.

The next dead body I spent time with was Russell Morgan. Russell is a friend who died at the age of 28 of AIDS, actually Kaposi's sarcoma lesions in his lungs. Russell died very shortly before effective treatments became available. I was visiting him at the time of his death. He had been in and out of the hospital. His breathing became uncomfortably difficult, and he decided to go back to the hospital. I helped carry him down the front steps and into the car. He never returned home. I was in the corridor outside his hospital room when he died. He was with his lover and his family. I knew he had died because I heard them wailing. Russell had been connected to oxygen, and still his breathing became more and more labored. As the scene was recounted to me, Russell removed the respirator mask, threw it to the floor, said, "Fuck this!" and dived bravely into the unknown beyond. I admire his courage. The hospital staff let us spend some time in the room with Russell's body. We built a shrine around Russell in the hospital bed, trying to create a ritual of transition in that denatured environment.

Most recently I helped bury my friend Crazy Owl, one of my fermentation mentors, who made the first homemade miso I tried. He lived a good long life, into his mid-80s, and as his illness became debilitating, he stopped most of his elaborate daily self-care routine and announced, "I'm ready to go." As friends arrived for his burial, we had the opportunity to view him, touch him, and talk to him. He looked more peaceful in death than he ever did in life. I got to share the moment with a young friend who had never seen a dead body, and saw how much more real this abstraction of death became for him.

These experiences have given me a vision for how I would like my own death to be handled. I'll be happy to live a good long time; but I have given death plenty of thought. I would like my body to be given a transition period, so my friends and family can be with me, to touch my clammy skin and say good-bye to my lifeless form and have death demystified a little bit. Then I want to be returned to the earth without resort to the impersonal industries of death. Just place me in a hole in the ground, no casket please, and let me compost fast.

Compost Happens

I love to watch the compost decompose. Recognizable forms with histories, such as onion skins from last night's soup, gradually melt back into the all-oneness of the Earth. I find the process itself so beautiful: poetry. Walt Whitman found inspiration in compost, too:

> The summer growth is innocent and disdainful above all those
>   strata of sour dead.
> What chemistry!
> That the winds are really not infectious.
>
> . . . .
>
> That all is clean forever and forever,
> That the cool drink from the well tastes so good,
> That blackberries are so flavorous and juicy,
> That the fruits of the apple-orchard and the orange-orchard, that
>   melons, grapes, peaches, plums, will none of them poison me,
> That when I recline on the grass I do not catch any disease,
> Though probably every spear of grass rises out of what was once
>   catching disease.
> Now I am terrified at the Earth, it is that calm and patient,
> It grows such sweet things out of such corruptions,
> It turns harmless and stainless on its axis, with such endless
>   succession of diseas'd corpses,
> It distills such exquisite winds out of such infused fetor,
> It renews with such unwitting looks its prodigal, annual,
>   sumptuous crops,
> It gives such divine materials to men, and accepts such leavings
>   from them at last.[3]

I use the term *compost* broadly, to describe the piles of kitchen scraps, the piles of weeds and prunings, the piles of goat "muck" (their excrement mixed with bedding straw), and the piles of our own human feces from our outhouse, mixed with toilet paper, sawdust, and ash. After a year or two, each of these piles looks the same. They are all broken down into simpler forms by microorganisms in the act of fermentation. Composting is a fermentation process.

There are many different ideas about the best composting methods. Gardeners are a passionate bunch, with strong opinions about the best ways to do things. Rodale's *Complete Book of Composting* describes gardeners who "spend years running from method to method, charting secret figures, constructing weird bins, boxes, ventilating pipes and watering systems, and carefully measuring each bit of material which is placed just right on the heap."[4] Certainly you can manipulate conditions to encourage compost to proceed faster, or hotter, or more odor-free. But even if you do nothing and let the food scraps just accumulate, compost happens. There is nothing you can do to stop it. Microorganisms decompose organic compounds. It is this process, as it breaks down fallen leaves, animal feces and carcasses, dead trees and other plants, and any other organic matter, that regenerates the soil. The transformative action of microorganisms is the basis of soil fertility.

In chapter 2, I referred to a 19th-century German chemist named Justus von Liebig, who staunchly opposed the idea that fermentation is a biological process. This same misguided man pioneered the idea of fertilizing soil with manufactured chemicals. Von Liebig's 1845 monograph *Chemistry and Its Application to Agriculture and Physiology* laid the groundwork for the chemical agricultural methods that have become standard practice and that are rapidly depleting soils everywhere. Fermentation is a natural, biological, self-generating process of decomposition that builds soil fertility and nurtures plant life. Chemical fertilization may be effective in terms of short-term yields, but it impairs the function of the soil as a self-regulating, biodiverse ecological system.

Thinking about mass food production makes me sad and angry. Chemical monocrop agriculture. Genetic modification of the most basic food crops to accommodate even heavier chemical usage. Ugly, inhumane factory animal breeding. Ultra-processed foods full of preservative chemicals, industrial by-products, and packaging. Food production is just one realm among many in which ever more concentrated corporate units extract profits from the Earth and the mass of humanity.

Historically, food has been our most direct and tangible ongoing connection to the Earth. Increasingly, though, food

Steam rising from an active compost pile.

has become a collection of mass-produced and aggressively marketed commodities. This is the song of progress: We have supposedly been freed, by technology and mass social organization, from the burdens of growing or procuring our own food. Just going to the supermarket and putting the food into the microwave is burden enough. Most people do not know or care where their food comes from.

Social Change

The astute reader will have noticed by now that my outlook can be rather bleak. Many current trends contribute to my pessimism, not only mass food production, but war, climate change, accelerating

species extinctions, the growing class divide, the persistence of racism, xenophobia, the horrifying number of people in prisons, high-tech militarization and social control, consumerism as patriotic duty, polarized media and politics, driven by greed, and so much more.

What gives me hope is the simple notion that current trends do not necessarily have to continue. It seems to me that they cannot possibly. The revolutionary spirit of liberation and hope always and everywhere remains, even dormant or confined to dreams, like a seed culture, ready anytime to multiply, thrive, and transform, given the right conditions.

Social change is another form of fermentation. Ideas ferment, as they spread and mutate and inspire movements for change. The *Oxford English Dictionary* offers as the second definition of *ferment*: "The state of being excited by emotion or passion, agitation, excitement . . . a state of agitation tending to bring about a purer, more wholesome, or more stable condition of things." The word *ferment* derives from the Latin *fervere*, to boil. *Fervor* and *fervent* are other words from the same root. Fermenting liquids bubble just like boiling liquids. Excited people can channel the same intensity, and use it to create change.

Though fermentation is a phenomenon of transformation, the change it renders tends to be gentle, slow, and steady. Contrast fermentation with another transformative natural phenomenon: fire. As I revised this book in 2015, fire seared itself into my consciousness in two separate events. First, my friend Dust's house burned down. It happened in the night, as he was sleeping. He awoke to smoke, and managed to escape, but not without severe burns. He lost everything, except his life. When he recounted the story, it was with a sense of being extremely grateful. Had he slept seconds longer, he may have perished with the house.

Then, a few months later, another fire destroyed the home of my friends Merril and Gabby. They are in their 70s and built the sprawling, funky house themselves decades ago for their large family. The house had enough artifacts to fill a museum, mementos of their unique and fascinating countercultural lives, all gone in an instant. Luckily, nobody was home, and so nobody was hurt, and their overwhelming reaction was gratitude for that. But the loss sinks in slowly, as they think of books, letters, photographs, artwork, clothes, and other cherished objects that are gone forever. Fire changes everything, in an instant.

In the realm of social change, fire is the revolutionary moment of upheaval; desperately sought, or dreaded and guarded against, depending upon your perspective. Fire spreads, destroying whatever lies in its path, and its path is unpredictable. Fermentation is not so dramatic. It bubbles rather than burns, and its transformative mode is gentle and slow. Steady, too. Fermentation is a force that cannot be stopped. It recycles life, renews hope, and goes on and on.

Your life and my life and everyone's lives and deaths are part of the endless biological cycle of life and death and fermentation. Wild fermentation is going on everywhere, always. Embrace it. Work with the material resources and life processes that are close at hand. As micro-organisms work their transformative magic and you witness the miracles of fermentation, envision yourself as an agent for change, agitating and releasing bubbles of transformation. Use your fermented goodies to nourish yourself and your family and friends and allies. The life-affirming power of these basic foods contrasts sharply with the lifeless, industrially processed foods that fill supermarket shelves. Draw inspiration from the action of bacteria and yeast, and make your life a transformative process.

appendix:
cultural resources

Sources for Starter Cultures

Network locally to find other fermentation enthusiasts who may have cultures to share. The SCOBY cultures (kefir, kombucha, and water kefir) are self-generating, and everyone who maintains them ends up with more than they can use.

The following are online databases that function as geographically organized culture exchanges, with users around the world posting the availability of cultures:

- International Kefir Community: "Real Live Kefir Grains shared by members worldwide": www.torontoadvisors.com/Kefir /kefir-list.php
- Cómo conseguir kefir: A Spanish site with international listings of sources for water kefir grains, milk kefir grains, and kombucha mothers: www.lanaturaleza.es/bdkefir.htm

The Internet has made finding, buying, and selling cultures much easier. You can find them for sale on platforms ranging from Craigslist to eBay to Amazon.

Sources of Starter Cultures

Cultures for Health: Kombucha, water kefir, yogurt, kefir, other milk cultures, tempeh starter, koji, and more: www.culturesforhealth.com

GEM Cultures: Kombucha, water kefir, kefir, other milk cultures, koji, koji starter, and more: www.gemcultures.com

Kombucha Kamp: Kombucha, water kefir, kefir, and more: www.kombuchakamp.com

Yemoos Nourishing Cultures: Kombucha, water kefir, kefir, and more: www.yemoos.com

Cultures Alive (Australia): Kombucha, water kefir, yogurt, kefir, other milk cultures, and more: www.culturesalive.com.au

The Kefir Shop (UK): Kombucha, water kefir, kefir, and more: www.kefirshop.co.uk

Additional Sources of Dairy Cultures

New England Cheesemaking Supply Co.: www.cheesemaking.com

Additional Source of Koji

South River Miso Company: www.southrivermiso.com

Additional Sources of Tempeh Starter

Short Mountain Cultures (my friend John Parker's new venture): www.shortmountaincultures.com

The other available sources of tempeh spores right now are in Belgium and Indonesia. Both sell online and ship internationally.

Tempeh Starter Shop (Indonesia): www.tempehstarter.com
Top Cultures (Belgium): www.topcultures.com

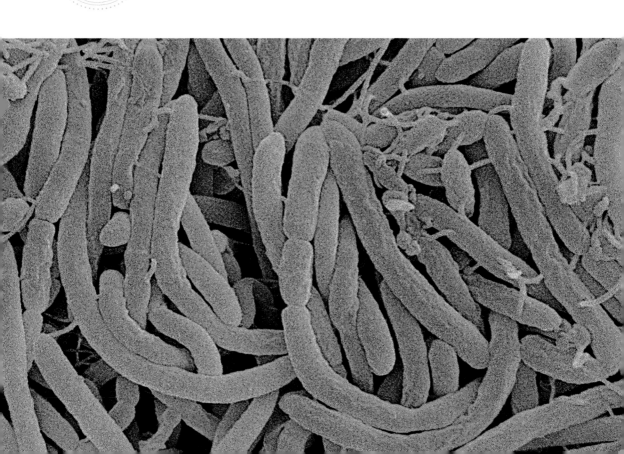

notes

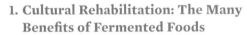

1. Cultural Rehabilitation: The Many Benefits of Fermented Foods

1. Chavan et al., United Nations Food and Agriculture Organization, *Fermented Fruits and Vegetables: A Global Perspective*, Agriculture Services Bulletin, 1999.

2. Bill Mollison, *The Permaculture Book of Ferment and Human Nutrition* (Tyalgum, Australia: Tagari Publications, 1993), 20.

3. Sally Fallon goes on at some length about phytic acid in *Nourishing Traditions* (Washington, DC: New Trends Publishing, 1999), 452. See also Paul Pitchford's *Healing with Whole Foods* (Berkeley, CA: North Atlantic Books, 1993), 184.

4. Mollison, *The Permaculture Book of Ferment and Human Nutrition*, 20.

5. Victor Herbert, "Vitamin B_{12}: Plant Sources, Requirements, and Assay," *American Journal of Clinical Nutrition* 48 (1988), 852–58.

6. L. A. Santiago, M. Hiramatsu, and A. Mori, "Japanese Soybean Paste Miso Scavenges Free Radicals and Inhibits Lipid Peroxidation," *Journal of Nutrition Science and Vitaminology* 38, no. 3 (June 1992).

7. S. Bengmark, "Immunonutrition: Role of Biosurfactants, Fiber, and Probiotic Bacteria," *Nutrition* 14, nos. 7–8 (1998).

8. Eeva-Liisa Ryhänen et al., "Plant-Derived Biomolecules in Fermented Cabbage," *Journal of Agricultural and Food Chemistry* 50, no. 23 (2002).

9. "New Chapter Health Report," 2000.

10. Cited in D. Gareth Jones, ed., *Exploitation of Microorganisms* (London: Chapman & Hall, 1993).

11. R. Binita and N. Khetarpaul, "Probiotic Fermented Food Mixtures: Possible Applications in Clinical Anti-Diarrhea Usage," *Nutritional Health* 12, no. 2 (1998).

12. Bengmark, "Immunonutrition."

13. Litjen Tan, Nancy H. Nielsen, Donald C. Young, Zoltan Trizna for the Council on Scientific Affairs, American Medical Association. "Use of Antimicrobial Agents in Consumer Products." *Archives of Dermatology* 138, no. 8 (2002), 1082–86.

14. Cited by Jane Brody, "Germ Paranoia May Harm Health," *London Free Press*, June 24, 2000.

15. Stephen Harrod Buhner, *The Lost Language of Plants* (White River Junction, VT: Chelsea Green Publishing, 2002), 134.

16. Mary Ellen Sanders, "Considerations for Use of Probiotic Bacteria to Modulate Human Health," *Journal of Nutrition* 130 (2000), 384S–390S.

17. Terence McKenna, *Food of the Gods* (New York: Bantam, 1992), 41.

18. Lynn Margulis and Karlene V. Schwartz, *Five Kingdoms* (New York: W. H. Freeman, 1999), 14. See also Lynn Margulis and

René Fester, eds., *Symbiogenesis as a Source of Evolutionary Innovation* (Cambridge, MA: MIT Press, 1991).

19. Elie Metchnikoff, *The Prolongation of Life: Optimistic Studies*, translated by P. Chalmers Mitchell (New York & London: G. P. Putnam's Sons, 1908), 182.

2. Cultural Theory: Human Beings and the Phenomenon of Fermentation

1. Maguelonne Toussaint-Samat, *A History of Food*, translated by Anthea Bell (Malden, MA; Oxford, UK; and Melbourne, Australia: Blackwell Publishing, 1992), 34.
2. Claude Levi-Strauss, *From Honey to Ashes*, translated by John and Doreen Weightman (New York: Harper & Row, 1973), 473.
3. Stephen Harrod Buhner, *Sacred and Herbal Healing Beers* (Boulder, CO: Siris Books, 1998), 141.
4. Ibid., 81–82.
5. Friedrich Nietzche, *The Birth of Tragedy*, translated by W. A. Haussmann (New York: MacMillan, 1923), 26.
6. Solomon H. Katz and Fritz Maytag, "Brewing an Ancient Beer," *Archaeology* (July/August 1991), 30.
7. *The Egyptian Book of the Dead*, translated by E. A. Wallis Budge (New York: Dover Publications, 1967), 23.
8. Sophie D. Coe, *America's First Cuisines* (Austin: University of Texas Press, 1994), 166.
9. American Heritage Dictionary, 2000.
10. "Symposium: Did Man Once Live by Beer Alone?" in *American Anthropologist*, New Series 55, no. 4, October 1953.
11. From Louis Pasteur's *Fermentation et Générations Dites Spontanées*, cited in Patrice Debre, *Louis Pasteur*, translated by Elborg Forster (Baltimore: Johns Hopkins University Press, 1998).
12. Leeuwenhoek cited in Daniel J. Boorstin, *The Discoverers: A History of Man's Search to Know His World and Himself* (New York: Random House, 1983).
13. Debre, *Louis Pasteur*, 95.
14. Justus Von Liebig's *Traité de Chimie Organique*, 1840, cited in Debre, *Louis Pasteur*, 92.
15. Louis Pasteur, *Oeuvres de Pasteur* 3:13, cited in Debre, *Louis Pasteur*, 101.
16. Jacob G. Lippman, *Bacteria in Relation to Country Life* (New York: MacMillan, 1908), vii–viii.
17. Cited in Madeleine Parker Grant, *Microbiology and Human Progress* (New York: Rinehart, 1953), 59.

3. Cultural Homogenization: Standardization, Uniformity, and Mass Production

1. Cocoa Research Institute.
2. "Cocoa," on *GMO Compass*, online at http://www.gmo-compass.org/eng/database/plants/43.cocoa.html, accessed August 25, 2015.
3. Mark Pendergrast, *Uncommon Grounds: The History of Coffee and How It Transformed Our World* (New York: Basic Books, 1999), 6.
4. McKenna, *Food of the Gods*, 186.
5. International Coffee Organization, "Coffee Production 2000."
6. My primary source of historical information about the tea trade is Henry Hobhouse, *Seeds of Change: Five Plants that Transformed Mankind* (New York: Harper & Row, 1985), 95–137.
7. Kaison Chang (Secretary, FAO Intergovernmental Group on Tea), "World Tea Production and Trade: Current and Future Development," Rome: Food and Agriculture Organization of the United Nations, 2015, online at http://www.fao.org/3/a-i4480e.pdf.
8. McKenna, *Food of the Gods*, 185–86.
9. Hobhouse, *Seeds of Change*, 64.
10. Sidney W. Mintz, *Sweetness and Power: The Place of Sugar in Modern History* (New York: Viking, 1985), 46.
11. Ibid., 95.

12. This and most of my other historical information about sugar is culled from Mintz, *Sweetness and Power*.

13. Medicinally, sugar was mixed with unpleasant-tasting herbs to make them more palatable and applied topically to wounds. As a spice, sugar was grouped with the other varied and much-desired flavorings of the East, and it was used in combination with them in cooking, to spice up the monotonous and bland medieval European diet.

14. Sudarsan Raghavan and Sumana Chatterjee, "Slave Labor Taints Sweetness of World Chocolate," *Kansas City Star*, June 23, 2001.

15. Mintz, *Sweetness and Power*, 214.

16. José Bové, "Who Really Makes the Decisions About What We Eat?" *The Guardian* (London), June 13, 2001, excerpted from his book *The World Is Not for Sale: Farmers Against Junk Food*.

17. Wendell Berry, *What Are People For?*, 1990, excerpted as "The Pleasures of Eating," *The Sun* (January 2002), 18.

18. Vandana Shiva, *Stolen Harvest: The Hijacking of the Global Food Supply* (Cambridge, MA: South End Press, 2000), 127.

4. Cultural Manipulation: A Do-It-Yourself Guide

1. Personal correspondence with USDA Agricultural Research Service microbiologist Fred Breidt, February 19, 2010.

2. Mikal Aasved, "Alcohol, Drinking, and Intoxication in Preindustrial Society: Theoretical, Nutritional, and Religious Considerations," unpublished PhD dissertation, University of California, Santa Barbara, 1988, cited in Buhner, *Sacred and Herbal Healing Beers*, 73.

3. Annie Hubert, "A Strong Smell of Fish?" *Slow 22* (Summer 2001), 56.

5. Vegetable Ferments

1. Susun S. Weed, *Healing Wise* (Woodstock, NY: Ash Tree Publishing, 1989), 96.

7. Dairy Ferments (and Vegan Alternatives)

1. Oskar Adolfsson et al., "Yogurt and Gut Function," *American Journal of Clinical Nutrition* 80, no. 245 (2004).

2. Susun S. Weed, *Breast Cancer? Breast Health! The Wise Woman Way* (Woodstock, NY: Ash Tree Publishing, 1996), 45.

3. Irma S. Rombauer and Marion Rombauer Becker, *The Joy of Cooking* (New York: Signet, 1964), 486–87.

4. Dominic N. Anfiteatro, *Kefir: A Probiotic Gem Cultured with a Probiotic Jewel* (Adelaide, Australia: self-published, 2001).

5. Burkhard Bilger, "Raw Faith," *The New Yorker*, August 19 & 26, 2002, 157.

6. Cited in Pierre Boisard, "The Future of a Tradition: Two Ways of Making Camembert, the Foremost Cheese of France," in *Food and Foodways* 4 (1991), 183–84.

7. Marlene Cimons, "Food Safety Concerns Drive FDA Review of Fine Cheeses," *American Society for Microbiology News*, February 13, 2001.

8. European Alliance for Artisan and Traditional Raw Milk Cheese, "Manifesto in Defense of Raw-Milk Cheese." Online at www.bestofbridgestone.com/mb/nr/nr00/rmc.html.

9. Jeffrey Steingarten, "Cheese Crisis," *Vogue*, June 2000, 269.

10. Cited in Bilger, *Raw Faith*, 157.

8. Grain Ferments (Porridges, Soft Drinks, Soups, Flatbreads, and Breads)

1. Michael Pollan, *The Botany of Desire: A Plant's-Eye View of the World* (New York: Random House, 2001), 204.

2. Shiva, *Stolen Harvest*, 17.

3. http://sekituwahnation.tripod.com/index/recipes.htm#hominydrink; http://web.archive.org/web/20090426080317/http://www.wisdomkeepers.org/nativeway/soup/nwsh0004.html.

4. Solomon H. Katz, M. L. Hediger, and L. A. Valleroy, "Traditional Maize Processing Techniques in the New World," *Science* 184 (May 17, 1974).

5. Coe, *America's First Cuisines*, 14.

6. Bruno Latour, *The Pasteurization of France*, translated by Alan Sheridan and John Law (Cambridge, MA: Harvard University Press, 1988), 82.

7. Ruth Allman, *Alaska Sourdough: The Real Stuff by a Real Alaskan* (Anchorage: Alaska Northwest Publishing, 1976).

8. Peter Schumann, *Bread* (Glover, VT: Bread and Puppet, 1984).

9. Bean Ferments

1. Analects of Confucius, scroll 2, chapter 10, cited in William Shurtleff and Akiko Aoyagi, *The Book of Miso* (Berkeley, CA: Ten Speed Press, 2001), 214.

2. Weed, *Healing Wise*, 224.

10. Wines (Including Mead, Cider, and Other Alcoholic Beverages Made from Simple Sugars)

1. Toussaint-Samat, *A History of Food*, 36.

2. Buhner, *Sacred and Herbal Healing Beers*, 67.

3. From the website of the Vegetarian Resource Group, www.vrg.org.

4. Ben Watson, *Cider, Hard and Sweet* (Woodstock, VT: The Countryman Press, 1999), 89.

5. Ibid., 25.

11. Beers

1. Cited in Keith Steinkraus, ed., *Handbook of Indigenous Fermented Foods* (New York: Marcel Dekker, 1983).

2. Jeremy Geller, "Bread and Beer in Fourth-Millennium Egypt," *Food and Foodways* 5 (1993), 255–67.

3. Solomon H. Katz and Fritz Maytag, "Brewing an Ancient Beer," *Archaeology* (July/August 1991), 27.

4. United Nations Food and Agriculture Organization, "Sorghum and Millets in Human Nutrition" (Rome: Food and Nutrition Series No. 27, 1995), online at www.fao.org/docrep/T0818E/T0818E00.htm, accessed November 30, 2010.

5. Buhner, *Sacred and Herbal Healing Beers*, 429.

12. Vinegars

1. Terre Vivante, *Keeping Food Fresh: Old World Techniques and Recipes* (White River Junction, VT: Chelsea Green Publishing, 1999), 110.

13. Cultural Reincarnation: Fermentation in the Cycles of Life, Soil Fertility, and Social Change

1. Lippman, *Bacteria in Relation to Country Life*, 136–37.

2. Audre Lorde, *The Cancer Journals* (San Francisco: Aunt Lute Books, 1980), 16.

3. Walt Whitman, excerpt from "This Compost," *Leaves of Grass*, 1881.

4. J. I. Rodale, ed., *The Complete Book of Composting* (Emmaus, PA: Rodale Books, 1960), 44.

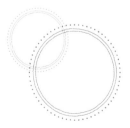

image credits

Unless noted below, all images are from the collection of Sandor Ellix Katz.

Page vi   Barry Blitt
Page viii   Andrew Syred / Science Source
Page xviii   © Catherine Opie
Pages 11 and 12   Kate Berry
Page 19   Mural by Noah Church, from the collection of Sandor Ellix Katz
Page 34   Science Source, colorization by Mary Martin
Page 65   Kate Berry
Page 69   Jessieca Leo
Page 80   Chris Baker, Isaac Plant, Tim Roth, and Denise Sirias
Page 102   Kate Berry
Page 108   Milos Kalab
Page 110   Bread and Puppet Press
Pages 128–129   Joseph Shuldiner
Page 217   Alison LePage
Page 258   Eileen Richardson
Pages 260–261   Pauline Lévêque / New Zealand Festival
Page 282   David Scharf / Science Source

Images on pages 4, 15, 22–23, 40–41, 53, 56–57, 70–71, 78–79, 81, 94, 100–101, 114, 125, 136, 156–157, 228–29, and 266 are used courtesy of Jacqueline Schlossman / READYLUCK.

Images on pages xiv, xx–xxi, xxii, 6–7, 8, 47, 73, 84, 97, 132–133, 140, 142–143, 148–149, 162, 175, 191, 206–207, 214–215, 224–225, 254–255, 273, 274, 277, and 280 are used courtesy of Shane Carpenter.

index

Note: Page numbers in *italics* refer to photographs.

about the author

© Catherine Opie

Sandor Ellix Katz is a fermentation revivalist. A self-taught experimentalist who lives in rural Tennessee, his explorations in fermentation developed out of overlapping interests in cooking, nutrition, and gardening. This book (originally published in 2003), along with *The Art of Fermentation* (2012) and the hundreds of fermentation workshops he has taught around the world, has helped to catalyze a broad revival of the fermentation arts. *Newsweek* called *Wild Fermentation* "the fermenting Bible," and *The New York Times* calls Sandor "one of the unlikely rock stars of the American food scene." For more information, check out his website www.wildfermentation.com.